100 D

5

William Congreve

THE WAY OF THE WORLD

William Congreve

THE WAY OF THE WORLD

[Edited with Introduction, Author's Information, Complete Text, Summary and Analysis and Study Questions]

Mansi Sachdeva
B.A. English (Hons), Delhi University;
M.A., M. Phil. (English), IGNOU

ANMOL PUBLICATIONS PVT. LTD.
NEW DELHI - 110 002 (INDIA)

ANMOL PUBLICATIONS PVT. LTD.

H.O.: 4374/4B, Ansari Road, Darya Ganj,
New Delhi-110 002 (India)
Ph.: 23278000, 23261597

B.O.: No. 1015, Ist Main Road, BSK IIIrd Stage
IIIrd Phase, IIIrd Block
Bangalore - 560 085 (India)
Visit us at: www.anmolpublications.com

The Way of the World
© Reserved by the Author
First Published, 2009

[All rights reserved. No part of this publication may be reproduced, stored in a retrieval system or transmitted, in my form or by any means, mechnical, photocopying, recording or otherwise, without prior written permission of the publisher.]

PRINTED IN INDIA

Printed at Balaji Offset Press, Delhi.

Contents

Preface

William Congreve was born in 1670 in Bardsey (a village near Leeds), Yorkshire. When his father was commissioned to command the garrison at Youghal four years later, the family moved to Ireland, where Congreve was enrolled at a famous school in Kilkenny.

In 1700, when The Way of the World was performed on the English stage at Lincoln's Inn Fields (a new theatre that William Congreve managed), it was not a popular success. This was the last play Congreve was to write, perhaps for that reason.

Author

Chapter 1

Introduction

Sir William Congreve, 2nd Baronet (May 20, 1772 – May 16, 1828), was an English inventor and rocket artillery pioneer distinguished for his development and deployment of Congreve rockets. He was son of Lt. General Sir William Congreve, 1st Baronet, the Comptroller of the Royal Laboratories at the Royal Arsenal, raised in Kent, England, educated at Singlewell School and educated in law at Trinity College, Cambridge.

Congreve died in Toulouse, France. Congreve was inspired to work on iron-cased gunpowder rockets for use by the British military, by their use against British troops in India by Tipu Sultan during the Anglo-Mysore Wars. He first demonstrated solid fuel rockets at the Royal Arsenal in 1805. He considered his work sufficiently advanced to engage in two Royal Navy attacks on the French fleet at Boulogne, France, one that year and one the next. Parliament authorized Congreve to form two rocket companies for the army in 1809. Congreve subsequently commanded one of these at the Battle of Leipzig in 1813.

Congreve rockets were used for the remainder of the Napoleonic Wars, as well as the War of 1812 the "rockets' red glare" in the American national anthem describes their firing at Fort McHenry during the latter conflict. They remained in the arsenal of the United Kingdom until the 1850s. Congreve was awarded the honorary rank of Lieutenant colonel in 1811 and was often referred to as "Colonel Congreve."

Chapter 2

Other Inventions

Besides his rockets, Congreve was a prolific (if indifferently successful) inventor for the remainder of his life. Congreve invented a gun-recoil mounting, a time-fuze, a rocket parachute attachment, a hydropneumatic canal lock and sluice (1813), a perpetual motion machine, a process of colour printing (1821) which was widely used in Germany, a new form of steam engine, and a method of consuming smoke (which was applied at the Royal Laboratory).

He also took out patents for a clock in which time was measured by a ball rolling along a zig-zag track on an inclined plane; for protecting buildings against fire; inlaying and combining metals; unforgeable bank note paper; a method of killing whales by means of rockets; improvements in the manufacture of gunpowder; stereotype plates; fireworks; and gas meters. Congreve was named as comptroller of the Royal Laboratory at Woolwich from 1814 until his death. (Congreve's father Sir William Congreve had also held the same post.)

Congreve's unsuccessful perpetual motion scheme involved an endless band which should raise more water by its capillary action on one side than on the other. He used capillary action of fluids that would disobey the law of never rising above their own level, so to produce a continual ascent and overflow. The device had an inclined plane over pulleys. At the top and bottom, there travelled an endless band of sponge, a bed, and, over this, again an endless band of heavy weights jointed together. The whole stood over the surface of still water. The capillary action raised the water, whereas the same thing could not happen in the part, since the weights would squeeze the water out. Hence, it was heavier than the other; but as "we know that if it were the same weight, there would be equilibrium, if the heavy chain be also uniform". Therefore the extra weight of it would cause the chain to move round in the direction of the arrow, and this would go on, supposedly, continually.

Chapter 3

Publications

In 1804 Congreve published A concise account of the origin and progress of the rocket system. Publication of A Concise Account of the Origin and Progress of the Rocket System by William Congreve was in 1807. In 1814 Congreve published The details of the rocket system. In 1827 The Congreve Rocket System was published in London. His other publications were: An Elementary Treatise on the Mounting of Naval Ordnance (1812); A Description of the Hydropneumatical Lock (1815); A New Principle of Steam-Engine (1819); Resumption of Cash Payments (1819) and Systems of Currency (1819).

Chapter 4

Life

WILLIAM CONGREVE, English dramatist, the greatest English master of pure comedy, was born at Bardsey near Leeds, where he was baptized on the 10th of February 1670, although the inscription on his monument gives his date of birth as 1672. He was the son of William Congreve, a soldier who was soon after his son's birth placed in command of the garrison at Youghal. To Ireland, therefore, is due the credit of his education — as a schoolboy at Kilkenny, as an undergraduate at Dublin, where he was a contemporary and friend of Swift. From college he came to London, and was entered as a student of law at the Middle Temple. The first-fruits of his studies appeared under the boyish pseudonym of "Cleophil," in the form of a novel whose existence is now remembered only through the unabashed avowal of so austere a moralist as Dr Johnson, that he "would rather praise it than read it."

In 1693 Congreve's real career began, and early enough by the latest computation, with the brilliant appearance and instant success of his first comedy, The Old Bachelor, under the generous auspices of Dryden, then as ever a living and immortal witness to the falsehood of the vulgar charge which taxes the greater among poets with jealousy or envy, the natural badge and brand of the smallest that would claim a place among their kind. The discrowned laureate had never, he said, seen such a first play; and indeed the graceless grace of the dialogue was as yet only to be matched by the last and best work of Etherege, standing as till then it had done alone among the barefaced brutalities of Wycherley and Shadwell.

The types of Congreve's first work were the common conventional properties of stage tradition; but the fine and clear-cut style in which these types were reproduced was his own. The gift of one place and the reversion of another were the solid fruits of his splendid success.

Next year a better play from the same hand met with worse fortune on the stage, and with yet higher honour from the first living poet of his nation. The noble verses, as faultless in the expression as reckless in the extravagance of their applause, prefixed by Dryden to The Double Dealer, must naturally have supported the younger poet, if indeed such support can have been required, against the momentary annoyance of assailants whose passing clamour left uninjured and secure the fame of his second comedy; for the following year witnessed the crowning triumph of his art and life, in the appearance of Love for Love (1695).

Two years later his ambition rather than his genius adventured on the foreign ground of tragedy, and The Mourning Bride (1697) began such a long career of good fortune as in earlier or later times would have been closed against a far better work. Next year he attempted, without his usual success, a reply to the attack of Jeremy Collier, the nonjuror, "on the immorality and profaneness of the English stage" — an attack for once not discreditable to the assailant, whose honesty and courage were evident enough to approve him incapable alike of the ignominious precaution which might have suppressed his own name, and of the dastardly mendacity which would have stolen the mask of a stranger's. Against this merit must be set the mistake of confounding in one indiscriminate indictment the levities of a writer like Congreve with the brutalities of a writer like Wycherley — an error which ever since has more or less perverted the judgment of succeeding critics.

The general case of comedy was then, however, as untenable by the argument as indefensible by the sarcasm of its most brilliant and comparatively blameless champion. Art itself, more than anything else, had been outraged and degraded by the recent school of the Restoration; and the comic work of Congreve, though different rather in kind than in degree from the bestial and blatant licence of his immediate precursors, was inevitably for a time involved in the sentence passed upon the comic work of men in all ways alike his inferiors. The true and triumphant answer to all possible attacks of honest men or liars, brave men or cowards, was then as ever to be given by the production of work unarraignable alike by fair means or foul, by frank impeachment or furtive imputation.

In 1700 Congreve thus replied to Collier with The Way of the World — the unequalled and unapproached masterpiece of English comedy, which may fairly claim a place beside or but just beneath the mightiest work of Molière. On the stage which had recently acclaimed with uncritical applause the author's more questionable appearance in the field of tragedy, this final and flawless evidence of his incomparable powers met with a rejection then and ever since inexplicable on any ground of conjecture. During the twenty-eight years which remained to him, Congreve produced little beyond a volume of fugitive verses, published ten years after the miscarriage of his masterpiece.

His even course of good fortune under Whig and Tory governments alike was counterweighed by the physical infirmities of gout and failing sight. He died, January 19, 1729, in consequence of an injury received on a journey to Bath by the upsetting of his carriage; was buried in Westminster Abbey, after lying in state in the Jerusalem Chamber; and bequeathed the bulk of his fortune to the chief friend of his last years, Henrietta, duchess of Marlborough, daughter of the great duke, rather than to his family, which, according to Johnson, was then in difficulties, or to Mrs Bracegirdle, the actress, with whom he had lived longer on intimate terms than with any other mistress or friend, but who inherited by his will only £200. The one memorable incident of his later life was the visit of Voltaire, whom he astonished and repelled by his rejection of proffered praise and the expression of his wish to be considered merely as any other gentleman of no literary fame. The great master of well-nigh every province in the empire of letters, except the only one in which his host reigned supreme, replied that in that sad case Congreve would not have received his visit.

The fame of the greatest English comic dramatist is founded wholly or mainly on but three of his five plays. His first comedy was little more than a brilliant study after such models as were eclipsed by this earliest effort of their imitator; and tragedy under his hands appears rouged and wrinkled, in the patches and powder of Lady Wishfort. But his three great comedies are more than enough to sustain a reputation as durable as our language. Were it not for these we should have no samples to show of comedy in its purest and highest form. Ben Jonson, who alone attempted to introduce it by way of reform among the mixed work of a time when comedy and tragedy were as inextricably blended on the stage as in actual life, failed to give the requisite ease and the indispensable grace of comic life and movement to the action and passion of his elaborate and magnificent work. Of Congreve's immediate predecessors, whose aim had been to raise on French foundations a new English fabric of simple and unmixed comedy, Wycherley was of too base metal and Etherege was of metal too light to be weighed against him; and besides theirs no other or finer coin was current than the crude British ore of Shadwell's brutal and burly talent. Borrowing a metaphor from Landor, we may say that a limb of Molière would have sufficed to make a Congreve, a limb of Congreve would have sufficed to make a Sheridan.

The broad and robust humour of Vanbrugh's admirable comedies gives him a place on the master's right hand; on the left stands Farquhar, whose bright light genius is to Congreve's as female is to male, or "as moonlight unto sunlight." No English writer, on the whole, has so nearly touched the skirts of Molière; but his splendid intelligence is wanting in the deepest and subtlest quality which has won for Molière from the greatest poet of his country and our age the tribute of exact and final definition conveyed in that perfect phrase which salutes at once and denotes him — "ce moqueur pensif comme un apotre." Only perhaps in a single part has Congreve half consciously touched a note of almost tragic depth and suggestion; there is something wellnigh akin to the grotesque and piteous figure of Arnolphe himself in the unvenerable old age of Lady Wishfort, set off and relieved as it is, with grace and art worthy of the supreme French master, against the only figure on any stage which need not shun comparison even with that of Celimene.

Chapter 5

Chronology

1659 The Protectorate collapses in May when the Army deposes Richard Cromwell and re-establishes the old Rump Parliament. A Royalist rebellion in August is easily crushed, but is a sign of an increasingly strong popular movement towards the restoration of the monarchy. In October, the Army becomes dissatisfied with the Rump and expels it in a coup d'etat. General George Monck, commander of the English army of occupation in Scotland, opposes the coup, and begins to move his army south towards the English border. Anti-army riots break out in London, as Royalist sentiment grows. On 26 December, military control of London collapses, and the Rump Parliament reconvenes.

1660 On 2 January, Monck's forces cross the River Tweed at Coldstream into England, and begin a slow but deliberate march on London. An army under General Lambert, sent to oppose his advance, disintegrates without firing a shot. Monck enters London on 3 February; on 11 February, amid scenes of great rejoicing in the City, he demands that the Rump prepare for its own dissolution, and the election of a new Parliament. On 22 February, Monck backs up his demand by enforcing the readmission of the (mostly Royalist) "secluded" members of Parliament, ejected 12 years earlier in Pride's Purge. On 16 March, the Long Parliament is finally dissolved; a new election brings in the "Convention Parliament" in April. On 4 April, the Declaration of Breda, outlining Charles II's intentions, is published; on May 8, the King is proclaimed in London. He lands at Dover on 25 May, and arrives in London on the 29th.

The Army is disbanded.

The new "Cavalier Parliament" begins to seek revenge on supporters of the Interregnum regimes.

The secret marriage of Anne Hyde to James, Duke of York, is revealed.

Birth of Daniel Defoe and Thomas Southerne.

Theatrical Patents granted to Wir William D'Avenant and Thomas Killigrew, who form the Duke of York's Company, and the King's Company, respectively.

Publication of Dryden's Astræa Redux and Robert Wild's Iter Boreale.

1661 Venner's Rising: revolt of Fifth Monarchy Men led by Thomas Venner.

Beginning of Cavalier Parliament. Enactment of the so-called Clarendon Code, really a series of measures repressing religious dissent, imposed by the Cavalier Parliament. Birth of Anne Finch, Countess Winchilsea

Publication of Edmund Waller's A Poem on St. James's Park.

Publication of Abraham Cowley's A Proposition for the Advancement of Experimental Philosophy.

1662 The Act of Uniformity ends attempts to include Presbyterians in the Church: despite efforts by the King to moderate its severity, the act results in some 900 Presbyterian clergy being deprived of their livings. The king responds with a Declaration of Toleration, which fails in the face of Parliamentary intransigence.

Charles II marries a Catholic Portugese princess, Catherine of Braganza.

Birth of Mary (the future Queen Mary), daughter of James, Duke of York, and his first wife, Anne Hyde.

Introduction of the Licensing Act, restricting publication, and reducing number of printers and presses.
Restoration of the Book of Common Prayer.
Royal Society granted charter by King.
Birth of Richard Bentley.
Publication of Samuel Butler's Hudibras, Part I, and of Rump, a two volume collection of royalist satires from the Civil War and Interregnum.

1663 Appointment of Sir Roger L'Estrange as "Surveyor of the Imprimery," giving him primary power over licensing of works for publication.
Publication of Butler's Hudibras, Part II, and Abraham Cowley's Verses upon Several Occasions.
Publication of John Dryden's To My Honor'd Friend, Dr. Charleton on His Learned and Useful Works; And More Particularly this of Stonehenge Restor'd to the True Founders, in Chorea Gigantum.
Probable date of birth of Walter Shandy.

1664 Death of Katherine Philips.
Birth of Sir John Vanbrugh and Matthew Prior.
Publication of Charles Cotton's Scarronides.
Publication of first edition of John Evelyn's Silva.

1665 Beginning of Second Dutch War, which begins well, but ends disastrously in 1667.
Birth of Anne (the future Queen Anne), daughter of James, Duke of York, and his first wife, Anne Hyde.
The plague makes one final and devastating visit to London. Theatres closed 5 June, due to plague.
Publication of Andrew Marvell's Character of Holland.
Publication of Philosophical Transactions of the Royal Society commences. Publication of Robert Hooke's Micrographia

1666 The Great Fire of London.
The French join the Dutch in the war against the English.
Suppression of the Covenanters in the Pentland Rising in Scotland.

Death of James Shirley.
Thomas Hobbes's works censured by Parliament.
Publication of Edmund Waller's Instructions to a Painter. Publication of Nicholas Boileau's influential Satires.
Publication of John Bunyan's Grace Abounding.

1667 A Dutch naval force launches a surprise attack on the English shipyards at Chatham, at the mouth of the Thames: the Dutch destroy many ships, and then proceed to blockade the river.
Charges of mismanagement and corruption against Edward Hyde, Earl of Clarendon and Charles' Lord Chancellor, lead to a move to impeach him; he flees the country, and dies in France in 1674, having written his autobiography, and his History of the Great Rebellion. Birth of Jonathan Swift. Death of Abraham Cowley.
Publication of John Milton's Paradise Lost, Dryden's Annus Mirabilis, and Marvell's Last Instructions to a Painter. Publication of Katherine Philip's Poems.
Publication of Thomas Sprat's The History of the Royal Society, including a prefatory ode "To the Royal Society," by Abraham Cowley.

1668 Sir William Temple negotiates the Triple Alliance, between England, Holland, and Sweden, aimed against France. Charles II has little actual intention of abiding by this alliance, and pursues a pro-French policy, and French alliance, secretly.
Death of Sir William D'Avenant. Dryden appointed Poet Laureate.
Dryden publishes Of Dramatick Poesie: An Essay.
Publication of Abraham Cowley's Works, edited by Thomas Sprat, and including "An Account of the Life and Writings of Mr. Abraham Cowley." Publication of Sir John Denham's Poems and Translations.
Performances of Sir George Etherege's She Wou'd if she Cou'd and Sir Charles Sedley's The Mulberry Garden.

1669 Parliament prorogued by Charles II after it launches an inquiry into royal expenditures.
Death of the Queen Mother, Henrietta Maria.
Birth of Susannah Centlivre. Death of Sir John Denham.
Performance of Dryden's Tyrannic Love.

1670 Formation of the "Cabal" ministry, led by the Earl of Arlington.
Charles II signs the Treaty of Dover with the French; secret clauses to the treaty provide for clandestine financial aid from the French in exchange for a pro-French foreign policy, and a pro-Catholic domestic policy. Charles is supposed to announce his own conversion to the Roman Church, but puts it off indefinitely.
Arrival of Louise de Kerouaille (soon to be mistress to the King, and Duchess of Portsmouth) in London.
Incorporation of the Hudson's Bay Company.
Births of William Congreve and Sarah Fyge.
Publication of Milton's The History of Britain and Samuel Parker's A Discourse of Ecclesiastical Polity.
Performances of Dryden's The Conquest of Granada, Part I, and Aphra Behn's The Forced Marriage.

1671 Death of Anne, Duchess of York, mother of both the future Queen Mary and Queen Anne.
Opening of Dorset Garden Theatre. Birth of Colley Cibber. Publication of Milton's Paradise Regained and Samson Agonistes.
Performances of Dryden's The Conquest of Granada, Part II, and The Duke of Buckingham's The Rehearsal.

1672 Charles issues a stop of Exchequer in January, representing a virtual admission of royal bankruptcy.
Beginning of the Third Dutch War, with England this time allied with France against the Dutch; the war ends inconclusively in 1674.
Charles attempts a second time to issue a Declaration of Indulgence offering widespread religious

toleration, but is foiled again by Parliament, which passes the Test Act in 1673, requiring all office holders to take the Anglican sacrament.
James, Duke of York, marries a Catholic, Mary of Modena; his own secret conversion to the Roman Church is widely suspected when he resigns from his offices rather than subscribe to the Test Act.
Death of Anne Bradstreet.
Births of Joseph Addison and Richard Steele.
Publication of Marvell's The Rehearsal Transpros'd.
Performances of Dryden's Marriage à la Mode and Thomas Shadwell's Epsom Wells.

1673 Revocation of the Declaration of Indulgence, and imposition of the Test Act.
Shaftesbury dismissed as Lord Chancellors, and enters into opposition. Publication of Sir William D'Avenant's Works. Milton's 1645 Poems reissued.

1674 Peace concluded with the Dutch.
Collapse of the "Cabal" ministry. The Duke of Buckingham dismissed from office, and enters into opposition.
Death of the Earl of Clarendon, in exile. Birth of Nicholas Rowe. Death of Milton, Robert Herrick, and Thomas Traherne.
Opening of New Drury Lane Theatre.

1675 Royal Proclamation enforces punitive laws against Nonconformity.
Work begins on Sir Christopher Wren's St. Paul's Cathedral. Orders for the suppression of coffee-houses issued, and quickly revoked.
Performance of William Wycherley's The Country Wife.

Chapter 6

The Drama in the 18th Century

Everywhere in Europe the modern drama has been evolved from out the drama of the middle ages; but the development had been slower in France than in Spain and in England; and this retarding of its evolution was fortunate for the French, since the golden days of their dramatic literature arrived only after the conditions of the theater had become far less medieval than they had been during the golden days of the Spanish and of the English dramatic literatures. It was natural that the more modern form of play should be taken as a model by the poets of other countries, the more especially at the beginning of the eighteenth century, when the French were everywhere accepted as the arbiters of art, the custodians of taste, and the guardians of the laws by which genius was to be gaged. In England the Puritans had closed the places of amusement and had thus broken off the theatrical traditions that ran far back into the middle ages; and when the playhouses opened again after the Restoration, the managers had to gratify new likings which king and courtiers had brought back with them from France.

Even though the plain people in London continued to prefer the plays of Shakespeare to belauded adaptations from Corneille or Racine and to icily decorous imitations like the CATO of Addison, and even though the plebeian folk in Madrid still relished the plays of Lope de Vega and Calderon, the English men-of-letters and the Spanish men-of-letters were united in taking an apologetic tone toward the earlier dramas which had pleased their less cultivated forefathers. In England as in Spain the learned critic was willing to admit that these earlier dramas had a certain rough power which might move the uneducated, but he had no desire to deny that they wanted art. For instance, Doctor Johnson, when he brought out his edition of Shakespeare in the middle of the eighteenth century and when he ventured a timid suggestion that possibly the so-called rules of the theater were not absolutely infallible, seems to have felt almost as though he was taking his life in his hands.

In Italy and in Germany, as in England and in Spain, the men-of-letters maintained the necessity of conforming to the theatrical theory of the French because they believed the French to be the only true exponents of the Greek tradition, which it was the bounden duty of every dramatic poet to follow blindly. The rules of the theater as the French declared them had only a remote connection with the Greek tradition; and they consisted mainly of purely negative restrictions. They told the dramatic poet what he was forbidden to do, and they declared what a tragedy must not be. To accord with the demands of the French theory a tragedy should not have more or less than five acts and it should not be in prose; it should deal only with a lofty theme, having queens and kings for its chief figures, and avoiding all visible violence of action or of speech, and all other breaches of decorum; it should eschew humour, keeping itself ever serious and stately, and never allowing any underplot; and, above all, it should permit no change of scene during the whole play, and it should not allow the time taken by the story to extend over more than twenty-four hours.

These were the rules to conform to which Corneille cramped himself and curbed his indisputable genius, with the result that he is to Shakespeare "as a clipped hedge is to a forest,"—to quote an unsympathetic British critic. A certain likeness to the virgin woods is discoverable in the Elizabethan drama, whereas the drama of Louis XIV resembles rather a pleasure-park laid out by some such architect as Lenôtre. French tragedy had a graceful symmetry of its own, but it was lacking in bold variety and in imaginative energy. Here is an added reason why it was widely accepted in the eighteenth century, which has been termed "an age whose poetry was without romance" and "whose philosophy was without insight." The century itself, rather than the French example, is to blame if it has left so few poetic plays deserving to survive. What Lowell called "its inefficacy for the higher reaches of poetry, its very good breeding that made it shy of the raised voice and the flushed features of enthusiasm," enabled the century to make its prose supple for the elegancies of the social circle and for the literature which sought to reflect those elegancies. "Inevitably, as human intercourse in cities grows more refined, comedy will grow more subtle," so De Quincey declared; "it will build itself on distinctions of character less grossly defined and on features of manners more delicate and impalpable."

II

A flexible prose is plainly the fittest instrument for the comedy-of-manners; and the comedy-of-manners is as plainly the kind of drama best suited to the limitations of the eighteenth century. By their comedies rather than by their tragedies are the dramatists of that century now remembered. Their comedies, like their tragedies, were composed in imitation of french models; but the influence of molière was as stimulating as the influence of corneille and racine had been stifling. Within a few years after molière's death the type of comedy which he had elaborated to suit his own needs and to contain his veracious portrayal of life as he saw it, had been taken across to england by the comic dramatists of the restoration, some of whom had borrowed plots from him and all of whom had tried to absorb his method.

No one of the english dramatists had molière's insight into character or his sturdy morality. Congreve and wycherley, farquhar and vanbrugh helped themselves to molière's framework only to hang it about with dirty linen. At times molière had been plain of speech, but he was ever clean-minded; whereas the english dramatists of the restoration were often foul in phrase and frequently filthy in thought also.

Clever as these restoration comedies were and brilliant in their reflection of the glittering immorality, their tone was too offensive for our modern taste, and scarcely one of them now survives on the stage. Yet the form they had copied from molière they firmly established in england, where the conditions of the theater had come to be like those in france; and this form has been accepted by all the later comic dramatists of our language, who have never cared to return to the looser and more medieval form which had to satisfy the humorous playwrights under elizabeth. Steele and fielding and, later in the century, goldsmith and sheridan continue in english comedy the tradition established by molière. In she stoops to conquer and in the rivals there is an element of rolicking farce not quite in keeping with the elevation of high comedy but not unlike the joyous gaiety which laughs all through the ibourgeois gentilhomme. In the school for scandal we have an english comedy with something like the solid structure of the femmes savantes, but narrower in its outlook, not so piercing in its insight, and far more metallic in its luster.

The english followers of molière are many, but they are not more numerous or more amusing than those who in his own country profited by the example he had left. Regnard is almost the equal of his master in adroitness of versification and even in comic force, in the power of compelling laughter. Monsieur de pourceaugnac has hardly added more to the mirth of the french than has the légataire universal. But regnard is fantastic and arbitrary in the conduct of his plots; and he lacks the truth to life and the penetration which characterize molière. Lesage comes nearer, in his knowledge of human nature and in his appreciation of its frailties, although it is in his novels rather than in his plays that he reveals himself most fully as a disciple of molière. Like fielding in england, lesage in france carried over into prose fiction the method of character-drawing which he had acquired from the greatest of all comic dramatists.

In the dépit amoureux and in the école des femmes molière had shown how to set on the stage certain more delicate phases of feminine personality; marivaux pushed the analysis still further, thereby enriching French comedy with a series of studies of women in love,—women at once ethereal, sophisticated, and fascinating. Broader than Marivaux was Beaumarchais, broader and franker; his psychology was swifter, his action more direct, and his stagecraft was more obvious. It was tartuffe and the éto ırdi that he had taken as his models, but he was only clever and wily where molière was transparently sincere; and instead of the large liberality of the dramatist under louis xiv the dramatist under louis xvi had a caustic skepticism. The career of beaumarchais was as varied in its vicissitudes as that of his own figaro; he was an adventurer himself, like sheridan, his contemporary on the other side of the channel. The barber of seville was as lively and as vivacious as the rivals; and the marriage of figaro was as scintillating and as hard as the school for scandal.

There was a disintigrating satire in these comedies of beaumarchais, a daring bitterness of attack like that of a reckless journalist who might happen also to be an ingenious and witty playwright. Where Molière had assaulted hypocrisy in religion and humbug in medicine, Beaumarchais made an onslaught on the Ancient Regime as a whole. No doubt a portion of the vogue Beaumarchais enjoyed among his contemporaries was due to their covert sympathy with the thesis he was so cleverly sustaining on the stage. He knew how to profit by the scandal aroused by his scathing insinuations against the established order. Yet he was not dependent on these factitious aids, and his solidly constructed comedies re /eal remarkable dramaturgic felicity. They have established themselves firmly on the French stage, where they are still seen with pleasure, although certain polemic passages here and there strike us now as extraneous and as over-vehement. Beaumarchais is the connecting-link between the French comedy of the seventeenth century and that of the nineteenth, between Molière and Augier.

III

Although the french theorists insisted on a complete separation of the comic and the tragic, disapproving fiercely of any humorous relief in a tragedy, they also maintained that comedy should hold itself aloof from vulgar subjects, that it should ever be genteel; and there were some who held that it ought to be unfailingly dignified. Even in england goldsmith was reproached for having disfigured she stoops to conquer with scenes of broad humour "to low even for farce"; and sheridan in the prologue of the rivals felt forced to make a plea for laughter as a not unnatural accompaniment of comedy. without asserting categorically that the drama should be strenuously didactic, many critics considered that it was the duty of comedy, not first of all to depict human nature as it is with its foibles and its failings, and not to clear the air with hearty laughter wholesome in itself, but chiefly to teach, to set a good example, to hold aloft the standards of manners and of morals. Dryden had declared that the general end of all poetry was "to instruct delightfully"; and not a few later writers of less authority were willing enough to waive the delight if only they could make sure of their instruction.

Thus there came into existence a new dramatic species, which flourished for a little space on both sides of the English Channel and which was known in London as sentimental-comedy and in Paris as tearful-comedy, comédie larmoyante. The most obvious characteristic of this comedy was that it was not comic; and in fact it was not intended to be comic, but pathetic. It was a mistake that a play of this new class should call itself comedy, which was precisely what it was not, and that by this false claim it should hinder the healthy growth of true comedy with its ampler pictures of life and its contagious gaiety. But the new species, however miscalled, responded to a new need of the times. It was the result of that awakening sensibility of the soul, of that growing tenderness of spirit, of that expansion of sympathy, which was after a while to bring about the Romanticist upheaval.

In England this sentimental-comedy never amounted to much, even though it had for one of its earliest practitioners Steele, who claimed that a certain play of his had been "damned for its piety." But Steele, undeniable humorist as he was, lacked the instinctive touch of the born playwright, and his humour was too delicate to adjust itself easily to the huge theaters of London. Steele's is the only interesting name in all the list of writers for the English stage who intended to edify rather than to amuse and who did not regret that their comedies called for tears rather than laughter. That the liking for sentimental-comedy was more transient in England than in France perhaps was due to the fact that the Londoners had already wept abundantly over dramas of an irregular species, not comedies of course, nor yet true tragedies, but dealing pathetically with the humbler sort of people. Of this irregular species lillo's george barnwell and moore's gamester may serve as specimens. Difficult to classify as these plays may have been, they were moving in their appeal to the emotions of the London citizens; and they must be accepted as spontaneous attempts at a kind of play which the French later in the century were to strive for under the name of tragédie bourgeoise, the tragedy of common life, with no vain tinsel of royalty and no false perspective of antiquity.

In France, where comedy and tragedy were more rigorously restricted than in England, the vogue of sentimental-comedy was less fleeting, sustained as it was by the sudden success of the pathetic plays of La Chaussée and by the ardent proclamations of Diderot. With all his intelligence, Diderot failed to write a single good play of his own; but he was swift to see that the prescribed molds of tragedy and comedy, as the French theorists had established them, were not only too narrow but above all too few for a proper representation of the infinite variety of human life. Envying the larger liberty of the English theater and approving of the comédie larmoyante and the tragédie bougeoise, he demanded a frank recognition of the right of these new species not only to exist but also to be received as the equals of tragedy and comedy. Unfortunately Diderot could not sustain precept by example; his own attempts at play-writing were painfully unsatisfactory, and the tearful-comedies of La Chaussée were poor things at best, even though they had won favour for a little while. Perhaps the most pleasing example of French sentimental-comedy was Sedaine's PHILOSOPHE SANS LE SAVOIR; and in spite of its amiable optimism and its touching situations, the tone of this innocent little play was thin, and its manner was rather argumentative than appealing.

IV

IF we needed proof of the temporary popularity of the ingenuous domestic drama which pretended to be comedy, although it preferred tears to laughter, we could find this in the fact that it tempted even Voltaire to essay it. Yet for sentimental-comedy it would seem as though Voltaire had few natural qualifications, since he was deficient in sentiment, in pathos, and in humour. Wit he had in profusion,—indeed, he was the arch-wit of the century; and he was so amazingly clever that when he attempted tragedy he was able to make his wit masquerade even as poetry. In the drama, as in almost every other department of literature, Voltaire is the dominating figure of this time. He was very fond of the theater, and he had possessed himself of some of the secrets of the dramaturgic art. He could devise an ingenious story; but he had no firm mastery of human motive. However artfully his plots might be put together, they were generally improbable in the main theme and arbitrary in the several episodes.

Even his best tragedy, zaïre, which is less of an improvisation than most of his other plays, and which still has an intermittent vitality on the French stage, was little more than a melodrama, as the characters existed soley for the situations by which they were created. Although his versification was feeble, and although he was never truly a poet, he was sometimes really eloquent. As a dramatist he was often self-conscious, not to say insincere; his mind was on the minor effects of the stage and not on the larger problems of the soul. His conception of tragedy was petty; it was without elevation or austerity; and yet he thought that the French had been able to improve on the type of tragedy which they had borrowed from the Greeks. He did not see that French tragedy, vaunting itself so absolutely Greek, had acquired from the Spanish drama a trick of complicating its plot with ingenious surprises, than which nothing could be more foreign to the large simplicity of the Athenian drama. He did not percieve that what his countrymen had been trained to expect and to admire in the tragic drama "was a set of circumstances peculiar to that play, with a set of characters common to all French plays in general, the mesdames et seigneurs of the spanish cid of corneille, the jewish athalie of racine, and the grecian mérope of voltaire" himself.

How widely the ideal of tragedy upheld by the french dramatists under louis xv differed from that pursued by the English playwrights under Elizabeth, and also from that followed by the Greek poets under Pericles, was made plain by Voltaire's own formal declaration in which he set up a standard of tragedy as he understood it:

"To compact an illustrious and interesting event into the space of two or three hours; to make the characters appear only when they ought to come forth; never to leave the stage empty; to put together a plot as probable as it is attractive; to say nothing unnecessary; to instruct the mind and move the heart; to be always eloquent in verse with the eloquence proper to each character represented; to speak one's tongue with the same purity as in the most chastened prose, without allowing the effort of rhyming to seem to hamper the thought; to permit no single line to be hard or obscure or declamatory; these are the conditions which nowadays one insists upon in a tragedy." From this explicit definition it is evident that Voltaire regarded tragedy as a work of the intelligence rather than of the imagination; and it might even be inferred that he distrusted the imagination, and that he thought that the intelligence could be aided in the accomplishment of its task by the rules.

The rules of the theater, including that of the Three Unities, had been adopted in France in the seventeenth century largely because Corneille had given his adhesion to them, although they held him in bondage he could not but feel; and they were maintained in France in the eighteenth century very largely because of the authority of Voltaire, who was ever ready to reproach Corneille for every chance dereliction and to denounce Shakespeare for every open disregard of dramatic decorum. The weight of Voltaire's authority was acknowledged not only in France but throughout Europe. His plays were translated and acted in the various languages of civilization; and his opinions about the theater were received with acquiescence in Italy, in Germany, and in England. It is true that in England, while the professed critics deplored the lamentable lack of taste shown by their rude forefathers, they themselves continued to enjoy the actual performances of the vigorous plays of the Elizabethan dramatists. It is true that in Italy the men-of-letters who accepted the rulings of Voltaire could take little more than an academic interest in the drama, since their theater was not flourishing, and even the comedy-of-masks seemd to be wearing itself out. It is true that in Germany also the theater was in a sorry condition, and that the German actors were often forced to perform in adaptations of French plays in default of native dramas worthy of consideration.

Charming as are certain of the comedies of Goldoni, they are slight in texture and superficial in character; and it is significant that Goldoni himself felt it advisable to leave his native land and to go to Paris to push his fortunes. Significant is it also of the increasing cosmopolitanism of the theater toward the end of the century that the plot of one of Goldoni's Italian comedies was utilized by Voltaire, whose French play was adapted into English by the elder Colman. Lofty as are the tragedies of Alfieri they have a scholarly rigidity as if they were intended rather for the closet than the stage, although the simplicity of their structure has made it possible to present them in the actual theater. Italy in the eighteenth century was sunk in corruption or busy with petty intrigue; and it was devoid of the energy of will which is the vital element of the drama. Not only was there little expectation or even hope of national unity; there was in fact but little solidarity of feeling among those who spoke the language.

The French people, and the English also, were each of them conscious of their nationality and proud of it; but the Italians were like the Germans in having neither pride nor consciousness. Italy was only a geographical expression then; and no fervid lyrist had yet proclaimed the large limits of the German fatherland. The Italians and the Germans, whatever their merits as individuals, were then as peoples too infirm of purpose and too lax of will to be ripe for an outflowering of the drama such as might follow hard upon the achievement of national unity and the establishment of a national capital. Very important indeed is the contribution which a city can make to the development of a dramatic literature; and not only in Athens but also Madrid, London, and Paris have deserved well of all lovers of the drama.

V

Although the Germans had then no centre of national life and had not yet felt the need of it, they had given more proof of resolution than the Italians; and it was in the eighteenth century that Frederick laid the firm foundation of the national unity to be achieved more than a century later. It was in Germany again that there arose a stalwart antagonist to withstand Voltaire, to destroy the universal belief in the infallibility of French criticism, and to disestablish the pseudo-classicism which needed to be swept aside before a rebirth of the drama was possible. Lessing was the best equipped and the most broad-minded critic of aesthetic theory who had come forward since Aristotle; and he had not a little of the great Greek's commingled keenness and common sense.

The German critic was not so disinterested as Aristotle; indeed, what strikes us now as the sole defect of his stimulating study of the drama is its polemic tone. It was in the stress of a contemporary controversy that Lessing set forth eternal principles of the dramatic art. He went into the arena with the zest of a trained athlete; and he was never afraid to try a fall with Voltaire himself. In fact, it was especially in the hope of a grapple with the French dictator of the republic of letters that the German kept his loins girded.

Lessing had not only a courage of his own: he had also the solid learning of his race. He was a scholar, thoroughly grounded and widely read. He knew at first hand the Greek drama and the Latin; he was acquainted with Shakespeare and with Lope de Vega in the original; he was thoroughly familiar with the French theater, and with the criticisms made against it in Paris itself. Original as Lessing was, he profited by the suggestions of his predecessors, and there is no reason now to deny his immediate indebtedness to Diderot. The French critic it was who pointed out the path, but only the German critic was able to attain the goal. What Diderot had happened merely to indicate in passing, Lessing, with his wider knowledge of life, of literature, and of art, was able to accomplish. He took up the French rules of theater with their insistence on the alleged Three Unities, and he was able to show the baselessness of the claim that they are derived from the practice or the precepts of the ancients. Then he went further and pointed out the inherent absurdity of these factitious restrictions and their fettering effect upon the French dramatic poet, even when they were kept only in letter and broken in spirit.

Lessing destroyed the superstitious reverence for the French theories; but he could build up as well as tear down. German literature was then at its feeblest period; and such original German pieces as might exist were almost as pitiful as the week limitations of French tragedy. The German theater was battling for life; it was barren of plays worthy of good acting; it was almost as deficient in good actors capable of doing justice to a fine drama; and it attracted scant and uncultivated audiences without standards of comparison and therefore with little appreciation of either the dramaturgic art or the histrionic. Like Aristotle, Lessing had grasped the complex nature of the dramatic art, with the necessary correlations of playwright and player; and, like Aristotle again, he never thought of a drama as a work of pure literature but always as something intended to be performed by actors, in a theater, before an audience. The French imitations Lessing strove to eliminate by substitution,—by providing plays of his own which should be native to Germany in motive and in temper, and which might serve as the foundation for a national drama. He was almost as successful in this constructive effort as he had been in his destructive labors.

A critic Lessing was, no doubt, but a critic who had the rare ability to practice what he preached. It at least three plays he revealed himself as a true dramatist, as a man who had mastered the craft of play-making, and who could present on the stage the essential scenes of a struggle between contending forces embodied in vital characters. The proof of the play is in the acting always; and lowell did not hesitate to assert that minna von barnhelm and emilia galotti act "better than anything of goethe or schiller." In justification of lowell's assertion it may be noted that these two plays are nowadays seen in the german theaters quite as often as any two dramas of either goethe or schiller.

Emilia galotti and miss sara sampson are tragedies of middle-class life, tragédies bourgeoises, owing something to the precept of diderot and owing perhaps more to the practice of the english dramatists, whom lessing had also admired. Although his style is noble and direct, he is not primarily a poet, with a poet's instinctive happiness in finding the illuminative phrase. His culture, his formidable instruction, his resolute thinking, unite to give certain of his dramas a richness of texture uncommon enough in popular plays. Minna von barnhelm is a comedy, not tearful exactly, nor yet mirthful, rather cheerful, even if grave in spirit. Lessing was scarcely every gay, although he could be witty enough on occasion. His dialogue has sometimes a Gallic ease, and it has always a Teutonic sincerity. MINNA is the best of his plays; it is brisk in action, lively in incident, and ingeniously contrived throughout.

Perhaps the model of which Lessing availed himself unconsciously when his serious plays were taking shape in his mind, was that suggested by Molière's larger and later comedies. But with his practicality and his perfect comprehension of the conditions of the modern theater, Lessing made one important modification in the form of the drama which Molière had supplied. Where the Frenchman, dealing only with the crisis of Tartuffe's career in Orgon's house, had no difficulty in concentrating the action into a single day and a single spot, the German, rejecting the Unity of Time and the Unity of Place, held himself at liberty to protract the action over so long a period as he might find advisable, and to change the scene as often as he might see fit. But Lessing perceived the advantage of not distracting the attention of the audience by changes of scene during the progress of the act; and he therefore made his removals from place to place while the curtain was down. He was apparently the first playwright who gave to each act its own scenery, not to be changed until the fall of the curtain again. Here he supplied an example now followed by the most accomplished playwrights of the twentieth century.

VI

In this avoiding of the confusion resulting from frequent shifting of the scenery before the eyes of the spectators, Lessing was more modern than either goethe or schiller, both of whom—especially in their earlier dramatic efforts, in the goetz of the one and in the robbers of the other—appeared to hold that the example of shakespeare warranted their returning to the more medieval practice of making as many changes of place as a loosely constructed plot might seem to require. Lowell suggested that there was "in the national character an insensibility to proportion" which would "account for the perpetual groping of german imaginative literature after some foreign mold in which to cast its thought or feeling, now trying a louis quatorze pattern, then something supposed to be Shakespearian, and at last going back to ancient Greece."

Nowadays Goethe's surpassing genius is everywhere acknowledged,—his comprehensive and insatiable curiosity, his searching interrogation of life, his power of self-expression in almost every department of literature. But great poet as he was, a theater-poet he was not. He was not a born playwright, seizing with unconscious certainty upon the necessary scenes, the scènes a faire, to bring out the conflict of will against will which was the heart of his theme. He lacked the instinctive perception of the exact effect likely to be produced on the audience, and he was deficient in the intuitive knowledge of the best method to appeal to the sympathies of the spectators. In fact, the time came in Goethe's career as a dramatic poet when he refused to reckon with the playgoers who might be present at the performance of his plays,—an attitude inconceivable on the part of a true dramatist and as remote as possible from that taken by Sophocles, by Shakespeare, and by Molière. When he was director of the theater in Weimar he did not hesitate to assert that "the public must be controlled." A more enlightened tyrant than Goethe no theater could ever hope to have; and yet little more than sterility and emptiness was the net result of his theatrical dictatorship and of his refusal to consider the native preferences of the Weimar playgoers.

It was Victor Hugo who once declared that the audience in a theater can be divided into three classes, the crowd which expects to see action, women, who are best pleased with passion, and thinkers, who are hoping to behold character. The main body of playgoers has always wanted to be amused by the spectacle of something happening before their eyes; and many of them, including nearly all women, desire to have their sympathies excited; but it is only a chosen few who go to the theater seeking food for thought and ready, therefore, to welcome psychologic subtlety and philosophic profundity. The great dramatists have been able to satisfy the demands of all three classes; and oedipus the king, hamlet, and tartuffe were popular with the plain people from their first performance. But goethe seemed to care for the approval of only the smallest class of the three; and only in faust did he reveal the dramaturgic skill needed to devise an action interesting enough in itself to bear whatever burden of philosophy he might wish to lay upon it.

Even in his early plays, in goetz von berlichingen, for example, in which there is action enough and emotion also, there is no felicity of stagecraft. It purports only to be a chronicle-play; but although afterward reshaped for the stage, it was not conceived to suit the conditions of the actual theater. Clavigo, however, which is only a dramatized anecdote, an unpretending improvisation, swift in its action and clear in its handling of contending motives, is effective on the boards; and as a stage-play it is perhaps the most satisfactory of all goethe's dramatic attempts, trifle as it is after all, devoid of either poetry or philosophy. Iphigenia is a dramatic poem rather than a play; and egmont is little more than a novel in dialogue. So fraternal a critic as schiller confessed that he found iphigenia to be wanting in "the sensuous power, the life, the agitation, and everything which specifically belongs to a dramatic work." But if final proof is needed that goethe, however various and powerful as a poet, was not a born playwright, it can be found, outside his own attempts at dramatic form, in his alteration of romeo and juliet. In this he not only modified and condensed both mercutio and the nurse, but he also substituted a tame narrative for shakespeare's skillful and spirited exposition by which the quarrel of the two families was brought bodily before our eyes.

VII

A theater-poet schiller was, even if goethe was not; yet schiller's first drama, the robbers, was not written for performance,—although it soon found its way to the stage-door, after the poet had somewhat restrained its boyish extravagance. Schiller rejected the model he could have found in lessing's tragedies of middle-class life, a model too severe for the tumultuous turbulence of the storm-and-stress period. He followed goethe, who, in goetz, had claimed the right to be formless as shakespeare was supposed to be. There is in the robbers a certain resemblance to the crude elizabethan tragedy-of-blood with its perfervid grandiloquence and its frequent assassination.

In this first play schiller's stagecraft was primitive and unworthy; he shifted his scenes with wanton carelessness, and he let his absurd villain turn himself inside out in interminable soliloquies. But however reckless the technique, the play revealed schiller's abundant possession of genuine dramatic power. The conflict of contending passions was set before the spectator in scenes full of fire and action. The antithesis of moor's two sons, one strenuously noble and the other unspeakably vile, was rather forced, but it was at least obvious even to the stupidest playgoer. The hero lacked common sense, no doubt; but he had energy to spare; and at the end he rose to tragic elevation in his willingness to expiate his wrong-doing.

Dramatist as Schiller was by native gift, he was but a novice in the theater when the ROBBERS was written, and it was the fitting of that play to the actual stage which drew his attention to the inexorable conditions of theatrical performance. In his later dramas, in william tell, for example, and in mary stuart, the technique is less elementary and more in accord with the practice of the contemporary playhouse. But schiller appears to have been thinking rather of his readers than of the spectators massed and expectant in the theater. He seems to have taken no keen interest in spying out the secrets of the stage. His plays are what they are by sheer dramatic power, and not by reason of any adroitness of technique. Indeed, in Schiller's day the German theater was almost in chaos; and probably he never saw any satisfactory performance of a dramatic masterpiece, German or French or English, until he went to Weimar.

Despite his limitations, Schiller was the one dramatic poet of the eighteenth century; he is to be compared, not with Sophocles and Shakespeare, the supreme masters, but rather with Calderon and Hugo. He lacked their conscious control of theatrical effect, but he had something of their rhetorical luxuriance and their exuberant lyricism. He was intellectually deeper than the Spaniard and he was more masculine than the Frenchman. Schiller's influence on the later development of the drama would have been fuller if his structure had been more modern and if he had profited earlier by the example of Lessing, emulating the great critic's certainty of artistic aim and imitating his rigorous self-control.

But self-control was rarely a characteristic of German poets in those days of impending cataclysm. Lessing had emancipated his countrymen from the tyranny of French taste, from the despotism of pseudo-classicism. Other despotisms survived in Germany, not in literature but in life itself; and a younger generation was ardent for the destruction of these survivals from the middle ages. In Lessing's play the father of Emilia Galotti slew his daughter to preserve her honor, while the evil ruler who was responsible escaped scot-free. In GOETZ and in the ROBBERS the aggrieved hero was ready to turn outlaw on slight provocation, and to revenge individual injuries on society at large. The ROBBERS especially had the super-saturated sentimentality of the last half of the eighteenth century; and it was filled with the clamor of revolt, which was to reverberate louder and louder throughout Europe until at last the tocsin tolled in the streets of Paris and the French Revolution was let loose to sweep away feudalism forever.

VIII

THE most of the German dramas of this period of unrest were not intended for the actual theater, although many of them did manage to get themselves acted here and there. With all their wild bombast and with all their overstrained emotionalism, they were not without a significance and a vitality of their own, a freshness of self-expression wholly lacking on the German stage before Lessing had inspired it. If these dramas had been controlled by something of Lessing's self-restraint, if they had been less excessive in their violence, they might have afforded shelter for the growth of a dramatic literature native to the soil and national in spirit. But they were not healthy enough, and they soon fell into decay; and what did burgeon from their matted roots was the melodrama of Kotzebue, with its exaggeration of motive, its hollow affectation, and its tawdry pathos. Kotzebue's taste is dubious and his methods now outworn; but his play-making gift is as undeniable as that of heywood before him or that of scribe after him. Misanthropy and repentance, known in england as the stranger, has caused as many tears to flow as a woman killed with kindness; and whereas heywood's simply pathetic play was known to his contemporaries only in the land of its language, kotzebue's turgid treatment of the same theme was performed in all the tongues of europe, in paris and london and new york as well as in vienna and berlin.

Melodrama bears much the same relation to tragedy and to the loftier type of serious play that farce does to pure comedy. When we can recall more readily what the persons of a play do than what they are, then the probability is that the piece if gay is a farce, and if grave a melodrama. Even among the tragedies of the Greeks we can detect more than one drama which was melodramatic rather than truly tragic; and not a few of the powerful plays of the Elizabethans were essentially melodramas. So also were some of Corneille's, though they masqueraded as tragedies and conformed to the rules of the pseudo-classics. Yet it was only in the eighteenth century that melodrama plainly differentiated itself from every other dramatic species.

The "tradesmen's tragedies" of Lillo and Moore in England and the tearful-comedies of La Chaussée and Sedaine in France had helped along its development; but it was Kotzebue in Germany who was able at last to reveal its large possibilities. In the pieces which the German playwright was prolific in bringing forth there was something exactly suited to the temper of the times; and this helped to make his vogue cosmopolitan.

He was the earliest play-maker whose dramas were instantly plagiarized everywhere; and in this he was the predecessor of Scribe and Sardou. He influenced men like Lewis in England and like Pixérécourt and Ducange in France. In the works of the Parisian playwrights there was a deftness of touch not visible in the pieces of Kotzebue, who was heavy-handed; as Amiel once suggested, it is not unusual to see "the Germans heap the fagots for the pile, the French bring the fire." It was this French modification of eighteenth century German melodrama which was to serve as a model for French romanticist drama in the nineteenth century.

A century is only an artificial period of time adopted for the sake of convenience and corresponding to no logical division of literary history. None the less we are able to perceive in once century or another certain marked characteristics.

No doubt every century is more or less an era of transition; but surely the eighteenth century seems to deserve the description better than most. For nearly three quarters of its career, it appears to us as prosaic in many of its aspects, dull and gray and uninteresting; but it was ever a battle-ground for contending theories of literature and of life. In the drama more especially it was able to behold the establishment and the disestablishment of pseudo-classicism.

At its beginning the influence of the French had won wide-spread acceptance for the rules with their insistence on the Three Unities and on the separation of the comic and the tragic. At its end every rule was being violated wantonly; and the drama itself seemed almost as lawless as the bandits it delighted in bringing on the stage so abundantly. Throughout Europe, except in France, the theater had broken its bonds; and even in France, the last stronghold of the theorists, freedom was to come early in the nineteenth century. Lessing had undermined the fortress of pseudo-classicism; and the walls of its last citadel were to fall with a crash at the first blast on the trumpet of Hernani.

Chapter 7

The way of the World

William Congreve's The Way of the World is the best-written, the most dazzling, the most intellectually accomplished of all English comedies, perhaps of all the comedies of the world. But it has the defects of the very qualities which make it so brilliant. A perfect comedy does not sparkle so much, is not so exquisitely written, because it needs to advance, to develop. To The Way of the World may be applied that very dubious compliment paid by Mrs. Browning to Landor's Pentameron that, "were it not for the necessity of getting through a book, some of the pages are too delicious to turn over." The beginning of the third act, the description of Mirabell's feelings in the opening scene, and many other parts of The Way of the World, are not to be turned over, but to be re-read until the psychological subtlety of the sentiment, the perfume of the delicately chosen phrases, the music of the sentences, have produced their full effect upon the nerves. But, meanwhile, what of the action?

The reader dies of a rose in aromatic pain, but the spectator fidgets in his stall, and wishes that the actors and actresses would be doing something. In no play of Congreve's is the literature so consummate, in none is the human interest in movement and surprise so utterly neglected, as in The Way of the World. The Old Bachelor, itself, is theatrical in comparison. We have slow, elaborate dialogue, spread out like some beautiful endless tapestry, and no action whatever. Nothing happens, nothing moves, positively from one end of The Way of the World to the other, and the only reward of the mere spectator is the occasional scene of wittily contrasted dialogue, Millamant pitted against Sir Wilful, Witwoud against Petulant, Lady Wishfort against her maid. With an experienced audience, prepared for an intellectual pleasure, the wit of these polished fragments would no doubt encourage a cultivation of patience through less lively portions of the play, but to spectators coming perfectly fresh to the piece, and expecting rattle and movement, this series of still-life pictures may easily be conceived to be exasperating, especially as the satire contained in them was extremely sharp and direct.

Very slight record has been preserved of the manner in which The Way of the World was acted. The only part which seems to have been particularly distinguished was that of Mrs. Leigh in Lady Wishfort. Mrs. Bracegirdle, of course, was made for the part of Millamant, and her appearance in the second act, "with her fan spread and her streamers out, and a shoal of fools for tenders," was carefully prepared; yet we hear nothing of the effect produced. Mrs. Barry took the disagreeable character of Mrs. Marwood, and Betterton had no special chance for showing his qualities in Fainall. Witwoud and Petulant, who keep some of the scenes alive with their sallies, were Bower and Bowman, and Underhill played Sir Wilful. It is very tantalizing, and quite unaccountable, that no one seems to have preserved any tradition of the acting of this magnificent piece.

In The Way of the World, as in The Old Bachelor, Congreve essayed a stratagem which Molière tried but once, in Le Misanthrope. It is one which is likely to please very much or greatly to annoy. It is the stimulation of curiosity all through the first act, without the introduction of one of the female characters who are described and, as it were, promised to the audience. It is probable that in the case of The Way of the World it was hardly a success. The analysis of character and delicate intellectual writing in the first act, devoid as it is of all stage-movement, may possibly have proved very tedious to auditors not subtle enough to enjoy Mirabell's account of the effect which Millamant's faults have upon him, or Witwoud's balanced depreciation of his friend Petulant. Even the mere reader discovers that the whole play brightens up after the entrance of Millamant, and probably that apparition is delayed too long. From this point, to the end of the second act, all scintillates and sparkles; and these are perhaps the most finished pages, for mere wit, in all existing comedy. The dialogue is a little metallic, but it is burnished to the highest perfection; and while one repartee rings against the other, the arena echoes as with shock after shock in a tilting-bout. In comparison with what we had had before Congreve's time that was best—with The Man of Mode, for instance, and with The Country Wife the literary work in The Way of the World is altogether more polished, the wit more direct and effectual, the art of the comic poet more highely developed. There are fewer square inches of the canvas which the painter has roughly filled in, and neglected to finish; there is more that consciously demands critical admiration, less that can be, in Landor's phrase, pared away.

Why, then, did this marvellous comedy fail to please? Partly, no doubt, on account of its scholarly delicacy, too fine to hold the attention of the pit, and partly also, as we have seen, because of its too elaborate dialogue and absence of action. But there was more than this. Congreve was not merely a comedian, he was a satirist also—asper jocum tentavit. He did not spare the susceptibilities of his fine ladies. His Cabal-Night at Lady Wishfort's is the direct original of Sheridan's School for Scandal; but in some ways the earlier picture is the more biting, the more disdainful. Without posing as a Timon or a Diogenes, and so becoming himself an object of curious interest, Congreve adopted the cynical tone, and threads the brightly-coloured crowd of social figures with a contemptuous smile upon his lips. When we come to speak of his plays as a whole, we shall revert to this trait, which is highly characteristic of his genius; it is here enough to point out that this peculiar air of careless superiority, which is decidedly annoying to audiences, reaches its climax in the last of Congreve's comedies.

We have spoken with high praise of the end of the second act; but perhaps even this is surpassed in the third act by Lady Wishfort's unparalleled disorder at the sight of her complexion, "an arrant ash-colour, as I'm a person," and her voluble commands to her maid; or, in the fourth act, by the scene in which Millamant walks up and down the room reciting tags from the poets, not noticing Sir Wilful, the country clodpole squire, "ruder than Gothic," who takes the ejaculation, "Natural easy Suckling!" as a description of himself. It is to be noticed, as a proof that this play, in spite of its misfortunes, has made a deep impression on generations of hearers and readers, that it is fuller than any other of Congreve's plays of quotations that have become part of the language. It is from The Way of the World, for instance, that we take—"To drink is a Christian diversion unknown to the Turk and the Persian"; while it would be interesting to know whether it is by a pure coincidence that Tennyson, in perhaps the most famous of all his phrases, comes so near to Congreve's "'Tis better to have been left, than never to have been loved."

Chapter 8

The Comedies of William Congreve

Before repeating such known facts of Congreve's life as seem agreeable to the present occasion, and before attempting (with the courage of one's office) to indicate with truth what manner of man he was, and what are the varying qualities of his four comedies, it seems well to discuss and have done with two questions, obviously pertinent indeed, but of a wider scope than the works of any one writer. The first is a stupid question, which may be happily dismissed with brief ceremony. Grossness of language the phrase is an assumption—is a matter of time and place, a relative matter altogether. There is a thing, and a generation finds a name for it. The delicacy which prompts a later generation to reject that name is by no means necessarily a result of stricter habits, is far more often due to the flatness which comes of untiring repetition and to the greater piquancy of litotes. I am told that there are, or were, people in America who reject the word 'leg' as a gross word, but they must have found a synonym. So there is not a word in Congreve for which there is not some equivalent expression in contemporary writing. He says this or that: your modern writers say so-and-so. One man may even think the monosyllables in better taste than the periphrases. Another may sacrifice to his intolerance thereof such enjoyment as he was capable of taking from the greatest triumphs of diction or observation: he is free to choose. It may be granted that to one unfamiliar with the English of two centuries since the grossness of Congreve's language may seem excessive—like splashes of colour occurring too frequently in the arrangement of a wall. But that is merely a result of novelty: given time and habit, a more artistic perspective will be achieved.

The second question is more complex. Since Jeremy Collier let off his _Short View of the Immorality and Profaneness of the English Stage_, there has never lacked a critic to chastise or to deplore the more effective and irritating course—not simply the coarseness but, the immorality of our old comedies, their attitude towards and their peculiar interests in life. Without affirming that we are now come to the Golden Age of criticism, one may rejoice that modern methods have taught quite humble critics to discriminate between issues, and to deal with such a matter as this with some mental detachment. The great primal fallacy comes from a habit of expecting everything in everything. Just as in a picture it is not enough for some people that it is well drawn and well painted, but they demand an interesting story, a fine sentiment, a great thought: so since our national glory is understood to be the happy home, the happy home must be triumphant everywhere, even in satiric comedy. The best expression of this fallacy is in Thackeray. Concluding a most eloquent, and a somewhat patronising examination of Congreve, 'Ah!' he exclaims, 'it's a weary feast, that banquet of wit where no love is.' The answer is plain: comedy of manners is comedy of manners, and satire is satire; introduce 'love'—an appeal, one supposes, to sympathy with strictly legitimate and common affection and a glorification of the happy home—and the rules of your art compel you to satirise affection and to make the happy home ridiculous: a truly deplorable work, which the incriminated dramatists were discreet enough for the most part to avoid.

The remark brings us to the first of the half-truths, which cause the complexity of the subject. The dramatists whose withers the well-intentioned and disastrous Collier wrung seem to have thought their best answer was to pose as people with a mission—certainly Congreve so posed—to reform the world with an exhibition of its follies. An amusing answer, no doubt, of which the absurdity is obvious! It does, however, contain a half-truth. The idea of _The Way of the World's_ reforming adulterers—observe the quotation from Horace on the title-page—is a little delicious; yet the exhibition in a ludicrous light of the thing satirised is surely an end of satiric comedy? The right of the matter is indicated in a sentence which occurs in the dedication of _The Double- Dealer_ far more wisely than in Congreve's answer to Collier: 'I should be very glad of an opportunity to make my compliment to those ladies who are offended: but they can no more expect it in a comedy, than to be tickled by a surgeon, when he's letting 'em blood.' Something more than a half-truth is in Charles Lamb's theory, that the old comedy 'has no reference whatever to the world that is': that it is 'the Utopia of Gallantry' merely. Literally, historically, the theory is a fantasy.

What the Restoration dramatists did not borrow from France was inspired directly by the court of Charles the Second, and nobody conversant with the memoirs of that court can have any difficulty in matching the fiction with reality. I imagine that Congreve in part accepted a tradition of the stage, but I am also perfectly well assured that he depicted what he saw. How far the virtues we should associate with the Charles the Second spirit may atone for its vices is a question which would take us far into moral philosophy. It is enough to remark that those vices are the exclusive possession of no period: so long as society is constituted in anything like its present order, there must be a section of it for which those vices are the main interest in life. But Charles Lamb's gay and engaging defiance of the kill-joys of his day has this value: it is most certainly just to say that, in appreciating satiric comedy, 'our coxcombical moral sense' must be 'for a little transitory ease excluded.'

For one may apprehend the whole truth to be somewhat thus. Satiric comedy, or comedy of manners, is the art of making ludicrous in dramatic form some phase of life. The writers of our old comedy thought that certain vices—gambling, adultery, and the like—formed a phase of life which for divers reasons, essential and accidental, lent itself best to their purpose. They may, or may not, have thought they were doing society a service: their real justification is that, as artists, they had to take for their art that material they could use best. They used it according to their lights: Wycherley with a coarse and heavy hand, so that it became nauseous; Etherege with a light touch and a gay perception; Congreve with an instinct of good-breeding, with a sure and extensive observation, and with an incomparable style.

But all were justified in choosing for their material just what they chose. They sinned artistically, now here, now there; but to complain of this old comedy as a whole, that vice in it is crammed too closely, is to forget that a play is a picture, not a photograph, of life—is life arranged and coloured—and that comedy of manners is composed of foibles or vices condensed and relieved by one another. In so far as they overdid this work, the comic writers were artistically at fault, and Jeremy Collier was a good critic; but when he and his successors go beyond the artistic objection, one takes leave to say, they misapprehend the thing criticised.

To complain that 'love' and common morality have no place in satiric comedy is either to contemplate ridicule of them or to ask comedy to be other than satiric. We know what happened when the dramatists gave way: there followed, Hazlitt says, 'those _do-me-good_, lack-a-daisical, whining, make-believe comedies in the next age, which are enough to set one to sleep, and where the author tries in vain to be merry and wise in the same breath.' These in place of 'the court, the gala day of wit and pleasure, of gallantry, and Charles the Second!' And all because people would not keep their functions distinct, and remember that at a comedy they were in a court of art and not in a court of law! The old comedy is dead, and its spirit gone from the stage: I have but endeavoured to show that no harm need come to our phylacteries, if a flame start from its ashes in the printed book.

II

William Congreve was born at Bardsey, near Leeds, and was baptized on 10th February 1669 [1670]. The Congreves were a Staffordshire family, of an antiquity of four hundred years at the date of the poet's birth. Richard, his grandfather, was a redoubtable Cavalier, and William, his father, an officer in the army. The latter was given a command at Youghal, while his son was still an infant, and becoming shortly afterwards agent to Lord Cork, removed to Lismore. So it chanced that the poet had his schooling at Kilkenny, and proceeded to Trinity College, Dublin, in 1685, rejoining Swift, and like his friend becoming a pupil of St. George Ashe, the mathematician. In 1688 he left Dublin, remained with his people in Staffordshire for some two years, entered himself at the Temple, and came upon the town with _The Old Bachelor_ in January 1692. _The Double-Dealer_ was produced in November 1693.

In 1694 a storm in the theatre led to a secession of Betterton and other renowned players from Drury Lane: with the result that a new playhouse was opened in Lincoln's Inn Fields, on 30th April 1695, with _Love for Love_. In the same year Congreve was appointed 'Commissioner for Licensing Hackney Coaches.' _The Mourning Bride_ was produced in 1697, and was followed, oddly enough, by the controversy, or rather 'row,' with Jeremy Collier. In March 1700 came _The Way of the World_. The poet was made Commissioner of Wine-Licences in 1705, and in 1714 with his Jamaica secretaryship and his places in the Customs and the delightful 'Pipe-Office,' he had an income of twelve hundred pounds a year. He died at his house in Surrey Street, Strand, on 19th January 1728 [1729].

One or two comments on these dates are obvious. They dissipate the Thackerayan fable that on the production of _The Old Bachelor_, the fortunate young author received a shower of sinecures, 'all for writing a comedy.' 'And crazy Congreve scarce could spare A shilling to discharge a chair,' writes Swift, and 'crazy' indicates that Congreve was gouty before he was rich. But then, the gout was a very early factor in his life, and one may call the line an exaggeration. Another couplet: 'Thus Congreve spent in writing plays, And one poor office, half his days:' probably expresses the truth. With his plays and his hackney coaches he doubtless got through his twenties and thirties with no very hardly grinding poverty, and at forty or so was comfortably secure. But another fact, which the dates bring out very sharply, has a different interest. At an age when Swift was beginning to try his powers, Congreve's work was done. A few odes, a few letters he was still to write, but no more comedies. Was it ill-health? or because the town had all but damned his greatest play? or because he cared more for life than for art?

III

The question brings one to an attempted appreciation of the man. Mr. Gosse, for whose _Life_ I would express my gratitude, confesses that 'it is not very easy to construct a definite portrait of Congreve.' But that it baffled that very new journalist, Mrs. Manley, in his own day, and Mr. Gosse, with his information, in ours, to give 'salient points' to Congreve's character, proves in itself an essential characteristic, which need be negatively stated only by choice. That no amusing eccentricities are recorded, no ludicrous adventures, no persistent quarrels, implies, taken with other facts we know, that he was a well-bred man of the world, with the habit of society: that in itself is a definite personal quality. One supposes him an ease-loving man, not inclined to clown for the amusement of his world. He was loved by his friends, being tolerant, and understanding the art of social life. He was successful, and must therefore have had enemies, but he was careless to improve hostilities.

For the temperament which is so plain in the best of his writings must have been present in his life—an unobtrusive, because a never directly implied, superiority and an ironical humour. The picture of swaggering snobbishness which Thackeray was inspired to make of him is proved bad by all that we know. A swaggerer could not have made a fast friend of Dryden—grown mellow, indeed, but by no means beggared of his fire—on his first coming to town, nor kept the intimacy of Swift, nor avoided the fault-finding of Dennis. It is quite unnecessary to suppose that Congreve's famous remark to Voltaire, that he wished to be visited as a plain gentleman, was the remark of a snob: it was clearly a legitimate deprecation, spoken by a man who had written nothing notable for twenty-six years, which Voltaire misunderstood in a moment of stupidity, or in one of forgetfulness misrepresented. His superiority and his irony came from a just sense of the perspective of things, and, not preventing affection for his friends, left him indifferent to his foes. Probably, also, a course of dissipation (at which Swift hints) in his youth, acting on a temperament not particularly ardent, had left him with such passions for war and love as were well under control. The two women with whom his name is connected were Mrs. Bracegirdle and the Duchess of Marlborough; but nobody knew—though the latter's mother hinted the worst—how far the intimacy went. That is to say, no patent scandal was necessary to the connexion, if in either case Congreve was a lover. And Congreve was a gentleman.

But why did he become sterile at thirty? Where, if not in dealing with motives and causes, may one be fancy-free? Here there are many, of which the first to be given is mere conjecture, but conjecture, I fancy, not inconsistent with such facts as are known. When Congreve produced his first comedy, he was but twenty-three, fresh from college and the country, ignorant, as we are told, of the world. He discovered very soon that he had an aptitude for social life, that, no doubt, living humours and follies were as entertaining as printed ones, that for a popular and witty man the world was pleasant. But no man may be socially finished all at once.

In the course of the seven years between _The Old Bachelor and The Way of the World, Congreve must have found his wit becoming readier, his tact surer, his appreciation of natural comedy finer and (as personal keenness decreased) more equable, his popularity greater, and—in fine the world more pleasant and the attractions of the study waning and waning in comparison. He was a finished artist, he was born, one might almost say, with a style; but his inclination was to put his art into life rather than into print. Even in our days (thank God for all His mercies!) everybody is not writing a book. There are people whose talk has inimitable touches, and whose lives are art, but who never sit down to a quire of foolscap. I believe that Congreve naturally was one of these, that his literary ambition was a result of accidental necessity, and that had he lived as a boy in the society he was of as a very young man—for all its literary ornaments—we should have had of him only odes and songs. His generation was idler and took itself less seriously than ours. The primal curse was not imposed on everybody as a duty.

In seven years of growing appreciation Congreve came to think the little graces and humours the better part. That I believe to have been the first cause of his early sterility; but others helped to determine the effect. A certain indolence is of course implied in what has been said. There was the gout, and there were his unfortunate obesity and his failing sight. There was Henrietta, Duchess of Marlborough, an absorbing dame. There were the success of_Love for Love_ and the failure of The Way of the World.

For all that may be said of the indifference of the true artist to the verdict of the many-headed beast—and Congreve's contempt was as fine as any—it is not amusing when your play or your book falls flat, and Congreve must have known that he might write another, and possibly a better, _Way of the World_, but no more _Love for Loves_. Not to anticipate a later division of the subject, it may be said here that a man of thirty, of a fine intellect and a fine taste, of a languid habit withal, and with an invalided constitution, while he might repeat the triumphs of diction and intellect of _The Way of the World_, was most unlikely to return to the broader humours and the more popular gaiety of the other play. Congreve, like Rochester before him, despised the judgment of the town in these matters, but by the town he would have to be judged.

He was a witty, handsome man of the world, of imperturbable temper and infinite tact, who could make and keep the friendship of very various men, and be intimate with a woman without quarrelling with her lovers. He had a taste for pictures and a love for music. He must have hated violence and uproar, and liked the finer shades of life. He wore the mode of his day, and was free from the superficial protests of the narrow- minded. Possibly not a very 'definite portrait,' possibly a very negative characterisation. Possibly, also, a tolerably sure foundation for a structure of sympathetic imagination.

IV

Passing from necessarily vague and not obviously pertinent remarks to criticism, which may fairly be less diffident, we leave Congreve's life and come to his work, to his 'tawdry playhouse taper,' as Thackeray called it. It is only after the man has appeared that we recognise that he came at the hour; but the nature of the hour is in this case not difficult to be discerned. The habit of playgoing was well-established; the turmoil of the Revolution was over; De Jure was at a comfortable distance, and De Facto's wife was a patroness of the arts. But playgoers had but to be shown something better than that they had, to discover that the convention of the Restoration needed new blood. A justification of its choice of material has been attempted: there is no inconsistency in affirming that the tendency to use it with a mere monotony of ribaldry was emphatic. Of this tendency the most notable and useful illustration is Wycherley, because in point of wit and dramatic skill he dwarfed his colleagues.

As Mr. Swinburne has said, the art of Congreve is different in kind, not merely in degree, from the cruder and more boisterous product of the 'brawny' dramatist. Happily, however, for his success, the difference was not instantly clear. His first play links him with Wycherley, not with that rare and faint embryo of the later Congreve, George Etherege. 'You was always a gentleman, Mr. George,' as the valet says in _Beau Austin_. Happily for his popularity Congreve first followed the more popular man. It is not, indeed, until he wrote his last play that he was a whole Etherege idealised, albeit a greater than Etherege in the meantime. The peculiar effect which Etherege achieved in _Sir Fopling Flutter_—at whom and with whom you laugh at once—was not sublimated (the fineness left, the faintness become firmness) until Congreve created Witwoud, the inimitable, in _The Way of the World.

At the very first Congreve had good fortune in his players. It was a brave time for them. True, their salaries were not wonderfully large. Colley Cibber complains of the days before the revolt in 1694: 'at what unequal salaries the hired actors were held by the absolute authority of their frugal masters, the patentees.' But the example was not faded of those gay days when they were the pets of the most artistic court that England has known: when great ladies carried Kynaston in his woman's dress to Hyde Park after the play, and the King was the most persistent and the most interested playgoer in his realm. They were not thus petted for irrelevant reasons—for their respectability, their piety, or their domestic virtues; and their recognition as artists by an artistic society did not spoil their art.

When Congreve started on his course of play- writing, Queen Mary kept up, in a measure, the amiable custom of her uncle. He was very fortunate in his casts. There was Betterton, first of all, the versatile, the restrained, and, witness everybody, the incomparable. There was Underhill, 'a correct and natural comedian'—one must quote Cibber pretty often in this connexion—not well suited, one must suppose, to play Setter to Betterton's Heartwell in _The Old Bachelor_, but by reason of his admirable assumption of stupidity to make an excellent Sir Sampson in _Love for Love_. There were Powel, Williams, Verbruggen, Bowen, and Dogget (Fondlewife in the first play: afterwards Ben Legend, a part which made his fame and turned his head)—all notable comedians. Kynaston, graceful in old age as he had been beautiful in youth, was not in _The Old Bachelor_, but created Lord Touchwood in _The Double-Dealer_. Mountfort had been murdered by my Lord Mohun, and Leigh had followed him to the grave, but their names lived in their wives. Mrs. Mountfort 'was mistress of more variety of humour than I ever knew in any one woman actress... nothing, though ever so barren, if within the bounds of nature, could be flat in her hands.'

Indeed 'she was so fond of humour, in what low part soever to be found, that she would make no scruple of defacing her fair form to come heartily into it'—assuredly a rare actress! About Mrs. Leigh Cibber is less enthusiastic, but grants her 'a good deal of humour': her old women were famous. Mrs. Barry was a stately, dignified actress, best, no doubt, in tragedy. Lastly, there was Mrs. Bracegirdle, the innocent _publica cura_, whom authors courted through their plays, and who had all the men in the house for longing lovers. Who shall say how far 'her youth and lively aspect' influenced the criticisms that have come down to us? She played Millamant to Congreve's satisfaction.

V

It is not difficult to understand how it was that Dryden thought _The Old Bachelor_ the best first play he had seen, and the town applauded to the echo. But it is a little hard to understand why later critics, with the three other comedies before them, have not more expressly marked the difference between the first and those. There is no new tune in _The Old Bachelor_: it is an old tune more finely played, and for that very reason it met with immediate acceptance. It is not likely that Dryden a great poet and a great and generous critic, it may be, but an old man—would have bestowed such unhesitating approval on a play which ignored the conventions in which he had lived. As it was, he saw those conventions reverently followed, yet served by a master wit. The fact that Congreve allowed Dryden and others to 'polish' his play, by giving it an air of the stage and the town which it lacked, need not of course spoil it for us. The stamp of Congreve is clearly marked on the dialogue, though not on every page.

You may see its essentials in two passages taken absolutely at random. 'Come, come,' says Bellmour in the very first scene, 'leave business to idlers and wisdom to fools; they have need of 'em: wit be my faculty and pleasure my occupation, and let Father Time shake his glass.' Or Fondlewife soliloquises: 'Tell me, Isaac, why art thee jealous? Why art thee distrustful of the wife of thy bosom? Because she is young and vigorous, and I am old and impotent. Then why didst thee marry, Isaac? Because she was beautiful and tempting, and because I was obstinate and doating....' In the one passage is the gay and skilfully light paradox, in the other the clean, rhythmical, and balanced, yet dramatic and appropriate English that are elements of Congreve's style. It is in the conventions of its characterisation that _The Old Bachelor_ belongs, not to true Congrevean comedy but, to that of the models from which he was to break away. The characterisation of _The Way of the World_ is light and true, that of _The Old Bachelor_ is heavy and yet vague. Vainlove indeed, the 'mumper in love,' who 'lies canting at the gate,' is individual and Congrevean. But Heartwell, the blustering fool, Bellmour, the impersonal rake, Wittol and Bluffe, the farcical sticks, Fondlewife, the immemorial city husband, and the troop of undistinguished women—what can be said of them but that they are glaring stage properties, speaking better English than the comic stage had before attracted?

Germs, possibly, of better things to come, that is all, so far as characterisation goes. The Fondlewife episode, in particular, which doubtless was mightily popular—what is there more in it than the mutton fisted wit and brutality of Wycherley, with some of Congreve's English? Such scenes as these, it may be hazarded, so contemptible in the light of Congreve's better work, are ineffective now because they fall between two stools: between the comedy of a crude physical fact, naked and impossible, as in Rochester, and the comedy of delicately-phrased intrigue. The latter was yet to come when this play was produced, and meantime such episodes went very well, and their popularity is intelligible.

For the rest _The Old Bachelor_, though to us in these days its plot appear a somewhat uninspiring piece of fairyland, was a good acting play, fitted with great skill to its actual players. The part of Fondlewife, created by Dogget, was on a revival played (to his own immense satisfaction) by Colley Cibber. In Araminta Mrs. Bracegirdle began (in a faint outline as it were) the series of lively, sympathetic, intelligent heroines which Congreve wrote for her. Lord Falkland's Prologue is as funny as it is indecently suggestive, which is saying a great deal. The one actually spoken gave an opportunity of the merriest archness to Mrs. Bracegirdle, and was calculated to put the audience in the best of good humours.

The faults of _The Double-Dealer_ are obvious on a first reading, and were very justly condemned on a first acting. The intrigue is wearisome: its involutions are ineffectively puzzling. Maskwell's villainy and Mellefont's folly are both unconvincing. The tragedy of Lady Touchwood, less tragic than that of Lady Wishfort in _The Way of the World_, is more obviously than that out of the picture. The play is, in fact, not pure comedy of manners: it is that _plus_ tragedy, an element less offensive than the sentimentality which spoils _The School for Scandal_, but yet a notable fault. For while you can resolve the tragedy of Lady Wishfort into wicked and very grim comedy, you can do nothing with the tragedy of Lady Touchwood but try to ignore it.

In his epistle dedicatory to Charles Montague, Congreve admits that his play has faults, but does not take in hand those adduced above, with the exception of the objections to Maskwell and Mellefont. 'They have mistaken cunning in one character for folly in another': an ineffectual answer, because the extremity of cunning is equally destructive of dramatic balance. He defends his use of soliloquy very warmly: of which it may be said that, so long as his rule—that no character may overhear the soliloquiser—is observed, it is a tolerable convention, but a confession of weakness in construction. He declares he 'would rather disoblige all the critics in the world than one of the fair sex,' and, having made his bow, he turns upon the ladies and rends them. An author campaigning against his critics is always a pleasant spectacle, but Congreve's defence of _The Double-Dealer_ is rather amusing than convincing.

It needed no defence; for with all its faults, such as they are, upon it, there are in it scenes and characters which only Congreve could have made. Brisk is a worthy forerunner of Witwoud, Sir Paul Plyant a delicious old credulous fool; while the tyrannical and vain Lady Plyant is so drawn that you almost love her. But the triumph is Lady Froth, 'a great coquet, pretender to poetry, wit, and learning,' and one would almost as lief have seen Mrs. Mountfort in the part as the Bracegirdle's Millamant. Her serious folly and foolish wisdom, her poem and malice and compliments and babbling vivacity—set off, it is fair to remember, by a pretty face—are atonement for a dozen Maskwells. She is a female Witwoud, her author's first success in a sort of character he draws to perfection. The scene between Mellefont and Lady Plyant, where she insists on believing that the gallant, under cover of a marriage with her stepdaughter, purposes to lead her astray, and where she goes through a delightful farce of answering her scruples before the bewildered man the scene that for some far-fetched reason led Macaulay's mind to the incest in the _Oedipus Rex_—is perhaps the best comedy of situation in the piece.

But the scene of defamation between the Froths and Brisk is notable as (with the Cabal idea in _The Way of the World_) the inspiration of the Scandal Scenes in Sheridan's play. When we remember that less than two years were gone since the production of _The Old Bachelor_, the improvement in Congreve is remarkable. Almost his only concession to the groundlings is the star-gazing episode of Lady Froth and Brisk: a mistake, because it spoils her inconsequent folly, but a small matter. In his second play Congreve was himself, the wittiest and most polished writer of comedy in English.

In the face of this fact 'the public' conducted itself characteristically: it more or less damned _The Double-Dealer_ until the queen approved, when it applauded lustily. That occasion gave Colley Cibber his first chance as Kynaston's substitute in Lord Touchwood. When one remembers Dryden's long, struggling, cudgelling and cudgelled life, it is impossible to read without emotion his tribute to a very young and successful author in the verses prefixed to this play:

Firm Doric pillars found your solid base:
The fair Corinthian crowns the higher space;
Thus all below is strength, and all above is grace. ...
We cannot envy you, because we love.
Time, place, and action may with pains be wrought,
But Genius must be born, and never can be taught.
This is your portion, this your native store;
Heav'n, that but once was prodigal before.

To Shakespeare gave as much; she could not give him more. The tribute is indubitably sincere; in point of Congreve's wit and diction it is as indubitably true. _Love for Love_ was the most popular of Congreve's comedies: it held the stage so long that Hazlitt could say, 'it still acts and is still acted well.' Being wise after the event, one may give some obvious reasons. It is more human than any other of his plays, and at the same time more farcical. By 'more human' it is not meant that the characters are truer to life than those in _The Way of the World_, but that they are truer to average life, and therefore more easily recognisable by the average spectator.

Tattle, for instance, is so gross a fool, that any fool in the pit could see his folly; Witwoud might deceive all but the elect. No familiarity—direct or indirect—with a particular mode of life and speech is necessary to the appreciation of _Love for Love_. Sir Sampson Legend is your unmistakable heavy father, cross-grained and bullying. Valentine is no ironical, fine gentleman like Mirabell, but a young rake from Cambridge, all debts and high spirits. Scandal is a plain railer at things, especially women; Ben Legend a sea-dog who cannot speak without a nautical metaphor; Jeremy an idealised comic servant; and Foresight grotesque farce.

Angelica is a shrewd but hearty 'English girl,' and Miss Prue a veritable country Miss; while Mrs. Frail and Mrs. Foresight are broadly skittish matrons. There is nothing in the play to strain the attention or to puzzle the intellect, and it is full of laughter: no wonder it was a success. It is, intellectually, on an altogether different plane from _The Way of the World_, on a slightly lower one than _The Double-Dealer_. But in its own way it is irresistibly funny, and by reason of its diction it is never for a moment other than distinguished.

I imagine the bodkin scene will always take the palm in it for mere mirth. Delightful sisters! I suppose you would not go alone to the World's End? The World's End! What, do you mean to banter me? Poor innocent! You don't know that there's a place called the World's End? I'll swear you can keep your countenance purely; you'd make an admirable player.... But look you here, now—where did you lose this gold bodkin?—Oh, sister, sister! My bodkin? Nay, 'tis yours; look at it. Well, if you go to that, where did you find this bodkin? Oh, sister, sister!—sister every way.

Broad, popular comedy, it is admirable; but it is not especially Congrevean. Tattle's love-lesson to Miss Prue and his boasting of his duchesses are in the same broad vein. Valentine's mad scene is more remarkable, in that Congreve gives rein to his fancy, and that his diction is at its very best. 'Hark'ee, I have a secret to tell you. Endymion and the Moon shall meet us upon Mount Latmos, and will be married in the dead of night. But say not a word. Hymen shall put his torch into a dark lanthorn, that it may be secret; and Juno shall give her peacock poppy-water, that he may fold his ogling tail, and Argus's hundred eyes be shut, ha? Nobody shall know, but Jeremy.'

TATTLE. Do you know me, Valentine?

VALENTINE. You? Who are you? No, I hope not.

TATTLE. I am Jack Tattle, your friend.

VALENTINE. My friend, what to do? I am no married man, and thou canst not lie with my wife. I am very poor, and thou canst not borrow money of me. Then, what employment have I for a friend?

ANGELICA. Do you know me, Valentine?

VALENTINE. Oh, very well.

ANGELICA. Who am I?

VALENTINE. You're a woman, one to whom Heaven gave beauty when it grafted roses on a briar. You are the reflection of Heaven in a pond, and he that leaps at you is sunk. You are all white, a sheet of lovely, spotless paper, when you first are born; but you are to be scrawled and blotted by every goose's quill. I know you; for I loved a woman, and loved her so long, that I found out a strange thing: I found out what a woman was good for. Imagine Betterton, the greatest actor of his time, delivering that last speech, with its incomparable rhythm! I like to think that he gave the spectators an idea that Valentine's self-sacrifice for Angelica was nothing but a bold device, a calculated effect; otherwise the sacrifice is an excrescence in this comedy, which, popular and broad though it be, is cynical in Congreve's manner throughout.

One is consoled, however, by the pleasant fate of the ingenious Mr. Tattle and the intriguing Mrs. Frail, who are left tied for life against their will. The trick, by the way, of a tricked marriage is constant in Congreve, and reveals his poverty of construction. He can devise you comic situations unflaggingly, but when he approaches the end of a play his _deus ex machina_ is invariably this flattest and most battered old deity in fairyland.

The dedication to Lord Dorset contains nothing of interest beyond the confession that the play is too long, and the information that part of it was omitted in the playing. A line in the prologue, 'We grieve One falling Adam and one tempted Eve,' is explained by Colley Cibber to refer to Mrs. Mountford, who, having cast her lot with Betterton and migrated to Lincoln's Inn Fields, threw up her part on a question of cash, and to Williams, an actor who 'loved his bottle better than his business,' who deserted at the same time. It serves to show the interest the town took in the players, that the fact was referred to on the stage. The lady's part was taken by Mrs. Ayliff; Mrs. Leigh played the nurse a very poor part after Lady Plyant; Dogget's success as Ben Legend has been noted. Mrs. Bracegirdle's Angelica was doubtless ravishing: a 'virtuous young woman,' as our ancestors phrased it, but quite relieved from insipidity.

It would need a greater presumption than the writer is gifted withal to add his contribution to the praises critics have lavished on _The Way of the World_. It is better to quote Mr. Swinburne. 'In 1700 Congreve replied to Collier with the crowning work of his genius the unequalled and unapproached masterpiece of English comedy. The one play in our language which may fairly claim a place beside, or but just beneath, the mightiest work of Moliere, is _The Way of the World_.' But he continues: 'On the stage, which had recently acclaimed with uncritical applause the author's more questionable appearance in the field of tragedy,'—_The Mourning Bride_,—'this final and flawless evidence of his incomparable powers met with a rejection then and ever since inexplicable on any ground of conjecture.'

There the critics are not unanimous. Mr. Gosse, for instance, has his explanation: that the spectators must have fidgeted, and wished 'that the actors and actresses would be doing something.' Very like, indeed: the spectators, then as now, would no doubt have preferred 'knock-about farce.' But, I venture to think, the explanation is not complete. The construction of the play is weak, certainly, but the actors and actresses do a great deal after all. For that matter, audiences will stand scenes of still wit—but they like to comprehend it; and the characters in _The Way of the World_, or most of them, represent a society whose attitude and speech are entirely ironical and paradoxical, a society of necessity but a small fraction of any community.

Some sort of study or some special experience is necessary to the enjoyment of such a set. It is not the case of a few witticisms and paradoxes firing off at intervals, like crackers, from the mouths of one or two actors with whom the audience is taught to laugh as a matter of course: the vein is unbroken. Now, literalness and common sense are the qualities of the average uninstructed spectator, and _The Way of the World_ was high over the heads of its audience.

To come to details. The tragedy of Lady Wishfort has often been remarked the veritable tragedy of a lovesick old woman. All the grotesque touches, her credulity, her vanity, her admirable dialect ('as I'm a person!'), but serve to make the tragedy the more pitiable. Either, therefore, our appreciation of satiric comedy is defective, or Congreve made a mistake. To regard this poor old soul as mere comedy is to attain to an almost satanic height of contempt: the comedy is more than grim, it is savagely cruel. To be pitiless, on the other hand, is a satirist's virtue. On the whole, we may reasonably say that the tragedy is not too keen in itself, but that it is too obviously indicated.

Witwoud is surely a great character? The stage is alive with mirth when he is on it. His entrance in the very first part of the play is delightful. 'Afford me your compassion, my dears; pity me, Fainall; Mirabell, pity me.... Fainall, how does your lady? Gad, I say anything in the world to get this fellow out of my head. I beg pardon that I should ask a man of pleasure, and the town, a question at once so foreign and domestic. But I talk like an old maid at a marriage, I don't know what I say.' But one might quote for ever. Witwoud, almost as much as Millamant herself, is an eternal type. His little exclamations, his assurance of sympathy, his terror of the commonplace—surely one knows them well? His tolerance of any impertinence, lest he should be thought to have misunderstood a jest, is a great distinction.

But Congreve's gibe in the dedication at the critics, who failed 'to distinguish betwixt the character of a Witwoud and a Truewit,' is hardly fair: as Dryden said of Etherege's Sir Fopling, he is 'a fool so nicely writ, The ladies might mistake him for a wit.' Then, Millamant is the ultimate expression of those who, having all the material goods which nature and civilisation can give, live on paradoxes and artifices. Her insolence is the inoffensive insolence only possible to the well-bred. 'O ay, letters,—I had letters,—I am persecuted with letters,—I hate letters,—nobody knows how to write letters; and yet one has 'em, one does not know why, they serve one to pin up one's hair.' 'Beauty the lover's gift!—Lord, what is a lover, that it can give?

Why one makes lovers as fast as one pleases, and they live as long as one pleases, and they die as soon as one pleases; and then if one pleases one makes more.' In parts of its characterisation _The Way of the World_ is extremely bold in observation, extremely careless of literary types and traditions. Mrs. Fainall, a woman who is the friend, and assists in the intrigues, of a man who has ceased to be her lover, is most unconventionally human. Of all the inimitable scenes, that in which Millamant and Mirabell make their conditions of marriage is perhaps the most unquestionable triumph. 'Let us never visit together, nor go to a play together, but let us be very strange and well-bred' there is its keynote. The dialogue is as sure and perfect in diction, in balance of phrases, and in musical effectiveness as can be conceived, and for all its care is absolutely free in its gaiety.

It is the ultimate expression of the joys of the artificial. As for the prologue, it is an invitation to the dullards to damn the play, and is anything but serenely confident. The dedication, to 'Ralph, Earl of Mountague,' has an interesting fact: it tells us that the comedy was written immediately after staying with him, 'in your retirement last summer from the town,' and pays a tribute to the influence of the society the dramatist met there. 'Vous y voyez partout,' said Voltaire of Congreve, 'le langage des honnetes gens avec des actions de fripon; ce qui prouve qu'il connaissait bien son monde, et qu'il vivait dans ce qu'on appelle la bonne compagnie.' The want of dramatic skill which has been alleged against Congreve is simply a question of construction—of the construction of his plays as a whole.

His plots hang fire, are difficult to follow, and are not worth remembering. But many things besides go to the making of good plays, and few playwrights have had all the theatrical virtues. Do we not pardon a lack of incident in a novel of character? In this connexion it is worth while to contrast Congreve with Sheridan, who in the matter of construction was a far abler craftsman. But is there not in the elder poet enough to turn the scale, even the theatrical scale, ten times over? Compare the petty indignation, with which the dramatist of _The School for Scandal_ deals with his scandalmongers, and the amused indifference of Congreve towards the cabalists in _The Way of the World_. Or take any hero of Congreve's and contrast him with that glorification of vulgar lavishness and canting generosity, that very barmaid's hero, Charles Surface. It is all very well to say that Joseph is the real hero; but Sheridan made it natural for the stupid sentimentality of later days to make him the villain, and Congreve would have made it impossible.

Of wit there is more in a scene of Congreve than in a play of Sheridan. Moreover, faulty in construction as his main plots are, in detail his construction is often admirable: as in play of character upon character, in countless opportunities for delightful archness and cruelty in the women, for the display of every comic emotion in the men. He lived in the playhouse, and his characters, true to life though they be, have about them as it were an ideal essence of the boards. With Hazlitt, 'I would rather have seen Mrs. Abington's Millamant than any Rosalind that ever appeared on the stage.' A lover and a constant frequenter of the theatre—albeit the plays he sees bore him to death—cannot, in reading Congreve, choose but see the glances and hear the intonations of imaginary players.

VI

Congreve's choice of material has been defended at an early stage of these remarks. There is the further and more interesting question of his point of view, his attitude towards it. Mr. Henley speaks of his 'deliberate and unmitigable baseness of morality.' Differing with deference, I think it may be shown that his attitude is a pose merely, and an artistic and quite innocent pose. It is the amusing pose of the boyish cynic turned into an artistic convention. The lines: 'He alone won't betray in whom none will confide, And the nymph may be chaste that has never been tried:' which conclude the characteristic song in the third act of _Love for Love_, are typical of his attitude. Does anybody suppose that an intelligent man of the world meant that sentiment in all seriousness? 'Nothing's new besides our faces, Every woman is the same'— those lines (in his first play), which seemed so shocking to Thackeray, what more do they express than the green cynicism of youth? When Mr. Leslie Stephen speaks of his 'gush of cynical sentiment,' he speaks unsympathetically, but the phrase, to be an enemy's, is just.

It is cynical sentiment, and the hostility comes from taking it seriously. I think it the most artistic attitude for a writer of gay, satiric comedies, and that its very excess should prevent its being taken for more than a convention. We are not called upon to see satiric comedies all day long, and the question, everlastingly asked by implication of every work of art—'Would you like to live with it?'—is here, as in most other cases, irrelevant. One is reminded that there is more in life than intrigues and cynical comments on them.

And one is inclined to put the questions in answer: 'Does a man who really feels the sorrowful things of life, its futile endeavours and piteous separations, find relief in seeing his emotions mimicked on the stage in a 'wholesome' play of sentiment with a happy ending? Is he not rather comforted by the distractions of cheerful frivolity, of conventional denial of his pains?' The demand is as inartistic and irrelevant as the criticism which suggested it, but it returns a sufficient reply. It does not touch the 'catharsis' of tragedy, which is another matter. For the rest, Congreve's attitude, cynicism apart, is an attitude of irony and superiority over common emotions, the attitude, artificial and inoffensive, of the society he depicts in his greatest play. He enjoys the humours of his puppets, he is never angry with them. It is the attitude of an artist in expounding human nature, of an expert in observation of life: an attitude attainable but by very few, and disliked as a rule by the rest, who want to clap or to hiss—who can laugh but who cannot smile.

VII

When Congreve left the stage, said Dennis the critic, 'comedy left it with him.' Vanburgh and Farquhar were left to expound comedy of manners, the one with a vigorous gusto, the other with a romantic gaiety. The peculiar perfume of _The Way of the World_ was given to neither, yet they wrote comedy of manners. But if Congreve left colleagues, he left no sons, and most certainly, one may say, that when those colleagues died, English comedy took to her bed. 'The Comic Muse, long sick, is now a- dying,' wrote Garrick in his prologue to _She Stoops to Conquer_, and she had not to apologise, like Charles the Second, for the unconscionable time she was about it. It is a little crude to attribute her demise to Jeremy Collier and his _Short View_ a block painted to look like a thunderbolt. It is not a matter of decency, of alteration or improvement in manners.

A comedy might be wholly Congrevean without a coarse word from beginning to end. It is a matter of the exclusion (not the stultification), the suspension of moral prepossessions, the absence of sympathetic sentimentalism, the habit of shirking nothing and smiling at all things. These qualities are not characteristic of the average Englishman. Now, satiric comedy did not in its initiation depend upon the average Englishman. It took its cue from the court of Charles the Second, who—with a dash of thoroughly English humour—

was more than half- French in temperament, and attracted to himself all that was artistically frivolous in his kingdom. Questions of decency and morality—which after all are not perpetually amusing—apart, the social spirit typified in this exceptional king is one of sceptical humour and ironical smiles: it takes common emotions for granted—is bored by them, in fact—and is a foe to sentimentality and gush and virtuously happy endings. It was the spirit of Charles the Second that inspired English comedy, and inspired it most thoroughly in Congreve but a few years after Charles's death.

Under changed conditions, one is apt to underestimate the influence of the Court upon the Town two hundred years ago. Well, the Georges became our defenders of the faith, and they hated 'boets and bainters.' English comedy was thrown back upon the patronage and the inspiration of average England, and up to the time of writing has shown few signs of recovery. Of course, the decay was gradual: you may see it at a most interesting stage in _The School for Scandal_, a comedy of manners with a strong dash of common sentimentality. It would be just possible, one conceives, to play _The School for Scandal_ as Charles Lamb says he saw it played, with Joseph for a hero, as a comedy of manners: you can just imagine Sir Peter as a sort of Sir Paul Plyant, and as not played to raise a lump in your throat.

But Sheridan made it a difficult task. Perhaps you may see the evil influence at its worst in the so-called comedies which were our glory twenty-five years ago: in such a play as _Caste_, an even river of sloppy sentiment, where the acme of chivalrous delicacy is to refrain from lighting a cigarette in a woman's presence, where the triumph of humour is for a guardsman to take a kettle off the fire, and where the character of Eccles shows what excellent comedy the author might have written.

One is fain to ask if the spirit of Congrevean comedy will ever come back to our stage. An echo of it has been heard in dialogue once or twice in the last few years: not a trace has been seen in action. And yet we permit our dramatists a pretty wide range of subjects. We allow the subjects: it is the

Congrevean attitude towards them which we should condemn. But the stage would be all the merrier if we could only understand that that attitude is harmless; that to see the humorous aspect of a thing is not to ignore the pathetic or the sociological; and that we should return all the heartier to our serious and sentimental considerations of the problems of life for allowing them to be laughed at for an evening at a comedy.

Chapter 9

Restoration Drama

"Then came the gallant protest of the Restoration, when Wycherley and his successors in drama commenced to write of contemporary life in much the spirit of modern musical comedy.... A new style of comedy was improvised, which, for lack of a better term, we may agree to call the comedy of Gallantry, and which Etherege, Shadwell, and Davenant, and Crowne, and Wycherley, and divers others, labored painstakingly to perfect. They probably exercised to the full reach of their powers when they hammered into grossness their too fine witticisms just smuggled out of France, mixed them with additional breaches of decorum, and divided the results into five acts. For Gallantry, it must be repeated, was yet in its crude youth.... For Wycherley and his confreres were the first Englishmen to depict mankind as leading an existence with no moral outcome. It was their sorry distinction to be the first of English authors to present a world of unscrupulous persons who entertained no special prejudices, one way or the other, as touched ethical matters."

JAMES BRANCH CABELL, *Beyond Life.*

FROM 1642 onward for eighteen years, the theaters of England remained nominally closed. There was of course evasion of the law; but whatever performances were offered had to be given in secrecy, before small companies in private houses, or in taverns located three or four miles out of town. No actor or spectator was safe, especially during the early days of the Puritan rule. Least of all was there any inspiration for dramatists. In 1660 the Stuart dynasty was restored to the throne of England. Charles II, the king, had been in France during the greater part of the Protectorate, together with many of the royalist party, all of whom were familiar with Paris and its fashions. Thus it was natural, upon the return of the court, that French influence should be felt, particularly in the theater. In August, 1660, Charles issued patents for two companies of players, and performances immediately began. Certain writers, in the field before the civil war, survived the period of theatrical eclipse, and now had their chance. Among these were Thomas Killigrew and William Davenant, who were quickly provided with fine playhouses.

Appearance of Women on the English Stage

It will be remembered that great indignation was aroused among the English by the appearance of French actresses in 1629. London must have learned to accept this innovation, however, for in one of the semi-private entertainments given during the Protectorate at Rutland House, the actress Mrs. Coleman took the principal part. *The Siege of Rhodes*, a huge spectacle designed by Davenant in 1656 (arranged in part with a view of evading the restrictions against theatrical plays) is generally noted as marking the entrance of women upon the English stage. It is also remembered for its use of movable machinery, which was something of an innovation. The panorama of *The Siege* offered five changes of scene, presenting "the fleet of Solyman the Magnificent, his army, the Island of Rhodes, and the varieties attending the siege of the city."

Disappearance of National Types

By the time the theaters were reopened in England, Corneille and Racine in France had established the neo-classic standard for tragedy, and Molière was in the full tide of his success. These playwrights, with Quinault and others, for a time supplied the English with plots. The first French opera, *Cadmus and Hermione*, by Lully and Quinault, performed in Paris in 1673, crossed the channel almost immediately, influencing Dryden in his attempts at opera. The romantic, semi-historical romances of Madame Scudéry and the Countess de la Fayette afforded a second supply of story material, while Spanish plays and tales opened up still another. Sometimes the plots of Calderón or I ope de Vega came to the English at second-hand through Fren .h versions. Whatever the case, it was now evident that the national type of play had ceased to be written. From this time on every European nation was influence by, and exerted an influence upon, the drama of every other nation. Characters, situations, plots, themes these things traveled from country to country, always modifying and sometimes supplanting the home product.

Persistence of Elizabethan Plays

With this influx of foreign drama, there was still a steady production of the masterpieces of the Elizabethan and Jacobean periods. The diarist Samuel Pepys, an ardent lover of the theater, relates that during the first three years after the opening of the playhouses he saw *Othello, Henry IV, A Midsummer Night's Dream,* two plays by Ben Jonson, and others by Beaumont, Fletcher, Middleton, Shirley, and Massinger. It must have been about this time that the practice of "improving" Shakespeare was begun, and his plays were often altered so as to be almost beyond recognition. From the time of the Restoration actors and managers, also dramatists, were good royalists; and new pieces, or refurbished old ones, were likely to acquire a political slant. The Puritans were satirized, the monarch and his wishes were flattered, and the royal order thoroughly supported by the people of the stage.

Richard Boyle, Earl of Orrery, seems to have the doubtful glory of re-introducing the use of rhymed verse. Boyle was a statesman, as well as a soldier and a dramatist. During the ten years or so following the Restoration, he wrote at least four tragedies on historical or legendary subjects, using the ten-syllabled rhymed couplet which he borrowed from France. It runs like this:

"Reason's a staff for age, when nature's gone;
But youth is strong enough to walk alone."

No more stilted sort of verse could well be contrived for dialogue. Monotonous as well as prosy, it was well suited to Orrery's plots. He took a semi-historical story, filled it with bombastic sentiments and strutting figures, producing what was known as "heroic drama." Dryden, who identified himself with this type of play, described it as concerned not with probabilities but with love and valor. A good heroic play is exciting, with perpetual bustle and commotion. The characters are extricated out of their amazing situations only by violence. Deaths are numerous. The more remote and unfamiliar the setting the better; and the speech should be suited to the action: hence the "heroic couplet." Pepys saw *Guzman*, by Orrery, and with his engaging frankness said it was as mean a thing as had been seen on the stage for a great while.

Parody of Heroic Drama

Other writers, Davenant, Etherege, and Sir Robert Howard, had also produced specimens of heroic plays, and by the time *The Conquest of Granada* reached the stage these clever gentlemen had grown tired of the species. Compared to Dryden they were nobodies in the literary world; but among them they contrived a hilarious burlesque called *The Rehearsal*, in which these showy but shallow productions were smartly ridiculed. Dryden is represented as Bayes (in reference to his position as poet laureate), and his peculiarities of speech and plot are amusingly derided. Though *The Rehearsal* was condemned as "scurrilous and ill-bred," yet it served a useful turn in puncturing an empty and overblown style.

Nature of Restoration Comedy

In almost every important respect, Restoration drama was far inferior to the Elizabethan. Where the earlier playwrights created powerful and original characters, the Restoration writers were content to portray repeatedly a few artificial types; where the former were imaginative, the latter were clever and ingenious. The Elizabethan dramatists were steeped in poetry, the later ones in the sophistication of the fashionable world. The drama of Wycherley and Congreve was the reflection of a small section of life, and it was like life in the same sense that the mirage is like the oasis. It had polish, an edge, a perfection in its own field; but both its perfection and its naughtiness now seem unreal. The heroes of the Restoration comedies were lively gentlemen of the city, profligates and loose livers, with a strong tendency to make love to their neighbors' wives.

Husbands and fathers were dull, stupid creatures. The heroines, for the most part, were lovely and pert, too frail for any purpose beyond the glittering tinsel in which they were clothed. Their companions were busybodies and gossips, amorous widows or jealous wives. The intrigues which occupy them are not, on the whole, of so low a nature as those depicted in the Italian court comedies; but still they are sufficiently coarse. Over all the action is the gloss of superficial good breeding and social ease. Only rarely do these creatures betray the traits of sympathy, faithfulness, kindness, honesty, or loyalty. They follow a life of pleasure, bored, but yawning behind a delicate fan or a kerchief of lace. Millamant and Mirabell, in Congreve's *Way of the World*, are among the most charming of these Watteau figures.

Everywhere in the Restoration plays are traces of European influence. *The Plain Dealer* of Wycherley was an English version of *The Misanthrope* of Molière; and there are many admirable qualities in the French play which are lacking in the English. *The Double Dealer* recalls scenes from *The Learned Ladies (Les femmes savantes)*; and Mr. Bluffe, in *The Old Bachelor*, is none other than our old friend Miles Gloriosus, who has traveled through Latin, Italian and French comedy. The national taste was coming into harmony, to a considerable extent, with the standards of Europe. Eccentricities were curbed; ideas, characters, and story material were interchanged. The plays, however, were not often mere imitations; in the majority of them there is original observation and independence of thought. It was this drama that kept the doors of the theater open and the love of the theater alive in the face of great public opposition.

Women Playwrights

Soon after the Restoration women began to appear as writers of drama. Mrs. Aphra Behn was one of the first and most industrious of English women playwrights. Her family name was Amis (some writers say Johnson). As the wife of a wealthy Dutch merchant she lived for some time in Surinam. Her novel, *Oroonooko*, furnished Southerne with the plot for a play of the same name. After the death of her husband, Mrs. Behn was for a time employed by the British government in a political capacity. She was the author of eighteen plays, most of them highly successful and fully as indecent as any by Wycherley or Vanbrugh. Mrs. Manly and Mrs. Susannah Centlivre, both of whom lived until well into the eighteenth century, also achieved success as playwrights. The adaptations from the French, made by Mrs. Centlivre, were very popular and keep the stage for nearly a century.

Collier's Attack On The Stage

Although the Puritans had lost their dominance as a political power, yet they had not lost courage in abusing the stage. The most violent attack was made by the clergyman Jeremy Collier in 1698, in a pamphlet called *A Short View of the Immorality and Profaneness of the English Stage*, in which he denounced not only Congreve and Vanbrugh, but Shakespeare and most of the Elizabethans. Three points especially drew forth his denunciations: the so-called lewdness of the plays, the frequent references to the Bible and biblical characters, and the criticism, slander and abuse flung from the stage upon the clergy. He would not have any Desdemona, however chaste, show her love before the footlights; he would allow no reference in a comedy to anything connected with the Church or religion; and especially would he prohibit any portrayal of the clergy. Next to the men in holy orders, Collier had a tender heart for the nobility.

He said in effect that if any ridicule or satire were to be indulged in, it should be against persons of low quality. To call a duke a rascal on the stage was far worse than to apply such an epithet to plain Hodge, almost as libellous as to represent a clergyman as a hypocrite. Collier made the curiously stupid error of accusing the playwrights of glorifying all the sins, passions, or peculiarities which they portrayed in their characters. He had no understanding of the point of view of the literary artist, nor any desire to understand it.

Collier's attack, unjust as it was, and foolish as certain phases of it appear today, yet it made an impression. The king, James II, was so wrought up over it that he issued a solemn proclamation "against vice and profaneness.

"Congreve and Vanbrugh, together with other writers, were persecuted, and fines were imposed on some of the most popular actors and actresses. Dryden, Congreve and Vanbrugh made an attempt at a justification of the stage, but it did little good. D'Urfey, Dennis, and others entered the controversy, which raged for many years. The public buzzed with the scandal set forth in *The Short View*, but did not stay away altogether from the playhouses. The poets answered the attack not by reformation, but by new plays in which the laughter, the satire, and the ridicule were turned upon their enemies.

Chapter 10

A Survey of Restoration Comedy

Refinement meets burlesque in Restoration comedy. In this scene from George Etherege's *Love in a Tub*, musicians and well-bred ladies surround a man who is wearing a tub because he has lost his trousers.

Restoration comedy is the name given to English comedies written and performed in the Restoration period from 1660 to 1710. After public stage performances had been banned for 18 years by the Puritan regime, the re-opening of the theatres in 1660 signalled a rebirth of English drama. Restoration comedy is famous for its sexual explicitness, a quality encouraged by Charles II personally and by the rakish aristocratic ethos of his court. The socially diverse audiences included both aristocrats, their servants and hangers-on, and a substantial middle-class segment.

These playgoers were attracted to the comedies by up-to-the-minute topical writing, by crowded and bustling plots, by the introduction of the first professional actresses, and by the rise of the first celebrity actors. This period saw the first professional woman playwright, Aphra Behn.

Theatre Companies

Original Patent Companies, 1660–82

The sumptuously decorated Dorset Gardens playhouse in 1673, with one of the sets for Elkannah Settle's *The Empress of Morocco*. The apron stage at the front which allowed intimate audience contact is not visible in the picture (the artist is standing on it).

Charles II was an active and interested patron of the drama. Soon after his restoration, in 1660, he granted exclusive play-staging rights, so-called Royal patents, to the King's Company and the Duke's Company, led by two middle-aged Caroline playwrights, Thomas Killigrew and William Davenant. The patentees scrambled for performance rights to the previous generation's Jacobean and Caroline plays, which were the first necessity for economic survival before any new plays existed. Their next priority was to build new, splendid patent theatres in Drury Lane and Dorset Gardens, respectively. Striving to outdo each other in magnificence, Killigrew and Davenant ended up with quite similar theatres, both designed by Christopher Wren, both optimally provided for music and dancing, and both fitted with moveable scenery and elaborate machines for thunder, lightning, and waves.

The audience of the early Restoration period was not exclusively courtly, as has sometimes been supposed, but it was quite small and could barely support two companies. There was no untapped reserve of occasional playgoers. Ten consecutive performances constituted a smash hit. This closed system forced playwrights to be extremely responsive to popular taste. Fashions in the drama would change almost week by week rather than season by season, as each company responded to the offerings of the other, and new plays were urgently sought. The King's Company and the Duke's Company vied with one another for audience favour, for popular actors, and for new plays, and in this hectic climate the new genres of heroic drama, pathetic drama, and Restoration comedy were born and flourished.

United Company, 1682–95

Both the quantity and quality of the drama suffered when in 1682 the more successful Duke's Company ate the struggling King's Company, and the amalgamated *United Company* was formed. The production of new plays dropped off sharply in the 1680s, affected by both the monopoly and the political situation (see Decline of comedy below). The influence and the incomes of the actors dropped, too. In the late 80s, predatory investors converged on the United Company, while management was taken over by the lawyer Christopher Rich. Rich attempted to finance a tangle of "farmed" shares and sleeping partners by slashing salaries and, dangerously, by abolishing the traditional perks of senior performers, who were stars with the clout to fight back.

War of the Theatres, 1695–1700

The company owners, wrote the young United Company employee Colley Cibber, "who had made a monopoly of the stage, and consequently presum'd they might impose what conditions they pleased upon their people, did not consider that they were all this while endeavouring to enslave a set of actors whom the public were inclined to support." Performers like the legendary Thomas Betterton, the tragedienne Elizabeth Barry, and the rising young comedienne Anne Bracegirdle had the audience on their side and, in the confidence of this, they walked out.

The actors gained a Royal "licence to perform", thus bypassing Rich's ownership of both the original Duke's and King's Company patents from 1660, and formed their own cooperative company. This unique venture was set up with detailed rules for avoiding arbitrary managerial authority, regulating the ten actors' shares, the conditions of salaried employees, and the sickness and retirement benefits of both categories. The cooperative had the good luck to open in 1695 with the première of William Congreve's famous *Love For Love* and the skill to make it a huge box-office success.

London again had two competing companies. Their dash to attract audiences briefly revitalized Restoration drama, but also set it on a fatal downhill slope to the lowest common denominator of public taste. Rich's company notoriously offered Bartholomew Fair-type attractions — high kickers, jugglers, ropedancers, performing animals — while the cooperating actors, even as they appealed to snobbery by setting themselves up as the only legitimate theatre company in London, were not above retaliating with "prologues recited by boys of five, and epilogues declaimed by ladies on horseback". The demand for new plays stimulated William Congreve and John Vanbrugh into writing some of their best comedies, but also gave birth to the new genre of sentimental comedy, which was soon to replace Restoration comedy in the public favour.

First actresses

Nell Gwynn was one of the first actresses and the mistress of Charles II. Restoration comedy was strongly influenced by the introduction of the first professional actresses. Before the closing of the theatres, all female roles had been played by boys, and the predominantly male audiences of the 1660s and 1670s were both curious, censorious, and delighted at the novelty of seeing real women engage in risqué repartee and take part in physical seduction scenes. Samuel Pepys refers many times in his famous diary to visiting the playhouse in order to watch or re-watch the performance of some particular actress, and to how much he enjoys these experiences.

Daringly suggestive comedy scenes involving women became especially common, although of course Restoration actresses were, just like male actors, expected to do justice to all kinds and moods of plays. (Their role in the development of Restoration tragedy is also important, compare She-tragedy.)

A new speciality introduced almost as early as the actresses was the breeches role, which called for an actress to appear in male clothes (breeches being tight-fitting knee-length pants, the standard male garment of the time), for instance in order to play a witty heroine who disguises herself as a boy to hide, or to engage in escapades disallowed to girls. A quarter of the plays produced on the London stage between 1660 and 1700 contained breeches roles.

Playing these cross-dressing roles, women behaved with the freedom society allowed to men, and some feminist critics, such as Jacqueline Pearson, regard them as subversive of conventional gender roles and empowering for female members of the audience. Elizabeth Howe has objected that the male disguise, when studied in relation to playtexts, prologues, and epilogues, comes out as "little more than yet another means of displaying the actress as a sexual object" to male patrons, by showing off her body, normally hidden by a skirt, outlined by the male outfit. Successful Restoration actresses include Charles II's mistress Nell Gwyn, the tragedienne Elizabeth Barry who was famous for her ability to "move the passions" and make whole audiences cry, the 1690s comedienne Anne Bracegirdle, and Susanna Mountfort (a.k.a. Susanna Verbruggen), who had many breeches roles written especially for her in the 1680s and 90s. Letters and memoirs of the period show that both men and women in the audience greatly relished Mountfort's swaggering, roistering impersonations of young women wearing breeches and thereby enjoying the social and sexual freedom of the male Restoration rake.

First celebrity actors

Thomas Betterton played the irresistible Dorimant in George Etherege's *Man of Mode*. Betterton's acting ability was praised by Samuel Pepys, Alexander Pope, and Colley Cibber.

During the Restoration period, both male and female actors on the London stage became for the first time public personalities and celebrities. Documents of the period show audiences being attracted to performances by the talents of particular actors as much as by particular plays, and more than by authors (who seem to have been the least important draw, no performance being advertised by author until 1699). Although the playhouses were built for large audiences—the second Drury Lane theatre from 1674 held 2000 patrons — they were of compact design, and an actor's charisma could be intimately projected from the thrust stage.

With two companies competing for their services from 1660 to 1682, star actors were able to negotiate star deals, comprising company shares and benefit nights as well as salaries. This advantageous situation changed when the two companies were amalgamated in 1682, but the way the actors rebelled and took command of a new company in 1695 is in itself an illustration of how far their status and power had developed since 1660. The greatest fixed stars among Restoration actors were Elizabeth Barry ("Famous Mrs Barry" who "forc 'd Tears from the Eyes of her Auditory") and Thomas Betterton, both of them active in organising the actors' revolt in 1695 and both original patent-holders in the resulting actors' cooperative.

Betterton played every great male part there was from 1660 into the 18th century. After watching *Hamlet* in 1661, Samuel Pepys reports in his diary that the young beginner Betterton "did the prince's part beyond imagination." Betterton's expressive performances seem to have attracted playgoers as magnetically as did the novelty of seeing women on the stage. He was soon established as the leading man of the Duke's Company, and played Dorimant, the seminal irresistible Restoration rake, at the première of George Etherege's *Man of Mode* (1676). Betterton's position remained unassailable through the 1680s, both as the leading man of the United Company and as its stage manager and *de facto* day-to-day leader. He remained loyal to Rich longer than many of his coworkers, but eventually it was he who headed the actors' walkout in 1695, and who became the acting manager of the new company.

Comedies

Variety and dizzying fashion changes are typical of Restoration comedy. Even though the "Restoration drama" unit taught to college students is likely to be telescoped in a way that makes the plays all sound contemporary, scholars now have a strong sense of the rapid evolution of English drama over these forty years and of its social and political causes. The influence of theatre company competition and playhouse economics is also acknowledged.

Restoration comedy peaked twice. The genre came to spectacular maturity in the mid-1670s with an extravaganza of aristocratic comedies. Twenty lean years followed this short golden age, although the achievement of Aphra Behn in the 1680s is to be noted. In the mid-1690s a brief second Restoration comedy renaissance arose, aimed at a wider audience. The comedies of the golden 1670s and 1690s peak times are extremely different from each other. An attempt is made below to illustrate the generational taste shift by describing *The Country Wife* (1675) and *The Provoked Wife* (1697) in some detail. These two plays differ from each other in some typical ways, just as a Hollywood movie of the 1950s differs from one of the 1970s. The plays are not, however, offered as being "typical" of their decades. Indeed, there exist no typical comedies of the 1670s or the 1690s; even within these two short peak-times, comedy types kept mutating and multiplying.

Aristocratic comedy, 1660–80

The drama of the 1660s and 1670s was vitalised by the competition between the two patent companies created at the Restoration, as well as by the personal interest of Charles II, and the comic playwrights rose to the demand for new plays. They stole freely from the contemporary French and Spanish stage, from English Jacobean and Caroline plays, and even from Greek and Roman classical comedies, and combined the looted plotlines in adventurous ways.

Resulting differences of tone in a single play were appreciated rather than frowned on, as the audience prized "variety" within as well as between plays. Early Restoration audiences had little enthusiasm for structurally simple, well-shaped comedies such as those of Molière; they demanded bustling, crowded multi-plot action and fast pace. Even a splash of high heroic drama might be thrown in to enrich the comedy mix, as in George Etherege's *Love in a Tub* (1664), which has one heroic verse "conflict between love and friendship" plot, one urbane wit comedy plot, and one burlesque pantsing plot. Such incongruities contributed to Restoration comedy being held in low esteem in the 18th, 19th and early 20th centuries, but today the early Restoration total theatre experience is again valued on the stage, as well as by postmodern academic critics.

The unsentimental or "hard" comedies of John Dryden, William Wycherley, and George Etherege reflected the atmosphere at Court, and celebrated with frankness an aristocratic macho lifestyle of unremitting sexual intrigue and conquest. The Earl of Rochester, real-life Restoration rake, courtier and poet, is flatteringly portrayed in Etherege's *The Man of Mode* (1676) as a riotous, witty, intellectual, and sexually irresistible aristocrat, a template for posterity's idea of the glamorous Restoration rake (actually never a very common character in Restoration comedy).

Wycherley's *The Plain Dealer* (1676), a variation on the theme of Molière's *Le misanthrope*, was highly regarded for its uncompromising satire and earned Wycherley the appellation "Plain Dealer" Wycherley or "Manly" Wycherley, after the play's main character Manly. The single play that does most to support the charge of obscenity levelled then and now at Restoration comedy is probably Wycherley's *The Country Wife* (1675). William Wycherley, *The Country Wife*: "O Lord, I'll have some china too. Good Master Horner, don't think to give other people china, and me none. Come in with me too."

Example. William Wycherley, The Country Wife (1675)

The Country Wife has three interlinked but distinct plots, which each project sharply different moods:

> Horner's impotence trick provides the main plot and the play's organizing principle. The upper-class town rake Horner mounts a campaign for seducing as many respectable ladies as possible, first spreading a false rumour of his own impotence, in order to be allowed where no complete man may go. The trick is a great success and Horner has sex with many married ladies of virtuous reputation, whose husbands are happy to leave him alone with them. In one famously outrageous scene, the "China scene", sexual intercourse is assumed to take place repeatedly just off stage, where Horner and his mistresses carry on a sustained double entendre dialogue purportedly about Horner's china collection. *The Country Wife* is driven by a succession of near-discoveries of the truth about Horner's sexual prowess (and thus the truth about the respectable

ladies), from which he extricates himself by quick thinking and good luck. Horner never becomes a reformed character, but keeps his secret to the end and is assumed to go on merrily reaping the fruits of his planted misinformation, past the last act and beyond.

The married life of Pinchwife and Margery is based on Molière's *School For Wives*. Pinchwife is a middle-aged man who has married an ignorant young country girl in the hope that she will not know to cuckold him. However, Horner teaches her, and Margery cuts a swathe through the sophistications of London marriage without even noticing them. She is enthusiastic about the virile handsomeness of town gallants, rakes, and especially theatre actors (such self-referential stage jokes were nourished by the new higher status of actors), and keeps Pinchwife in a state of continual horror with her plain-spokenness and her interest in sex. A running joke is the way Pinchwife's pathological jealousy always leads him into supplying Margery with the very type of information he wishes her not to have.

The courtship of Harcourt and Alithea is a comparatively uplifting love story in which the witty Harcourt wins the hand of Pinchwife's sister Alithea.

Decline of Comedy, 1678–90

When the two companies were amalgamated in 1682 and the London stage became a monopoly, both the number and the variety of new plays being written dropped sharply. There was a swing away from comedy to serious political drama, reflecting preoccupations and divisions following on the Popish Plot (1678) and the Exclusion Crisis (1682). The few comedies produced also tended to be political in focus, the whig dramatist Thomas Shadwell sparring with the tories John Dryden and Aphra Behn. Behn's unique achievement as an early professional woman writer has been the subject of much recent study.

Comedy Renaissance, 1690–1700

During the second wave of Restoration comedy in the 1690s, the "softer" comedies of William Congreve and John Vanbrugh reflected mutating cultural perceptions and great social change. The playwrights of the 1690s set out to appeal to more socially mixed audiences with a strong middle-class element, and to female spectators, for instance by moving the war between the sexes from the arena of intrigue into that of marriage. The focus in comedy is less on young lovers outwitting the older generation, more on marital relations after the wedding bells. Thomas Southerne's dark *The Wives' Excuse* (1691) is not yet very "soft": it shows a woman miserably married to the fop Friendall, everybody's friend, whose follies and indiscretions undermine her social worth, since her honour is bound up in his. Mrs Friendall is pursued by a would-be lover, a matter-of-fact rake devoid of all the qualities that made Etherege's Dorimant charming, and she is kept from action and choice by the unattractiveness of all her options. All the humour of this "comedy" is in the subsidiary love-chase and fornication plots, none in the main plot.

In Congreve's *Love for Love* (1695) and *The Way of the World* (1700), the "wit duels" between lovers typical of 1670s comedy are underplayed. The give-and-take set pieces of couples still testing their attraction for each other have mutated into witty prenuptial debates on the eve of marriage, as in the famous "Proviso" scene in *The Way of the World* (1700). Vanbrugh's *The Provoked Wife* (1697) follows in the footsteps of Southerne's *Wives' Excuse*, with a lighter touch and more humanly recognizable characters.

Example. John Vanbrugh, The Provoked Wife (1697)

John Vanbrugh, *The Provoked Wife*: "These are good times. A woman may have a gallant and a separate maintenance too."

The Provoked Wife is something of a Restoration problem play in its attention to the subordinate legal position of married women and the complexities of "divorce" and separation, issues that had been highlighted in the mid-1690s by some notorious cases before the House of Lords.

Sir John Brute in *The Provoked Wife* is tired of matrimony. He comes home drunk every night and is continually rude and insulting to his wife. She is meanwhile being tempted to embark upon an affair with the witty and faithful Constant. Divorce is not an option for either of the Brutes at this time, but forms of legal separation have recently come into existence, and would entail a separate maintenance to the wife. Such an arrangement would not allow remarriage. Still, muses Lady Brute, in one of many discussions with her niece Bellinda, "These are good times. A woman may have a gallant and a separate maintenance too."

Bellinda is at the same time being grumpily courted by Constant's friend Heartfree, who is surprised and dismayed to find himself in love with her. The bad example of the Brutes is a constant warning to Heartfree to not marry.

The Provoked Wife is a talk play, with the focus less on love scenes and more on discussions between female friends (Lady Brute and Bellinda) and male friends (Constant and Heartfree). These exchanges, full of jokes though they are, are thoughtful and have a dimension of melancholy and frustration.

After a forged-letter complication, the play ends with marriage between Heartfree and Bellinda and stalemate between the Brutes. Constant continues to pay court to Lady Brute, and she continues to shilly-shally.

End of Comedy

The tolerance for Restoration comedy even in its modified form was running out at the end of the 17th century, as public opinion turned to respectability and seriousness even faster than the playwrights did. Interconnected causes for this shift in taste were demographic change, the Glorious Revolution of 1688, William's and Mary's dislike of the theatre, and the lawsuits brought against playwrights by the Society for the Reformation of Manners (founded in 1692). When Jeremy Collier attacked Congreve and Vanbrugh in his *Short View of the Immorality and Profaneness of the English Stage* in 1698, he was confirming a shift in audience taste that had already taken place. At the much-anticipated all-star première in 1700 of *The*

Way of the World, Congreve's first comedy for five years, the audience showed only moderate enthusiasm for that subtle and almost melancholy work. The comedy of sex and wit was about to be replaced by the drama of obvious sentiment and exemplary morality.

After Restoration comedy

Stage history

During the 18th and 19th centuries, the sexual frankness of Restoration comedy ensured that theatre producers cannibalised it or adapted it with a heavy hand, rather than actually performed it. Today, Restoration comedy is again appreciated on the stage. The classics, Wycherley's *The Country Wife* and *The Plain-Dealer,* Etherege's *The Man of Mode,* and Congreve's *Love For Love* and *The Way of the World* have competition not only from Vanbrugh's *The Relapse* and *The Provoked Wife,* but from such dark unfunny comedies as Thomas Southerne's *The Wives Excuse.* Aphra Behn, once considered unstageable, has had a major renaissance, with *The Rover* now a repertory favourite.

Literary criticism

Distaste for sexual impropriety long kept Restoration comedy not only off the stage but also locked in a critical poison cupboard. Victorian critics like William Hazlitt, although valuing the linguistic energy and "strength" of the canonical writers Etherege, Wycherley, and Congreve, always found it necessary to temper aesthetic praise with heavy moral condemnation. Aphra Behn received the condemnation without the praise, since outspoken sex comedy was considered particularly offensive coming from a woman author. At the turn of the 20th century, an embattled minority of academic Restoration comedy enthusiasts began to appear, for example the important editor Montague Summers, whose work ensured that the plays of Aphra Behn remained in print.

"Critics remain astonishingly defensive about the masterpieces of this period", wrote Robert D. Hume as late as

1976. It is only over the last few decades that that statement has become untrue, as Restoration comedy has been acknowledged a rewarding subject for high theory analysis and Wycherley's *The Country Wife*, long branded the most obscene play in the English language, has become something of an academic favourite. "Minor" comic writers are getting a fair share of attention, especially the post-Aphra Behn generation of women playwrights which appeared just around the turn of the 18th century: Delarivier Manley, Mary Pix, Catharine Trotter, and Susannah Centlivre. A broad study of the majority of never-reprinted Restoration comedies has been made possible by Internet access (by subscription only) to the first editions at the British Library.

Chapter 11

Love and Marriage in Three Restoration Comedies

The Restoration comedies can be a window into a unique period of English history. Following the political and social turmoil of the English Civil War, the Restoration Age was characterized by a sense of loss and cultural disillusion coupled with efforts to restore social stability and cohesion. These conditions were associated with a diminishment in the influence of traditional institutions such as religion and the aristocracy and the rise of new institutions to replace them. *The Country Wife* and *The Rover* were both produced during this period of uncertain social structures and transformations, and *The Wives' Excuse* heralds the period's end and the beginning of a new age with new dominant values. This study will examine this progression in terms of the portrayal of each play's hero, a look at each play's heroine and minor female characters, and how the plays comment on marriage and gender to see how, if at all, art and life intersect.

Joseph Wood Krutch contends that Restoration comedy "was derived from the union of certain elements of the old comedy of Humours with certain elements in the romantic plays of the same period. From the former it took its realism, and from the latter hints in the handling of dialogue...Ben Jonson had given a picture of the bottom of society, so that we may call his plays comedies of bad manners. Fletcher had elaborated the play of courtly characters...The writers of the Restoration borrowed from both, presenting a picture as realistic as that of Jonson, but of a society as cultivated as that in the imaginary courts of Fletcher". Though other critics may dispute Krutch's lineage, the point is that Restoration comedy did have its antecedents in English drama and was not an aberration, reflective of earlier forms as well as being a product of its time.

Restoration comedy had a vogue of approximately fifty years, from 1668 to the 1710's. Built around a central group of young men and women, "its essential ingredients are wit, urbanity and sophistication. The scene is almost invariably London-its streets, parks and coffee houses. The themes are, almost exclusively, love, sexual intrigue and cuckoldry". Also referred to as the Comedy of Manners because the chief characters are usually members of high society, the Restoration comedy tends to feature recurring types- "the graceful young rake, the faithless wife, the deceived husband, and perhaps, a charming young heroine who is to be bestowed in the end on the rake". Finally, great emphasis is placed on witty dialogue and repartee for its own sake.

Morrah remarks, "It was in this emphasis on wit, the insistence on elegance in writing, on tidiness of mind, that the age differed from its predecessor". Witty repartee is often operative in these plays, used as a device to ridicule and reveal the flaws of others as well as an aid in attaining one's own goals. As Krutch remarks, "The technique of wit [can] become that of rationalizing debauchery into a philosophical system and producing a great corpus of mock casuistry whose fine points are expounded with a zeal worthy of a theologian". Wit is also a comic and clever way to woo a member of the opposite sex, and one critic credits Dryden with first popularizing "the battle of wits between the emancipated young couple". *The Country Wife, The Rover*, and *The Wives' Excuse* collectively share a number of these themes, attributes and character types, and the degree and significance of these commonalities will form the basis of my analysis.

Social and Historical Context

Yet before proceeding to the plays themselves, I would like to "set the stage" as it were. No matter how realistic a work of art, its nature AS art prevents one from making a direct comparison with the particular society in which it is produced. Yet art and society do intersect and often a work can be more appreciated when considered in its historical context. The Restoration comedies in particular intersect with Restoration society at a number of vital points. Many critics remark on the efforts of the contemporary playwrights "to represent the actual manners of the times, and to show real characters in a familiar setting". Wilkinson concurs "that certain essential properties of the plays are derived directly and barely altered from gallant society". I will briefly focus on three areas of Restoration society in order to investigate their possible effects and influences on the characters and content of the Restoration comedies I am studying. These areas are King Charles II and his court, audience composition, and economic and cultural changes that pertain to audience and theme.

Charles II ascended the throne of England in 1660 at age thirty and reigned until his death in 1685. Charles himself was considered a "rake," a successful and skilled pursuer of women, and he boasted a string of beautiful mistresses throughout his reign. Patrick Morrah writes that Charles was especially influenced by the French Court of Louis XIV and wanted his own court to imitate its elegance and sophistication (40-4); thus, the emphasis was on fashion, art, wit, and love. Morrah qualifies that though "there was as much womanizing at the Louvre (and perhaps at the Vatican) as there ever was at Whitehall, certainly at this palace it was openly practiced for all to see", and goes on to point out that "royal mistresses were a phenomenon new to even the oldest of English observers; not since the far-off days of Henry VIII had there been so much as a mention of extra-marital adventures". Thus, the King and his mistresses helped to make the pursuit of love, and particularly sexual love, the main preoccupation of the gallant lords and ladies who made up Court society. The King's mistresses set the tones in women's dress which tended to emphasize sexual suggestiveness and sensuality and "the king set an example of promiscuity, and his followers emulated him with enthusiasm".

In consequence, Burns' charge rings true: "The atmosphere of the plays corresponded very closely with the atmosphere of a portion of society, that their heroes were drawn from the characters of Sedley, Rochester, and Charles himself, and that however shocking the incidents and speeches might be, they are to be matched in dissoluteness by what is to be found in the histories and memoirs". This allusion to Sedley, etc. draws attention to another vital connection between the Court and Restoration theatre: many playwrights of the age were also associated with the Court. "Of the five great comedy writers, Etherege, Wycherley, Congreve, Vanbrugh and Farquhar, four were distinguished men of fashion, and two were, in addition, knights". In fact, many were part of a loosely knit group of amateur writers known as the Court Wits and these included Sir George Etherege, Sir Robert Howard, his brother-in-law John Dryden, Sir Charles Sedley, and the Duke of Buckingham and the Earl of Rochester.

Hume declares that Wycherley was a fringe member and Aphra Behn was a close friend of Rochester. Obviously most of these writers knew each other and moved within the same social set so their "realistic" representations of fashionable characters and situations were certainly informed by actual knowledge and experience.

Two licensed theatres were opened in 1662 under the special patronage of the King and the Duke of York, and it was in "the theatre that the talents of the Restoration wits found their most prolific output" and became the centre of fashionable life. Professional actresses were allowed on the stage for the first time, and Morrah claims that the Restoration wits, and indeed the London theatrical scene, revolved around these beautiful ladies. Many became mistresses of playwrights, and an actress named Nell Gwyn became mistress to King Charles himself. In these various ways it is clear that the relationship between the Restoration Court and the theatre was an intimate one.

Not only were character portrayals and dramatic plotting influenced by the playwrights' close association with the Court, but it was to a large extent the society of the Court for which the plays were written. There are many reasons for this. King Charles was an enthusiastic patron of the theatre, and he saw over four hundred professional performances during his twenty-five year reign. Naturally, his entourage followed suit. As a centre of fashionable life, the theatre was a place to see fashionable people and to be seen and also a forum to pursue sexual intrigues. Yet of the ten or fifteen licensed theatres operating before the War, only two were reopened, and they became consolidated in 1682.

Obviously, the Restoration audiences were both much smaller and more homogeneous, composed disproportionately of the upper classes of London. Thus, audience composition may also provide an insight into some of the recurrent themes of Restoration comedy: pursuit of love and pleasure, cynical manipulation of others, and condemnation of marriage. The playwrights obviously wanted to please their audiences and the Court social set espoused rather different values than the majority of the British population; thus, they are reflected in the plays.

Krutch asserts the debauchery practiced at Court was due in part to a reactionary backlash against Puritan repressiveness, and Wilkinson highlights how the War promoted general anxiety regarding previously stable traditional institutions. But rather than clinging more tightly to tradition as much of the lower and middle classes seemed to do, court society was characterized by a rejection of traditional values. Both Wilkinson and Birdsall point out that philosophers like Machiavelli and Hobbes (who was also reacting to the Civil War) had an impact within the educated classes and that they "were worldly realists who understood force and compulsion to be the only efficacious means for attaining personal security and social order who preferred not to trust unless compelled by necessity".

Hobbes characterized all human behavior as arising from basic self-interest and a will to power. Hobbes' philosophy was individualistic and materialistic, and these same attitudes towards sensual enjoyment and manipulation of others can certainly be detected in Restoration Court society and in many of the heroes and heroines of the Restoration comedies they went to see. In general, the Restoration was a time of both political and social uncertainty and transformation. In addition to the factors above, the rise of a merchant middle-class and its aspirations of social mobility also threatened social hierarchies. The bourgeois values of personal acquisition, private judgment, and subjective self-assessment began to filter into the society and the literature of the period.

Individual self-expression became an increasingly popular value among educated men and women, and there was a growing awareness of the problems of arranged marriage. The Restoration comedies of manners both dealt with many of these new issues yet "the search for novelty, the ready resort to laughter, the conscious reducing of the significance of traditional codes" also helped the audience to evade them.

The Rakish Hero

One of the features unique to Restoration comedy is the figure of the rake as romantic hero. Birdsall points out that the rake- hero is a descendant of earlier comedic male characters who were rogues, "shrewd, double-dealing rascals dedicated to the cause of their own freedom and prosperity", but he is a sign of the times in that during this period he supplanted the traditional romantic hero in many of the age's theatrical productions. The rake-hero exhibits a number of attitudes and characteristics that one can detect in Horner, Willmore, and Lovemore.

He is unmarried, cynical, coarse but with the manners of a gentleman, witty, manipulative, and self-serving. He tends to create his own brand of morality which includes a belief in the open pursuit of sensual pleasure and a dismissal of marriage. His "wit consists not so much in his defiance of traditional notions of right conduct, as in the casual and unruffled manner in which he expresses the 'shocking' sentiments" since "the first major requirement for a reputation for wit is the appearance of being in complete control of one's feelings and/or of one's circumstances, whether one is or not".

Horner, the rake-hero of *The Country Wife*, illustrates this ideal more fully than either Willmore or Lovemore. The dominant plot is set in motion through his experiment: pretending impotence in order to discover which ladies of his acquaintance like sex and are willing to cuckold their husbands by having sex with him: "If I can but abuse the husbands, I'll soon disabuse the wives". His manipulation of the other characters and control of the situations is nearly total, only faltering in the last scene when the maid, Lucy, must step in and maintain his deception.

Within the context of the play, his social power derives from an awareness of 'real' human nature; he 'knows' that 'ladies of quality' want to have sex with men other than their husbands if they will not be found out, and he 'knows' enough about the hypocrisy of men like Pinchwife and Sir Jasper to conclude that they deserve to be cuckolded. He assumes people's inner motives are opposite to their outer behavior: "Ay, your arrantest cheat is your trustee or executor; your jealous man, the greatest cuckold; your churchman, the greatest atheist; and your noisy, pert rogue of a wit, the greatest fop". Horner mirrors this social 'insight' in his own behavior by feigning impotence to act out his lechery. The fact that he doesn't suffer any adverse consequences supports the idea that his knowledge must be valid.

Horner is also presented as smarter than the other male characters, presumably due to his wit. He knows how to outsmart the husbands, as when he sees through the disguise of Margery dressed as a boy and kisses and fondles her in front of her husband. His witty superiority informs his social insights and makes his social power possible. He aggressively uses his wit to undermine and reveal the foolishness and hypocrisy of the other characters.

Sparkish's vanity and Pinchwife's jealousy make them vulnerable to ridicule, and the lesson is "to be invulnerable one must be a wit". He expresses his superiority when he mocks and rails at anything that could be considered socially restrictive or dishonest, "Affectation is [nature's] greatest monster" but ironically uses affectation to get what he wants. He rails against marriage because it is conventional and limits one's freedom, and he makes cuckolds to express his hostility to marriage gone wrong. Horner illustrates the "social power and witty superiority" of the gallant wit.

Yet Horner's wit and social power are dedicated almost exclusively to the goal of sexual conquest for its own sake, and his intrigues are as much about power as they are about any genuine feeling he has for the women he sleeps with. His opinion of Lady Fidget and her friends, "pretenders to honour" does not deter him from having sex with them. All women appear the same to him, "Now I must wrong one woman for another's sake. But that's no new thing with me" and he only "converse[s] with 'em...to laugh at 'em and use 'em ill".

One of the consequences of the sexual and power impulses coming together in the rake-hero is that since men hold the power in Restoration society, the 'male fantasy' that is played out in which he has sex without the traditional restraints of society and marriage is as much to prove his superiority over other men as it is about sexual freedom and enjoyment. Though Horner ostensibly outwits the foolish and reveals the pretentious, he becomes limited and caught in his own game when he is used by the women he seeks to use, when he becomes the commodity, and becomes as much defined by the game's rules as the others.

Willmore, the rake-hero of *The Rover*, exemplifies many of the same traits as Horner, but he differs in significant ways. He too is cynical about love and is the most insightful of the characters when it comes to seeing through disguises; he recognizes Helena dressed as a boy in Act IV and gives away Belville's disguise earlier in the same scene. He refuses to buy into Angelica's self-deception and instead castigates her for "the Vanity of that Pride, which taught you how to set such a Price on Sin". Especially with Angelica, his purpose, like Horner's, is to reveal her illusions and hypocrisy. But unlike Horner, he doesn't practice deceit to reveal it. This is probably because his goal is to have sex rather than to cuckold. Thus, the balance between sex and power in Willmore's personality leans more towards the enjoyment of sex, and his manipulation extends only to the women in service of this goal.

Willmore epitomizes the libertine ideal of sexual freedom

more so than Horner. He likes Naples where there is "a kind of legal authoriz'd Fornication, where the Men are not chid for 't, nor the Women despis'd". He frankly asks both Helena and Angelica to sleep with him when he first meets each of them and declares to Belville, "Thou know'st there's but one way for a Woman to oblige me".

But like Horner, all women seem the same to him. He declares, "Oh for my Arms full of soft, white, kind-Woman!" and accosts Florinda in the garden for no other reason than that she is there and "'tis a delicate shining Wench". After the attempted rape is stopped by Belville, Willmore recalls Angelica lives nearby and blithely goes to her house. All this occurs after he has promised Hellena to be faithful, and he only renews his pursuit of Hellena when Angelica throws him over. Yet, though Willmore is careless and irresponsible (and sometimes dangerous) and his drunken and sexual excesses outstrip Horner's, he is less consciously manipulative than Horner. He also genuinely admires Helena for her wit and recognizes and appreciates she is as cynical as he: "We are so of one Humour, it must be a Bargain". Thus, he takes a step that Horner would never consider, he marries.

One can see the dimunition of the popularity of the witty rake-hero when one reads *The Wives' Excuse* published in 1691. From the ideal of Horner in *The Country Wife* (1675) to its variation in Willmore (1677), the power and influence of the rake in Restoration comedy can be seen waning in the portrayal of Lovemore. Like Horner, he conspires to cuckold Mr. Friendall and sleep with Mrs. Friendall. He perceives that Friendall is a coward and so arranges him to be publicly challenged to a duel. When Friendall wriggles out of it, Lovemore hopes that Mrs. Friendall will be so disgusted with her husband that she will sleep with him.

Again like Horner, he has an insight into the society: it is a formula that has worked for him before, "Thus, who a married woman's love would win/ Should with the husband's failings first begin:". But when Lovemore finally succeeds in publicly exposing Friendall with Mrs. Witwoud (and consequently humiliating Mrs. Friendall), she still frustrates

Lovemore's designs and refuses to have sex with him. Thus, Lovemore's social power as the witty rake in the style of Horner is diminished. He can disrupt but not control; his vision of society cannot account for everyone in it.

The character of the rake-hero is a product of Restoration society. Taking their clue from the activities and ideas that prevailed in the Restoration Court, the Restoration playwrights fashioned a character type who could be successful in an uncertain society by outwitting others without being hampered by an outmoded morality. "In a world in which honor is but a word and virtue but a pose, whoever dissimulates most successfully will acquire most power and will least likely be a victim of others' ruthless schemes". The audience was doubtless meant to admire Horner's resourcefulness and Willmore's freedom from convention, yet by the time Lovemore mounts the stage, the rake appears weak and rather pathetic, mechanically pursuing pleasure without knowing why. The rake's currency with the audience lessened with the change in the times, a new monarch, and changes in social and cultural values and mores.

Changing Ideals of the Feminine

The heroines of the three plays, Margery, Hellena, and Mrs. Friendall, also seem to chart the times with regard to the changing attitudes about proper female behavior and the nature of women in general. Like her rake counterpart, each heroine is to a certain extent frank about her sexual needs and desires. Margery sighs over Horner in her room and a "hot fit comes and [she] is all in a fever". Hellena declares to her sister that she has a healthy sexual appetite and curiosity and knows "how these ought to be employ'd to the best Advantage", and the fact that Mrs. Friendall acknowledges that she is tempted by Lovemore makes her rejection of him more admirable.

This acknowledgment of normal female sexual desire on the part of the playwrights indicates a shift from ideas found in earlier dramas of the century, (like *The Revenger's Tragedy*) that female expressions of sexual appetite automatically made a woman a whore. It is also a way for the heroines themselves to challenge the social limitations imposed by husbands, fathers, and brothers that parallels and competes with the rake-heroes' desire for freedom of sexual expression. Independence of spirit is expressed rhetorically by many of the female characters but only Hellena does so through her use of wit. The other two heroines express themselves through their choices, but these lack little force beyond the rhetorical.

Horner declares that "wit is more necessary than beauty; and [he] thinks no young woman ugly that has it", but Margery is too honest and ignorant to banter with Horner, and he later laments this lack in her and all that it implies in terms of a practical knowledge of the world. Likewise, Mrs. Friendall's dialogue is consistently sentimental, and her declarations of virtue are too serious and prosaic to be witty. Yet, these two women both make moral choices, and they reflect their times in choosing opposite outcomes. Margery chooses to lie to her husband and protect Horner and Mrs. Friendall chooses to reject Lovemore although she separates from her husband. Margery's choice reflects her newly discovered understanding that she must practice deceit in order to survive in a hypocritical and repressive society. Thus, the vision of society that *The Country Wife* presents remains enclosed for women and there is little questioning of the dominant values espoused by Horner. In *The Wives' Excuse,* Mrs. Friendall's choice and the play itself tend to undermine Restoration assumptions about women, marriage and the society. Regardless, both women still remain trapped in an unhappy marriage.

Of the three, only Hellena exemplifies the independent and witty Restoration comic heroine, a suitable counterpart to her rake-hero. She resourcefully pursues Willmore and wins him. Hellena aspires to the control of a Horner in displaying an equal ability to outwit other characters and determine plot as when she disguises herself as a boy and disrupts the relationship between Angelica and Willmore. Her use of wit helps her win her man by eliciting his admiration. Willmore muses, "I cannot get her out of my Head; Pray Heaven...she prove damnable ugly that I may fortify my self against her Tongue" and praises her, "Ah Rogue! such black Eyes, such a Face, such a Mouth, such Teeth,-and so much Wit!". She also wins the battle of the sexes, played out in the arena of wit in which his aim is seduction and hers is matrimony. Yet, as Wilkinson points out, the hero "accepts marriage often with witty excuses, [only] if she proves resolutely chaste," so in fact chastity is still the basis of female survival and the price of female victory in the battle of the sexes. Even Hellena, the most independent and aggressive of these three Restoration heroines, cannot free herself from the social necessities of female chastity and conventional marriage. Thus, for all three women, increased awareness of and ability to talk about their respective situations does not translate into increased freedom to act. The minor female characters also illustrate some of these same contradictions.

Both Alithea and Florinda, who conform to the more traditionally idealized heroine figures, must undergo some kind of education that involves disillusion. Alithea, witty and independently minded in a way that prefigures Hellena, discovers her extreme idealism is out-of-place and even dangerous in this new era in which traditional values are inverted or abandoned. She betrays her naive understanding of the realities of marriage when she says of Sparkish, her betrothed, "Love proceeds from esteem; he cannot distrust my virtue. Besides he loves me, or he would not marry me". Her overly zealous ideal of honoring her pledge to Sparkish almost leads to a disastrous match, and she learns that her ideals must be tempered by a practical evaluation of the society around her though she never slips into the deep cynicism of Lady Fidget and her cohorts. Alithea contrasts with Margery in that though both start out innocent, Alithea is lucky enough, albiet through the manipulations of Harcourt, to avoid an unhappy match like the Pinchwifes'.

Florinda too is characterized as an ideal heroine, chaste, modest, and beautiful. She is also independent, willing to defy her brother through intrigue and disguise in order to marry Belville. Yet, just as Alithea's reputation is temporarily endangered when Margery impersonates her, Florinda is physically endangered when both Willmore and Blunt nearly rape her. Though Florinda does not acknowledge these experiences as having a lasting or negative effect upon her, I think the audience is meant to take note of the level of male violence directed towards her. Perhaps she encounters danger because she cannot defend herself with wit like her sister, but perhaps it is also an indication that the ideal of woman as a morally elevated being as portrayed in *The Broken Heart* is also losing currency in the society. Women are no longer automatically respected if they cannot prove they are of a certain class.

In these dramatic presentations, all of these female characters seem to reflect an effort by women in Restoration society to both step up from the moral gutter and down from the pedastal and no doubt corresponds with the slow but continuing move in Britain from a religious society (with their dogmatic views on the nature of women) to a secular society. They also echo the male heroes in their desires for freedom and self-expression which may be linked to the growing popularity of middle-class values. Yet, as pointed out above, women's growing awareness of their limitations and their aspirations for more freedom in expression does not in the plays, and did not in society, translate into a change of female legal status until the following century.

The problem of aspiration and limitation, as with appearance and reality, is dealt with by the female use of masks and disguises which generalizes the female experience in all three plays. Through disguise Margery achieves her desire of meeting with Horner, and the carnival masks enable Hellena and Florinda to move freely around the city without male supervision in pursuit of their lovers. Mrs. Witwoud in *The Wives' Excuse* uses a mask when having sex with Mr. Friendall, but it also serves to reveal his true character to Mrs. Friendall. The use of disguise allows many of the female characters to skirt societal restrictions but it also reveals how repressive their conventional roles actually are.

Representations of Marriage

The dramatic representations of male and female characters come together in the way the three plays comment on marriage. Many critics take the view that marriage as an institution is more vilified in Restoration comedy than in the drama of other periods but this is not generally true. The rake-heroes and their friends do express the Hobbesian views of freedom to follow natural impulses and their raillery against marriage is due to it often being seen as a restriction on these impulses, all the more since divorces were practically impossible to obtain. Yet *The Country Wife* ends with one marriage and *The Rover* ends with two and though *The Wives' Excuse* ends bleakly with a failed marriage, the institution itself is still supported. One also has to bear in mind that the rake-hero's inversion of values was also a source of laughter and would not have been had the audience been meant to take his views completely seriously.

The kinds of marriages that are satirized and condemned are those based on economic or other considerations rather than love and mutual affection. Pinchwife marries Margery specifically because of her igorance and youth since, as he asks Horner, "What is wit in a wife good for, but to make a man a cuckold?". But Horner does cuckold him and Pinchwife's selfishness and jealousy are presented as reasons that he deserves to be. Willmore, in response to Angelica's charge that men never ask anything about a Lady proposed to them for marriage except the size of her fortune, responds, "It is a barbarous Custom, which I will scorn to defend in our Sex". Hellena rails at her brother for wanting to marry Florinda off to an old man for economic and political gain.

The Pinchwife marriage and Hellena's comments refer to a specific result of arranged marriage which was the high incidence of young women being married to older, sometimes much older, men. Hume maintains that "by the standards of comedies written after about 1670 old husbands with young wives are fair game for horning, especially if the wife entered the marriage under duress. Cuckoldom is punishment". This is the attitude expressed in *The Country Wife* by Horner and such a marriage is avoided for Florinda thanks to the manipulations of Belville and Willmore. Though not significantly older than his intended, Sparkish's economic motives for marrying Alithea are revealed and the marriage is likewise prevented by Harcourt. Unfortunately the same motives led to Mr. Friendall marrying Mrs. Friendall and even though they agree to part, Mrs. Frier dall must still be his wife "and still unhappy". All three plays explore the fact that such marriages rarely have a happy outcome. What Gills says of Behn, that her plays focus on "the contending claims of love and money" can rightly be said of *The Country Wife* and *The Wives' Excuse* as well.

Instead, the kind of marriages endorsed are those based on love in which each partner chooses the other freely. Florinda and Belville are portrayed as a love match from the first. Harcourt chooses Alithea and she responds when he believes in her innocence. Interestingly, Harcourt is something of a rake and in *The Rover*, of the three plays, we see the fully developed rake, Willmore, also succumb to marriage. Indeed, Hellena and Willmore provide the most full example of a type of match peculiar to the Restoration comedies because they both seek freedom but when they find each other and are mutually attracted, (as Hellena says to Willmore, "I see our Business as well as Humours are alike"), they express an attempt to establish a new kind of paradigm for marriage in which male and female meet on a more equal footing.

Hellena's and Willmore's lack of illusions regarding each other and marriage can help them avoid many of the pitfalls and disappointments encountered by couples enacting traditional roles and expectations. Yet, the fact that they do marry nevertheless reinstates a social order and it is Mrs. Friendall's situation, still so common at the end of the century, that restates the argument that some marriages may never work and may be best dissolved.

What is perhaps more interesting than their comments on marriage are the plays' treatment of male and female gender roles. In many ways, gender roles appear more rigidly defined than in the earlier plays. The rake-hero's activities have been narrowed to exclude the traditional romantic hero's roles of soldier, son, etc. (i.e., Hamlet, Philaster) and feature only social manipulations in the service of sexual conquest. Likewise, female characters may perhaps have more rhetorical freedom, but their goals are also primarily sex and pleasure-oriented (Alithea, Margery, Hellena) and when the goals are not, as with Mrs. Friendall, the woman finds there is no role for her within the society.

But the plays also contain gender uncertainty, ambiguity, and reversal. Horner's pretended emasculation leads him to be viewed as feminized by the men and, as he is treated more familiarly and demandingly by the women he wishes to dominate, they feminize him as well; they treat him more like an object or pet and pass him around like a "whore". Yet, the play itself seeks to portray Horner as the "superior man" who exposes and groups with the "defective" females like Lady Fidget the "young fops and old lechers...in obvious ways to feminize them also"; they are lesser men than the rake-hero.

The< Rover also subverts gender roles as when both Hellena and Florinda skillfully pursue their lovers as would a male rake though their goals must be marriage; yet the male is object and the female is subject, and the play concludes with Willmore being presented to Hellena as a prize she has won. Finally, at the conclusion of *The Wives' Excuse*, though Lovemore delivers the last lines, Mrs. Friendall speaks the epilogue, a speech which deflates male vanity, and the audience is left with the impression that her situation is more interesting and significant to the future society than Lovemore's repititious round of philandering; the play concludes with her replacing him on centre stage.

Remarking on Restoration drama, Hume claims that "social commentary is an altogether common phenomenon in these plays" and neither *The Country Wife*, nor *The Rover*, nor *The Wives' Excuse* presents an exception. As I think has been made clear, these three plays reflect the age in a number of ways. The increasing awareness of arranged marriages as a social problem paralleled a growing concern with women's rights since once a woman was married she had almost no legal recourse against a tyrannical or unfaithful husband. This is represented by a body of writing in books, newspapers, and magazines of the time, and the Restoration comedy's preoccupation with marriage reflected these concerns. The increasing representation in drama of the urban gentry and middle class rather than royalty or aristocracy also corresponded to shifts in the society in which the merchant middle-class was growing in numbers and wealth and introducing into the culture the middle-class values of private ownership and individual rights. The class and power structure was shifting downward, making possible the opening scene in *The Wives' Excuse* in which the servants all know what their employers are up to.

Yet the plays also reflect the society during these volatile times in promoting "reactionary" sentiments. Hume believes the rake-hero illustrates the upper class rebellion against the repressive morality of the puritans and the bourgeois middle-class which Gill also credits with trends towards a hardening of binary gender roles. Nevertheless, the rise of the gentleman from the new gentry contributed to the diminishment of influence of the court gallant, and the parallel can be seen in the rake's loss of influence from Horner to Lovemore. By the 1690's, the wit and explicit sexuality of *The Country Wife* and *TheRover* was being superceded by the beginning of the portrayal of more idealized figures like Mrs. Friendall, staid and virtuous, and these kinds of figures would become increasingly prevalent in the new sentimental comedies of the new century.

Adieu, bon vivants!

Chapter 12

Synopsis of the Play

A ribald tangle of deceit among upper-class English households is revealed as Mirabell, a philanderer, cynically comforts Mrs. Fainall, his mistress. Mrs. Fainall is complaining that she completely detests her husband, and asks why Mirabell compelled her to marry him.

Observing that it is well to "have just so much disgust for your husband as may be sufficient to relish your lover," Mirabell reminds her: "If the familiarities of our loves had proved that consequence of which you were apprehensive, where could you have fixed a father's name with credit but on a husband?" As for his choice of Fainall, he says: "A better person ought not to have been sacrificed to the occasion; a worse had not answered the purpose."

Mrs. Fainall's passion for Mirabell, nevertheless, leads her to help him in his next scheme, even though it involves her own mother, Lady Wishfort, also infatuated with Mirabell. Mirabell wants to marry the beautiful and wealthy Mrs. Millamant, niece of Lady Wishfort, but her aunt—who is also her guardian—is jealously withholding her consent. With Mrs. Fainall's connivance, Mirabell arranges to have his servant, Waitwell, in the guise of an uncle called Sir Rowland, pay court to Lady Wishfort. Then, since he already has accomplished a secret marriage between Waitwell and Lady Wishfort's maid, Foible, he proposes to expose the scandal. His pride for silence is to be Mrs. Millamant and her fortune.

The scheme perfected, Foible tells Lady Wishfort that Sir Rowland has seen her picture and is infatuated by her loveliness. A meeting is arranged, but the plot is overheard by Mrs. Marwood, another of Mirabell's conquests and herself no mean schemer. Desiring Mirabell for herself, she promptly influences Lady Wishfort to agree that Mrs. Millamant shall be married to Sir Wilfull, a rich and amiable dunce. Then Mrs. Marwood, to make sure of success, enlists the help of Fainall who is infatuated with her and jealous of Mirabell. Fainall is a willing tool, complaining: "My wife is an arrant wife, and I am a cuckold....'Sdeath! To be out-witted, out-jilted, out-matrimoney'd!... 'Tis scurvy wedlock!"

Deceived by her caresses and angered by her reminder that Mirabell, his foe, may otherwise get Mrs. Millamant's fortune, Fainall agrees to Mrs. Marwood's plan: she will write a letter to be delivered to Lady Wishfort when Waitwell, as Sir Rowland, is with her. The letter will expose the fraud and Mirabell, she says, will be ruined. Mrs. Marwood neglects to tell Fainall of her scheme to save Mirabell for herself.

Lady Wishfort is a-twitter as she awaits the bogus Sir Rowland. She is informed by Foible that candles are ready, that the footmen are lined up in the hall in their best liveries, and that the coachman and postillion, well perfumed, are on hand for a good showing.

Assured by Foible that she looks "most killing well," Lady Wishfort ponders: "Well, and how shall I receive him?... Shall I sit? No, I won't sit—I'll walk—ay, I'll walk down from the door upon his entrance, and then turn full upon him—No, that will be too sudden. I'll lie—ay, I'll lie down—I'll receive him in my little dressing room—yes, yes, I'll give him the first impression on a couch. I won't lie neither, but loll and lean upon one elbow, with one foot a little dangling off, jogging in a thoughtful way—yes—and then as soon as he appears, start, ay, start and be surprised, and rise to meet him in a pretty disorder."

Sir Rowland arrives. He and Lady Wishfort get along famously at once, and Sir Rowland begs for an early marriage, declaring that his nephew, Mirabell, will poison him for his money if he learns of the romance. The jealous Lady Wishfort promptly agrees, suggesting that Sir Rowland starve Mirabell "gradually, inch by inch." Then Mrs. Marwood's letter, denouncing Sir Rowland as Waitwell, arrives, but Sir Rowland deftly declares the letter to be the work of his nephew, and he hies himself off "to fight him a duel."

Lady Wishfort learns of the deception that is being practiced, and turns on Foible: "Out of my house! To marry me to a serving-man! To make me the laughing-stock of the whole town! I'll have you locked up in Bridewell Jail, that's what I'll do!"

The frightened Foible confesses that it is Mirabell who has conceived the whole plot, and Lady Wishfort is planning a dire revenge when more trouble comes: Fainall, her son-in-law, demands that his wife turn over her whole fortune to him, else he and Mrs. Marwood will reveal to the world that Mrs. Fainall was Mirabell's mistress before her marriage and that she still is. Lady Wishfort is dazedly reflecting upon this new humiliation when Mirabell comes to her with another plan.

"If," he says, "a deep sense of the many injuries I have offered to so good a lady, with a sincere remorse and a hearty contrition, can but obtain the least glance of compassion, I am too happy.... Consider, madam, in reality it was an innocent device, though I confess it had a face of guiltiness. It was at most an artifice which love contrived—and errors which love produces have ever been accounted pardonable."

The susceptible Lady Wishfort offers to forgive Mirabell if he will renounce his idea of marrying Mrs. Millamant. Mirabell offers a compromise: if she will permit her niece to marry him, he will contrive to save Mrs. Fainall's reputation and fortune. If he can do this, Lady Wishfort agrees, she will forgive anything and consent to anything. Mirabell then tells her: "Well, then, as regards your daughter's reputation, she has nothing to fear from Fainall. For his own reputation is at stake. He and Mrs. Marwood—we have proof of it—have been and still are lovers.... And as regards your daughter's fortune, she need have no fear on that score, either: acting upon my advice, and relying upon my honesty, she has made me the trustee of her entire estate.

Cries Fainall: "'Tis outrageous!"

Says Mirabell: "'Tis the way of the world."

In a closing observation to the audience, he adds:
"From hence let those be warned, who mean to wed,
Lest mutual falsehood stain the bridal bed;
For each deceiver to his cost may find,
That marriage frauds too oft are paid in kind."

Chapter 13

Character List

Scout (Jean Louise Finch)

Narrator of the story. The story takes place from the time Scout is aged 6 to 9, but she tells the story as an adult. Scout is a tomboy who would rather solve problems with her fists than with her head. Throughout the course of the book, Scout comes to a new understanding of human nature, societal expectations, and her own place in the world.

Atticus Finch

Maycomb attorney and state legislative representative who is assigned to represent Tom Robinson. A widower, Atticus is a single parent to two children: Jem and Scout.

Jem (Jeremy Atticus Finch)

Scout's older brother who ages from 10 to 13 during the story. He is Scout's protector and one of her best friends. As part of reaching young adulthood, Jem deals with many difficult issues throughout the story.

Aunt Alexandra

Atticus' sister. Aunt Alexandra lives at Finch's Landing, the Finch family homestead, but she moves in with Atticus and the children during Tom Robinson's trial. She is very concerned that Scout have a feminine influence to emulate.

Francis Hancock

Aunt Alexandra's grandson. He taunts Scout about Atticus, getting her in trouble.

Uncle Jack Finch

Atticus and Aunt Alexandra's bachelor brother who comes to visit every Christmas. He is a doctor who, like Atticus, was schooled at home.

Calpurnia

The Finch's African American housekeeper. She grew up at Finch's Landing and moved with Atticus to Maycomb. She is the closest thing to a mother that Scout and Jem have. One of the few Negroes in town who can read and write, she teaches Scout to write.

Zeebo

The town garbage collector who is also Calpurnia's son. He's one of four people who can read at the First Purchase African M.E. Church.

Boo Radley (Mr. Arthur Radley)

The mysterious neighbour who piques the children's interest. They've never seen him and make a game of trying to get him to come outside.

Nathan Radley

Boo Radley's brother who comes back to live with the family when Mr. Radley dies.

Mr. and Mrs. Radley

Boo and Nathan Radley's parents.

Dill (Charles Baker Harris)

Jem and Scout's neighborhood friend. Living in Meridian, Mississippi, Dill spends every summer with his aunt, Miss Rachel Haverford.

Miss Rachel Haverford

Dill's aunt who lives next door to the Finches.

Miss Maudie Atkinson

One of Maycomb's most open-minded citizens, Miss

Maudie lives across the street from Jem and Scout. An avid gardener, she often spends time talking with the children – especially Scout – helping them to better understand Atticus and their community.

Miss Stephanie Crawford

The neighborhood gossip.

Mrs. Henry Lafayette Dubose

A cantankerous, vile, elderly woman who teaches Jem and Scout a great lesson in bravery.

Mrs. Grace Merriweather

A devout Methodist, Mrs. Merriweather writes the Halloween pageant.

Mrs. Gertrude Farrow

The "second most devout lady in Maycomb" belongs to the local Missionary Society.

Tom Robinson

The black man who is accused of raping and beating Mayella Ewell.

Helen Robinson

Tom Robinson's wife.

Link Deas

Tom and Helen Robinson's employer. He makes sure that Helen can pass safely by the Ewell's after Tom is arrested. Bob Ewell The Ewell patriarch, Bob Ewell spends his welfare checks on alcohol.He claims to have witnessed Tom attacking Mayella.

Mayella Violet Ewell

Tom's 19-year-old accuser.

Burris Ewell:

One of Bob Ewell's children. He attends school only one day a year.

Reverend Skyes

The pastor at First Purchase African M.E. Church. He helps Jem and Scout understand Tom's trial and finds seats for them in the "colored balcony."

Judge John Taylor

The judge at Tom's trial. He appoints Atticus to represent Tom.

Mr. Horace Gilmer

The state attorney representing the Ewells.

Sheriff Heck

Tate Maycomb's sheriff who accompanies Atticus to kill the mad dog and who delivers the news about Bob Ewell.

Mr. Braxton Bragg Underwood

The owner, editor, and printer of The Maycomb Tribune. Although he openly dislikes blacks, he defends Tom's right to a fair trial.

Dolphus Raymond

Father to several biracial children, Mr. Raymond lives on the outskirts of town. When he comes into Maycomb, he pretends to be drunk.

Walter Cunningham, Sr.

One of the men who comes to lynch Tom Robinson, he's also one of Atticus's clients. After speaking with Scout, he calls off the mob.

Walter Cunningham, Jr.

One of Scout's classmates. Jem invites him to have lunch with them after Scout accosts Walter on the playground.

Miss Caroline Fisher

New to teaching and to Maycomb and its ways, Miss Caroline is Scout's first grade teacher.

Cecil Jacobs

A schoolmate of the Finch children, he scares Jem and Scout on the way to the Halloween pageant.

Little Chuck Little

One of Scout's classmates who stands up to Burris Ewell in defence of Miss Caroline.

Miss Gates

Scout's second grade teacher.

Lula

A parishioner at First Purchase African M.E. Church who is upset when Scout and Jem attend services there.

Eula May

The local telephone operator.

Mr. Avery

A boarder at the house across from Mrs. Dubose's.

Chapter 14

Character Analysis

Scout Finch

That the young narrator of To Kill a Mockingbird goes by the nickname "Scout" is very appropriate. In the story, Scout functions as both questioner and observer. Scout asks tough questions, certainly questions that aren't "politically correct," but she can ask these questions because she is a child. As a child, Scout doesn't understand the full implication of the things happening around her, making her an objective observer and a reporter in the truest sense. The reader should keep in mind, though, that To Kill a Mockingbird really presents two Scouts: the little girl experiencing the story and the adult Jean Louise who tells the story. The woman relating the story obviously recognizes that her father is exceptional. However, the child Scout complains "Our father didn't do anything...he never went hunting, he did not play poker or fish or drink or smoke. He sat in the living room and read." The child Scout marvels that her father knew she was listening to his conversation with Uncle Jack; the adult Jean Louise marvels that he wanted her to overhear the conversation.

Although the story takes place over the course of three years, Scout learns a lifetime's worth of lessons in that span. Here, too, the reader should remember that in many ways To Kill a Mockingbird is Scout's memoir — the adult Jean Louise can better understand the impact of various events than the child living through them.

Scout hates school because in many ways it actually inhibits her learning. Her teacher is appalled that she already knows how to read, instead of celebrating that fact. She is bored waiting for the rest of the class to catch up to her skill level, and she doesn't have more than a passing respect for either of the teachers she describes in the story.

The most sympathy she can muster toward a frazzled Miss Caroline is to remark "Had her conduct been more friendly toward me, I would have felt sorry for her." And she is offended by Miss Gates' comments about African Americans after her staunch and moving support for the Jew's in Hitler's Europe. As a sign of her maturity, though, at the end of the story she realizes that she doesn't have much more to learn "except possibly algebra" and for that she needs the classroom. Scout faces so many issues in the duration of the novel, but one of the most lingering for her is the question of what it means to "be a lady." Scout is a tomboy. Sometimes her brother criticizes her for "acting like a girl," other times he complains that she's not girlish enough. Dill wants to marry her, but that doesn't mean he wants to spend time with her. Many of the boys at school are intimidated by her physical strength, yet she is told she must learn to handle herself in a ladylike way. Oddly enough, the women in her life impose more rigid requirements on her than the men do.

Scout's tomboyishness drives Aunt Alexandra to distraction; Miss Caroline sees Scout's outspokenness and honesty as impertinence. Ironically, the person she most wants to please — Atticus — is least concerned about her acting in a certain way. In fact she tells Jem, "'I asked him [Atticus] if I was a problem and he said not much of one, at most one he could always figure out, and not to worry my head a second about botherin' him.'" In the end, though, when she explains why the sheriff can't charge Boo with Bob Ewell's murder, she's become the kind of person who makes her father very, very proud. The other lesson that Scout is truly able to incorporate into her worldview is the necessity of walking in someone else's shoes. Atticus begins teaching her the importance of looking at things from the other person's point of view very early in the story. He points out her own failings in this area and demonstrates his point in his own interactions with other people. At the end of the story, Scout can put herself in Boo Radley's shoes, the person she's feared most throughout the story.

Atticus Finch

Atticus represents morality and reason in To Kill a Mockingbird. As a character, Atticus is even-handed throughout the story. He is one of the very few characters who never has to rethink his position on an issue. His parenting style is quite unique in that he treats his children as adults, honestly answering any question they have. He uses all these instances as an opportunity to pass his values on to Scout and Jem. Scout says that "'Do you really think so?'... was Atticus's dangerous question" because he delighted in helping people see a situation in a new light. Atticus uses this approach not only with his children, but with all of Maycomb. And yet, for all of his mature treatment of Jem and Scout, he patiently recognizes that they are children and that they will make childish mistakes and assumptions. Ironically, Atticus's one insecurity seems to be in the child-rearing department, and he often defends his ideas about raising children to those more experienced and more traditional.

His stern but fair attitude toward Jem and Scout reaches into the courtroom as well. He politely proves that Bob Ewell is a liar; he respectfully questions Mayella about her role in Tom's crisis. One of the things that his longtime friend Miss Maudie admires about him is that "'Atticus Finch is the same in his house as he is on the public streets.'" The only time he seriously lectures his children is on the evils of taking advantage of those less fortunate or less educated, a philosophy he carries into the animal world by his refusal to hunt. And although most of the town readily pins the label "trash" on other people, Atticus reserves that distinction for those people who unfairly exploit others. Atticus believes in justice and the justice system. He doesn't like criminal law, yet he accepts the appointment to Tom Robinson's case. He knows before he begins that he's going to lose this case, but that doesn't stop him from giving Tom the strongest defence he possibly can. And, importantly, Atticus doesn't put so much effort into Tom's case because he's an African American, but because he is innocent. Atticus feels that the justice system should be colour blind, and he defends Tom as an innocent man, not a man of colour. Atticus is the adult character least infected by prejudice in the novel. He has no problem with his children attending Calpurnia's church, or with a black woman essentially raising his children. He admonishes Scout not to use racial slurs, and is careful to always use the terms acceptable for his time and culture. He goes to Helen's home to tell her of Tom's death, which means a white man spending time in the black community. Other men in town would've sent a messenger and left it at that. His lack of prejudice doesn't apply only to other races, however. He is unaffected by Mrs. Dubose's caustic tongue, Miss Stephanie Crawford's catty gossip, and even Walter Cunningham's thinly veiled threat on his life. He doesn't retaliate when Bob Ewell spits in his face because he understands that he has wounded Ewell's pride — the only real possession this man has. Atticus accepts these people because he is an expert at "climb[ing] into [other people's] skin and walking around in it."

Jem Finch

Jem ages from 10 to 13 over the course of To Kill a Mockingbird, a period of great change in any child's life. Jem is no exception to this rule. Interestingly, the changes he undergoes are seen from the point-of-view of a younger sister, which gives a unique perspective on his growth. Jem represents the idea of bravery in the novel, and the way that his definition changes over the course of the story is important. The shift that occurs probably has as much to do with age as experience, although the experiences provide a better framework for the reader. When the story begins, Jem's idea of bravery is simply touching the side of the Radley house and then only because "In all his life, Jem had never declined a dare." But as the story progresses, Jem learns about bravery from Atticus facing a mad dog, from Mrs. Dubose's fight with addiction, and from Scout's confrontation with the mob at the jail, among others. And along the way, he grows from a boy who drags his sister along as a co-conspirator to a young gentleman who protects his Scout and tries to help her understand the implications of the events around her.

His own sister finds Jem a genuinely likeable boy, if sometimes capable of "maddening superiority." He very much wants to be like his father, and plans to follow him into law. He idolizes Atticus and would rather risk personal injury than disappoint his father. As he grows older, he begins to do what is right even though his decision may not be popular. For instance, when Dill sneaks into Scout's bedroom after running away from home, Jem can only say, "'You oughta let your mother know where you are'" and makes the difficult decision to involve Atticus.

Afterward, he's temporarily exiled by his friends, but he maintains the rightness of his decision without apology. Like many adolescents, Jem is idealistic. Even after Atticus' long explanation about the intricacies of the Tom Robinson case, Jem is unable to accept the jury's conviction. In fact, he is ready to overhaul the justice system and abolish juries all together. Wisely, Atticus doesn't try to squelch or minimize Jem's feelings; by respecting his son, Atticus allows Jem to better cope with the tragedy. Still, Jem turns on Scout when she tells him about Miss Gates' racist remarks at the courthouse, shouting, "'I never wanta hear about that courthouse again, ever, ever, you hear me?'"

His coping skills are still developing, and his family is the one group that gives him the room that he needs to hone them. Ironically, Jem, who so strongly identifies with Tom Robinson, is the only person in the story who is left with physical evidence of the whole event. More ironic still is the fact that Jem's injury leaves "His left arm…somewhat shorter than the right" just like Tom Robinson's, and Tom Robinson sustained his injury at approximately the same age. That the man responsible for breaking Jem's arm was also responsible for sending Tom to prison (and indirectly, responsible for his death) serves to drive the irony home.

The adult Jean Louise doesn't provide much insight into

the adult Jeremy Atticus Finch, but from the fact that the story begins with their disagreement over when various events started, the reader can assume that they maintained a similar relationship into adulthood.

Dill Harris

Because he hails from Mississippi, Dill Harris is an outsider, but having relatives in Maycomb, as well as being a child, grants him immediate acceptance in the town. Dill is an interesting character because his personality is a compilation of many of the story's other characters. As such, Dill functions as a sort of moral thermometer for the reader in understanding Maycomb. Readers, especially those who don't live in the South, are as much strangers to Maycomb as Dill is, and so he paves the way for the reader's objective observance of the story Scout has to tell.

Dill is an observer much like Scout; however, he has no vested interest or innate understanding of the various folks he encounters. Dill doesn't know his biological father, just as Scout doesn't know her mother. In his attempts to lure Boo Radley outside, Dill's not much different than Bob Ewell with Tom Robinson, although admittedly, Dill's intentions are nowhere near as heinous. He tells enormous lies and concocts unlikely stories just as Mayella does during Tom's trial. He often pretends to be something he isn't, just like Dolphus Raymond does when he comes into town. He risks his safety to run away to Maycomb just as Jem risks his when he goes to collect his pants from the Radleys.

Dill's fantastic stories bring the question of lying to the forefront of To Kill a Mockingbird. Dill's lies incense Scout, but she learns that "one must lie under certain circumstances and at all times when one can't do anything about them," a statement that foreshadows Mayella's predicament. Ironically, Dill, who so easily lies, sobs when the Ewell's succeed in the lies they tell about Tom Robinson.

Boo Radley and Tom Robinson

Boo Radley and Tom Robinson share many similarities

in spite of fact that one man is white and the other black. By juxtaposing these two characters, Lee proves that justice and compassion reach beyond the boundary of colour and human prejudices. The novel's title is a metaphor for both men, each of whom is a mockingbird. In this case however, one mockingbird is shot, the other is forced to kill.

Boo and Tom are handicapped men. Lee hints that he may be physically unhealthy, and she makes statements that lead the reader to believe he may be mentally unstable. However, no character sheds any light on his actual condition, leaving the reader wondering whether Boo's family protects him or further handicaps him. Tom is physically handicapped, like a bird with a broken wing, but his race is probably a bigger "disability" in the Maycomb community. As a result of these handicaps, both men's lives are cut short. Whatever Boo's problems may be, the reader knows that something happened to Boo that has caused him to become a recluse. For all practical purposes, Tom's life ends when a white woman decides to accuse him of rape.

Boo sees Scout and Jem as his children, which is why he parts with things that are precious to him, why he mends Jem's pants and covers Scout with a blanket, and why he ultimately kills for them: "Boo's children needed him." Apparently his family disapproves of his affection for the children or Mr. Radley wouldn't have cemented the knothole. But Boo is undeterred and loves them, even with the probable knowledge that he is the object of their cruel, childish games.

Tom also recognizes Mayella as a person in need. On the witness stand, he testifies that he gladly helped her because "'Mr. Ewell didn't seem to help her none, and neither did the chillun.'" Tom helps Mayella at great personal expense. Both men know their town very well. Unbeknownst to the Finch children, Boo has watched them grow up. The reader can fairly assume that Boo is also familiar with the Ewells, and probably doesn't think much more of them than the rest of Maycomb. Boo and Tom have had minor skirmishes with the law, but that past doesn't tarnish the kindness they show to others in the story. The moment that Mayella makes a pass at Tom, he inherently knows that he's in serious danger. Truthfully, he probably knew that helping her without pay was not the safest thing for him to do, but the compassion of one human being for another won out over societal expectations. The children treat Boo with as much prejudice as the town shows Tom Robinson. They assign characteristics to Boo without validation; they want to see Boo, not as their neighbour, but as a carnival-freak-show-type curiosity. Ironically, watching the injustice that Tom suffers helps the children understand why Boo may choose to be a recluse: "'it's because he wants to stay inside.'"

Aunt Alexandra and Miss Maudie Atkinson

Aunt Alexandra and Miss Maudie are roughly the same age and grew up as neighbors at Finch's Landing. But for all the background these women share, they couldn't be more opposite. Lee uses the contrasts between these two characters to further delineate the theme of tolerance in To Kill a Mockingbird.

Aunt Alexandra is very conscious of Maycomb's social mores, chooses to live within its constrictions, and "given the slightest chance she would exercise her royal prerogative: she would arrange, advise, caution, and warn." Even her clothing is tight and restrictive. Miss Maudie, on the other hand, sets herself towards the outside of Maycomb's conventionality. Like Atticus, she stays within bounds, but follows her own code. Although Miss Maudie is quick to welcome Aunt Alexandra as her new neighbour, she's also quick to take her to task. When Aunt Alexandra states, "'I can't say I approve of everything he does, Maudie, but he's my brother,'"

Miss Maudie reminds her that Atticus is doing a wonderful thing and that many in the town support him, even if that support is quiet. Aunt Alexandra is also extremely critical of Atticus's parenting style, while Miss Maudie is much more sympathetic. But then, Miss Maudie has a delightful sense of humour, a trait Aunt Alexandra does not possess. Aunt Alexandra works hard at being feminine, but Miss Maudie doesn't seem to care about those things. She wears men's overalls when she works in the garden, but is equally comfortable in more traditional garb. Aunt Alexandra has a personal quest to make Scout "behave like a sunbeam," but Miss Maudie accepts her as she is. Consequently, Scout finds in Miss Maudie a kindred spirit who helps her make sense of being female and, with Atticus, helps Scout develop tolerance. Miss Maudie treats the children in an adult manner, much like Atticus does. She never laughs at Scout's mistakes and she trusts the children to play in her yard within the boundaries she's set for them.

Aunt Alexandra is "analogous to Mount Everest:...cold and there" while Miss Maudie is warm enough to pop out her dentures for Scout to see. Miss Maudie has a quiet spirituality that shows itself only when taunted by "'the foot-washers [who] think women are a sin by definition.'" Aunt Alexandra displays her beliefs much more publicly. She's active in the Missionary Society, which appears to be as much a social club as a religious organization. Tolerance isn't a big part of the Missionary Society meetings, either. The ladies' lamentations over the living conditions of the Mrunas, an African tribe, leads to a discussion about how ungrateful the women believe Maycomb's African-American community to be. Miss Maudie is the person who ends that line of conversation with two sentences. Aunt Alexandra may not always agree with the course of discussion, but she refuses to be confrontational outside of her own family.

Bob and Mayella Ewell

The Ewells know that they are the lowest of the low amongst the whites in Maycomb. They have no money, no education, and no breeding. The single thing that elevates them at any level in the community is the fact that they're white. Like most people in similar situations, Bob and Mayella would like to better their station in life. However, Bob is unwilling to put forth the effort necessary to change his family's lot and Mayella doesn't have the resources to change her own life. With her mother dead, Mayella becomes a surrogate wife for her father and mother for her younger siblings. The fact that

Mayella wants a better life for herself is evidenced by the red geraniums she grows so lovingly — they're the only sign of beauty in a dismal, filthy shack and yard. She can't attend school because she has to take care of her younger siblings, especially when her father leaves on days-long drinking binges. She's involved in an incestuous and abusive relationship, but she doesn't have anywhere to go or anyone to help her. At 19, her future is set. She will most likely stay with her family, continuing to be both sexually and physically abused, until she marries and starts the cycle anew.

The idea of having an affair with a black man is exciting in a dangerous sort of way, but more importantly, making advances toward Tom gives Mayella power. This completely powerless woman has total control over Tom in this situation. If he were to agree to a liaison with her, then he would remain at her beck and call for the rest of his life. Readers know what happened when he didn't agree. In an attempt to gain some power in a shabby, pitiful existence, Mayella costs a man his life. Ironically, when Atticus finally shows Mayella the respect she so craves, she accuses him of making fun of her and ultimately refuses to answer his questions.

Bob Ewell would also like to improve his family's station, but the fact that "he was the only man [Scout] ever heard of who was fired from the WPA for laziness" proves that he isn't willing to earn it. Ewell is a drunkard and an abuser who is despised throughout the community, and very likely by his own family. But in accusing Tom Robinson, he sees what he believes is a brass ring. In his mind, the town should think him a hero for saving Maycomb's white women from a "dangerous" black man. Defending his daughter by going to court should raise his family's stature.

If they don't gain more respect from the community, at least Bob won't have to live with talk in the black community about a white woman making a play for a married black man. Unfortunately, all of Ewell's plans backfire. By the end of the trial, he and his daughter are proven liars, he's been publicly identified as a sexually and physically abusive father who fails to provide for his family, and the entire town knows that

Mayella made sexual overtures toward Tom. Instead of improving his life, Ewell cements his family's horrible reputation once and for all.

In this situation, Bob Ewell can do little but try to recover his own pride. He makes good on his threats to harm the people who embarrassed him in court. He rejoices in Tom's death. Bob Ewell is the kind of person who actually seems to enjoy being despicable. Summary and Analysis

Summary and Analysis

Epigraph

Lee begins To Kill a Mockingbird with an epigraph by Charles Lamb: "Lawyers, I suppose, were children once." That she chose this epigraph is interesting on several levels. A good part of this story's brilliance lies in the fact that it's told from a child's point of view. Through Scout's eyes, Lee is able to present the story objectively. By having an innocent little girl make racial remarks and regard people of colour in a way consistent with the community, Lee provides an objective view of the situation. As a child, Scout can make observations that an adult would avoid or sugarcoat. Readers, too, are likely to be forgiving of a child's perception, whereas they would find an adult who makes these remarks offensive. Much of Harper Lee is in the character of Scout. Lee's father was an attorney, as is Scout's. Importantly, Lee herself studied law. Because Scout's personality is loosely autobiographical, the epigraph makes sense. Lee proves through the telling of the story that she was also once a child.

Also significant in understanding the epigraph is Atticus' answer to Jem's question of how a jury could convict Tom Robinson when he's obviously innocent: "'They've done it before and they did it tonight and they'll do it again and when they do it — it seems that only children weep.'" At various points in the story, Jem expresses his desire to become a lawyer, following in his father's footsteps. The lessons he learns during the course of the story will ultimately shape not only the kind of lawyer he will be, but also the kind of man he will become. Readers see this future lawyer as a child first.

Summary and Analysis by Chapter

Part 1: Chapter 1

Scout, the narrator, remembers the summer that her brother Jem broke his arm, and she looks back over the years to recall the incidents that led to that climactic event. Scout provides a brief introduction to the town of Maycomb, Alabama and its inhabitants, including her widowed father Atticus Finch, attorney and state legislator; Calpurnia, their "Negro" cook and housekeeper; and various neighbors. The story starts with the first summer that Scout and Jem meet Dill, a little boy from Meridian, Mississippi who spends the summers with his aunt, the Finch's next-door neighbour Miss Rachel Haverford.

From the children's point of view, their most compelling neighbour is Boo Radley, a recluse whom none of them has ever seen. Dill's fascination, in particular, leads to all sorts of games and plans to try and get Boo to come outside. Their attempts culminate in a dare to Jem, which he grudgingly takes. Jem runs into the Radley's yard and touches the outside of the house.

Summary and Analysis by Chapter

Part 1: Chapters 2–3

Dill goes back to Mississippi for the school year, and Scout turns her attention to starting first grade — something she's been waiting for all her life. However, Scout's first day at school is not at all the glorious experience she'd been expecting from the winters she spent "looking over at the schoolyard, spying on multitudes of children through a two-power telescope...learning their games,...secretly sharing their misfortunes and minor victories." Scout's teacher, Miss Caroline Fisher, is new to teaching, new to Maycomb, and mortified that Scout already knows how to read and write. When Miss Caroline offers to lend Walter Cunningham lunch money, Scout is punished for taking it upon herself to explain Miss Caroline's faux pas to her. (Walter refuses to take the money because his family is too poor to pay it back.)

Scout catches Walter on the playground, and starts to

pummel him in retaliation for her embarrassment, but Jem stops her and then further surprises her by inviting Walter to have lunch with them. Scout is then punished by Calpurnia for criticizing Walter's table manners. Back at school, Miss Caroline has a confrontation with Burris Ewell about his "cooties" and the fact that he only attends school on the first day of the year.

That evening, Scout tells Atticus about her day, hoping that she won't have to go back to school — after all, Burris Ewell doesn't. Atticus explains why the Ewells get special consideration and then tells Scout, "'You never really understand a person...until you climb into his skin and walk around in it.'" These words stick with Scout, and she will try with varying degrees of success to follow Atticus' advice throughout the course of the story.

Summary and Analysis by Chapter

Part 1: Chapters 4–5

The school year passes slowly for Scout. Her grade is released a half hour earlier than Jem's, so Scout has to pass Boo Radley's house by herself every afternoon. One day, Scout notices something shiny in a tree at the edge of the Radley yard. When she goes back to investigate, she finds a stick of gum. Jem admonishes her for taking the gum, but Scout continues to check the knothole daily. On the last day of school, she and Jem find some coins in the tree, which they decide to keep until the next school year starts. Dill arrives two days later to spend the summer. After an argument with Scout, Jem suggests they play a new game called "Boo Radley," which Scout recognizes as Jem's attempt to prove his bravery. Against Scout's better judgement, they enact Boo's life with great gusto until Atticus learns of the game. The children play the game less frequently after that, and Jem and Dill begin excluding Scout, spending more and more time together in the treehouse. Lonely, Scout begins spending more of her time with Miss Maudie.

When Scout insists that the boys include her in their plans, they tell her that they're going to deliver a note to Boo Radley asking him to come outside. She and Dill are posted as guards, while Jem tries to deliver the note, but Atticus intervenes, telling the children to leave the Radleys alone.

Summary and Analysis by Chapter

Part 1: Chapters 6–7

On Dill's last night in Maycomb, he and Jem decide to "peep in the window with the loose shutter to see if they could get a look at Boo Radley." Scout discourages them from going to the Radley house, but reluctantly decides to join them. Someone inside the Radley house comes out and fires a shotgun. The children scurry out of the yard, but Jem gets caught on the fence and is forced to remove his pants to get to safety. As the neighborhood gathers to discuss the gunfire, Dill concocts an unlikely explanation for Jem's lack of pants. Atticus tells Jem to get his pants from Dill and come home. At home, Jem confides in Scout that he's going back to the Radley's to get his pants. Scout literally fears for his life, but Jem would rather risk life and limb than admit to Atticus that he lied. School starts again. This year, Jem and Scout walk home together, and they again begin finding things in the Radley's tree. After receiving several increasingly valuable treasures, Jem and Scout decide to write a thank-you note to whoever is leaving the gifts. When they try to deliver the note, however, they find to their dismay that the knothole has been filled with cement.

Summary and Analysis by Chapter

Part 1: Chapters 8–9

For the first time in decades, Maycomb gets snow. School is closed, so Jem and Scout spend their day trying to build a snowman. That night, Miss Maudie's house burns to the ground. Jem and Scout are sent to wait in front of the Radley's while the fire is still raging. Boo Radley walks up and puts a blanket around a shivering Scout's shoulders, but both she and Jem are too engrossed in the fire to notice. The next day, Scout is surprised to find Miss Maudie in good spirits, working in her yard and talking about expanding her garden. Near

Christmastime, a classmate taunts Scout with the news that Atticus is defending a black man. Atticus asks Scout to promise to "'hold your head high, and keep those fists down....Try fighting with your head for a change,'" — a promise Scout tries to uphold, with limited success. Uncle Jack Finch comes for Christmas as he does every year; Scout and her family spend Christmas at Finch's Landing with Aunt Alexandra and her family. Alexandra's grandson, Francis, begins teasing Scout about Atticus defending a black man. She attacks Francis and is punished by Uncle Jack, who had warned her not to fight or curse. Christmas evening, she and Uncle Jack talk, and she explains to him where he went wrong in his discipline. The chapter ends as Scout overhears Atticus and Uncle Jack talking about Tom Robinson's trial, which will start soon.

Summary and Analysis by Chapter

Part 1: Chapters 10–11

Jem and Scout lament the fact that "Atticus was feeble: he was nearly fifty." The children believe that Atticus' "advanced" age keeps him from doing the sorts of things other children's fathers do. Their view of their father changes when they see him shoot a mad dog. As Tom Robinson's trial grows closer, Jem and Scout endure more slurs against their father. When their neighbour Mrs. Dubose, a mean, elderly woman confined to a wheel chair, makes a particularly stinging remark, Jem retaliates by destroying some of her flowers. Of course, Atticus hears what happened and he makes Jem apologize to Mrs. Dubose, letting her decide his punishment. Jem is sentenced to read to Mrs. Dubose after school for one month. Scout chooses to accompany Jem. Shortly after Jem is relieved from duty, Mrs. Dubose dies. Only then does Atticus tell the children that Mrs. Dubose was very sick and fighting an extremely valiant battle against addiction.

Summary and Analysis by Chapter

Part 2: Chapters 12–13

As summer begins, Jem is now too old to be bothered by his little sister, which causes Scout great dismay. To add to

Scout's disappointment, Dill won't be coming to Maycomb this summer, although Calpurnia eases her loneliness somewhat. With Atticus at a special session of the state legislature, Calpurnia takes the children to church with her. Upon their return from church, they find Aunt Alexandra waiting on the porch for them. She announces that at Atticus' request, she's coming to live with them for "a while." Aunt Alexandra goes to great pains to educate the children in the importance of the Finch breeding, going so far as to have Atticus deliver an uncharacteristic speech — a speech he ultimately recants — to Scout and Jem.

Summary and Analysis by Chapter

Part 2: Chapters 14–16

As Scout innocently recounts her trip to Calpurnia's church for Atticus, Aunt Alexandra is mortified and vehemently refuses Scout's request to go to Calpurnia's house. With Scout out of the room, she comments that they really don't need a housekeeper now that she's come to stay, recommending that Atticus let Calpurnia go. Now it's Atticus' turn to vehemently deny Alexandra's request. Jem and Scout retreat to let the adults work out their differences, but end up in a fistfight with each other. Sent to bed early, Jem and Scout get themselves ready for sleep. Crossing the floor in the darkened room, Scout feels what she thinks is a snake. Jem discovers that the "snake" is Dill with a fantastic story of his runaway voyage to Maycomb.

Jem calls Atticus who arranges for Dill to spend the night. Dill's mother gives him permission to spend the summer in Maycomb and the children begin to enjoy their time together. Then Sheriff Tate and a group of other men come by the house to tell Atticus that Tom Robinson is being moved to the county jail and that there may be trouble. That Sunday night, Atticus heads into town, which gives Jem a funny feeling. At bedtime, he, Scout, and Dill walk downtown themselves to see what's happening. They find Atticus sitting outside Tom Robinson's cell and turn to head home when a group of men arrive to confront Atticus. Not realizing the danger of the situation,

Scout runs into the middle of the mob. After a few tense moments, she begins a conversation with Walter Cunningham's father, which causes the men to retreat, and very likely saves Atticus' life. The next morning, the day the trial is set to begin, Atticus and Scout talk about mob mentality, and, over Aunt Alexandra's protests, he thanks the children for appearing when they did. He asks the children to stay away from the courthouse during the trial, but by noon, their curiosity has the better of them, and they, along with Dill, head for the courthouse where the trial is about to get underway. They can't find a seat in the courtroom, so Reverend Skyes offers them seats in "the Colored balcony," which they gladly accept. Finally, readers are introduced to Judge Taylor, who the children earlier discovered — much to their surprise — appointed Atticus to defend Tom Robinson.

Summary and Analysis by Chapter

Part 2: Chapters 17–20

The trial begins. Heck Tate is the first witness. Under cross-examination, he admits that a doctor was never called to the scene to examine Mayella Ewell. Bob Ewell takes the stand next and causes a stir in the courtroom with his bad attitude and foul language. Mr. Ewell is not shaken from his story, but Atticus carefully plants the seed that Mr. Ewell himself could've beaten Mayella. Mayella takes the stand next. Even though Atticus believes that she's lying, he treats her with courtesy and respect; Mayella thinks that he's making fun of her. Her testimony soon proves that Mayella is unused to gentility and common courtesy.

Atticus asks Tom to stand up so that Mayella may identify him; as he does, Scout notices that Tom's left arm is withered and useless — he could not have committed the crime in the way it was described. The state rests its case. Atticus calls only one witness — Tom Robinson. Tom tells the true story, being careful all the while not to come right out and say that Mayella is lying. However, Tom makes a fatal error when he admits under cross-examination that he, a black man, felt sorry for Mayella Ewell. Dill has a very emotional response to Mr.

Gilmer's questioning and leaves the courtroom in tears. Scout follows Dill outside, where they talk with Dolphus Raymond, who reveals the secret behind his brown bag and his drinking. Scout and Dill return to the courtroom in time to hear the last half of Atticus's impassioned speech to the jury. Just as Atticus finishes, Calpurnia walks into the courtroom and heads toward Atticus.

Summary and Analysis by Chapter

Part 2: Chapters 21–23

Calpurnia brings a note telling Atticus that Scout and Jem are missing, which causes him great concern until Mr. Underwood tells him that the children are in the courtroom — in the Colored balcony. Calpurnia scolds the children all the way home, but Atticus says that they can return to hear the jury's verdict. Jem is convinced that the jury will acquit Tom Robinson after the evidence Atticus presented. After the verdict, Jem leaves the courtroom stunned, angry, and crying. The African-American community loads the Finch family with food for defending Tom so valiantly, which surprises the children because Atticus didn't win.

Atticus tells Jem not to be disheartened because he will appeal Tom's case, and they stand a much better chance of winning on appeal. The neighborhood is abuzz with talk of the trial, and Miss Stephanie questions the children relentlessly until Miss Maudie sides with Atticus and puts an end to the discussion. In the days following the trial, Bob Ewell publicly threatens Atticus, which frightens the children. However, Atticus uses the opportunity to further educate his children on the ways of the world. As they look forward to the appeal, Scout asks if Walter Cunningham can come over to play, which Aunt Alexandra firmly refuses to allow. In the process, Aunt Alexandra hurts Scout's feelings horribly, prompting Jem to guess why Boo Radley chooses to stay inside.

Summary and Analysis by Chapter

Part 2: Chapters 24–26

Aunt Alexandra invites Scout to attend her Missionary

Society meeting. Scout helps Calpurnia serve refreshments and tries to join the ladies in conversation. The women, with the exception of Miss Maudie, gently corner Scout with their questions, taking great delight in her responses. Just about the time Scout decides that she prefers the company of men, Atticus interrupts the meeting with the news that Tom Robinson has been killed in an attempted escape.

In the kitchen, Atticus asks Calpurnia to accompany him to give the news to Tom's wife, Helen. Aunt Alexandra is almost apologetic for Atticus, but Miss Maudie takes her to task, defending him. Scout rejoins the party with Aunt Alexandra and Miss Maudie, determined to act like a lady in the face of grim circumstances. Helen takes the news about Tom badly; the rest of Maycomb has mixed reactions. Bob Ewell is vocal about his glee at Tom's death, saying, "it made one down and about two more to go."

School starts again with Jem in the seventh grade and Scout in the third. Scout notices that the Radley house is still stark and depressing, but no longer as frightening as it once was. She and Jem have been through too much to be rattled by the thought of Boo Radley. At school, Scout's teacher, Miss Gates, talks with the class about Adolph Hitler and laments the persecution of the Jews. Later, Scout remembers that she overheard Miss Gates making racist remarks about African Americans after Tom's trial. When Scout questions Jem about this dichotomy, he becomes very angry and tells Scout never to mention the trial again. Scout then goes to Atticus who provides some consolation.

Summary and Analysis by Chapter

Part 2: Chapters 27–28

Things settle down in Maycomb, although Bob Ewell publicly blames Atticus for him losing his job. Tom Robinson's old boss, Link Deas, gives Helen a job, but Bob Ewell makes it very difficult for her to safely walk to work. Deas puts an end to that, which makes Ewell angry. The ladies of Maycomb decide to organize a Halloween pageant in the high school auditorium this year. Scout is assigned the role of a ham. She has a great costume for the pageant, but she can't get out of her ham suit without help. Atticus and Aunt Alexandra don't go to the pageant because they're tired, so Jem agrees to take Scout and bring her home. On the way to the pageant, Cecil Jacobs frightens Jem and Scout. The children enjoy the festivities, but Scout embarrasses herself by making a very late entrance onstage. When it's time to go home, Scout tells Jem that she would rather leave her costume on than have to face people, and they head for home with Jem guiding Scout.

Jem hears something unusual and tells Scout to be very quiet. Suddenly, a scuffle occurs. Scout hears Jem scream, and then steel-like arms begin crushing her inside the costume. Someone — Scout assumes it's Jem — pulls the attacker off her. Scout calls for Jem but gets no answer other than heavy breathing. She heads toward the breath sounds, feeling for Jem. When she touches the man's stubble, she knows he isn't Jem. Scout works to reorient herself and finally sees a strange man carrying Jem to their front door. Aunt Alexandra calls for the doctor, and Atticus calls for the sheriff.

Scout fears that Jem is dead, but Aunt Alexandra tells her that he's only unconscious as she works to disentangle Scout from the chicken wire. Dr. Reynolds arrives, and after he examines Jem, Scout and Heck Tate go into Jem's room. With Atticus is the man who brought Jem home. Scout has never seen him before. Sheriff Tate then announces that he found Bob Ewell dead under the tree where Scout and Jem were attacked.

Summary and Analysis by Chapter

Part 2: Chapters 29–31

At the sheriff's request, Scout recounts what happened, realizing that one of the strange noises she heard was Jem's arm breaking. The sheriff notices knife marks on Scout's costume, and she understands that Bob Ewell had intended to kill her and Jem. She also recognizes that the stranger — the man who pulled Ewell off of her and saved both children's lives — is Boo Radley. Scout, Atticus, Heck Tate, and Boo retire to the front porch. Atticus begins defending Jem, insisting that killing Bob Ewell was clearly self-defence. Sheriff Tate corrects Atticus, saying that Bob Ewell fell on his own knife. Atticus appreciates what Heck is trying to do, but he doesn't want anyone to cover for Jem. The sheriff remains adamant, saying that he isn't protecting Jem. As the men argue, Atticus realizes that Boo Radley killed Ewell, and it is Boo who Tate is trying to protect. They finally agree that Ewell did fall on his own knife, a decision Scout fully understands.

Boo sees Jem one more time and then asks Scout to take him home. Scout allows him to escort her to his door. She returns to Jem's room and Atticus reads aloud to her until she falls asleep. He tucks her in her own bed, and then retreats to Jem's room, where he spends the night.

Chapter 15

Text

Prologue

Of those few fools, who with ill stars are curst,
Sure scribbling fools, called poets, fare the worst:
For they're a sort of fools which fortune makes,
And, after she has made 'em fools, forsakes.
With Nature's oafs 'tis quite a diff'rent case,
For Fortune favours all her idiot race.
In her own nest the cuckoo eggs we find,
O'er which she broods to hatch the changeling kind:
No portion for her own she has to spare,
So much she dotes on her adopted care.
Poets are bubbles, by the town drawn in,
Suffered at first some trifling stakes to win:
But what unequal hazards do they run!
Each time they write they venture all they've won:
The Squire that's buttered still, is sure to be undone.
This author, heretofore, has found your favour,
But pleads no merit from his past behaviour.
To build on that might prove a vain presumption,
Should grants to poets made admit resumption,
And in Parnassus he must lose his seat,
If that be found a forfeited estate.
He owns, with toil he wrought the following scenes,
But if they're naught ne'er spare him for his pains:
Damn him the more; have no commiseration
For dulness on mature deliberation.
He swears he'll not resent one hissed-off scene,

Nor, like those peevish wits, his play maintain,
Who, to assert their sense, your taste arraign.
Some plot we think he has, and some new thought;
Some humour too, no farce—but that's a fault.
Satire, he thinks, you ought not to expect;
For so reformed a town who dares correct?
To please, this time, has been his sole pretence,
He'll not instruct, lest it should give offence.
Should he by chance a knave or fool expose,
That hurts none here, sure here are none of those.
In short, our play shall (with your leave to show it)
Give you one instance of a passive poet,
Who to your judgments yields all resignation:
So save or damn, after your own discretion.

Dramatis Personae

MEN.
FAINALL, in love with Mrs. Marwood,—Mr. Betterton
MIRABELL, in love with Mrs. Millamant,—Mr. Verbruggen
WITWOUD, follower of Mrs. Millamant,—Mr. Bowen
PETULANT, follower of Mrs. Millamant,—Mr. Bowman
SIR WILFULL WITWOUD, half brother to Witwoud, and nephew to Lady
Wishfort,—Mr. Underhill
WAITWELL, servant to Mirabell,—Mr. Bright
WOMEN.
LADY WISHFORT, enemy to Mirabell, for having falsely pretended love to her,—Mrs. Leigh
MRS. MILLAMANT, a fine lady, niece to Lady Wishfort, and loves Mirabell,—Mrs. Bracegirdle
MRS. MARWOOD, friend to Mr. Fainall, and likes Mirabell,—Mrs. Barry
MRS. FAINALL, daughter to Lady Wishfort, and wife to Fainall, formerly friend to Mirabell,—Mrs. Bowman
FOIBLE, woman to Lady Wishfort,—Mrs. Willis
MINCING, woman to Mrs. Millamant,—Mrs. Prince
DANCERS, FOOTMEN, ATTENDANTS.
SCENE: London.

Complete Text

ACT I

Scene I.

A Chocolate-house.

MIRABELL and FAINALL rising from cards. BETTY waiting.

MIRABELL

You are a fortunate man, Mr. Fainall.

FAINALL

Have we done?

MIRABELL

What you please. I'll play on to entertain you.

FAINALL

No, I'll give you your revenge another time, when you are not so indifferent; you are thinking of something else now, and play too negligently: the coldness of a losing gamester lessens the pleasure of the winner. I'd no more play with a man that slighted his ill fortune than I'd make love to a woman who undervalued the loss of her reputation.

MIRABELL

You have a taste extremely delicate, and are for refining on your pleasures.

FAINALL

Prithee, why so reserved? Something has put you out of humour.

MIRABELL

Not at all: I happen to be grave to-day, and you are gay; that's all.

FAINALL

Confess, Millamant and you quarrelled last night, after I left you; my fair cousin has some humours that would tempt the patience of a Stoic. What, some coxcomb came in, and was well received by her, while you were by?

MIRABELL

Witwoud and Petulant, and what was worse, her aunt, your wife's mother, my evil genius—or to sum up all in her own name, my old Lady Wishfort came in.

FAINALL

Oh, there it is then: she has a lasting passion for you, and with reason.—What, then my wife was there?

MIRABELL

Yes, and Mrs. Marwood and three or four more, whom I never saw before; seeing me, they all put on their grave faces, whispered one another, then complained aloud of the vapours, and after fell into a profound silence.

FAINALL

They had a mind to be rid of you.

MIRABELL

For which reason I resolved not to stir. At last the good old lady broke through her painful taciturnity with an invective against long visits. I would not have understood her, but Millamant joining in the argument, I rose and with a constrained smile told her, I thought nothing was so easy as to know when a visit began to be troublesome; she reddened and I withdrew, without expecting her reply.

FAINALL

You were to blame to resent what she spoke only in compliance with her aunt.

MIRABELL

She is more mistress of herself than to be under the necessity of such a resignation.

FAINALL

What? though half her fortune depends upon her marrying with my lady's approbation?

MIRABELL

I was then in such a humour, that I should have been better pleased if she had been less discreet.

FAINALL

Now I remember, I wonder not they were weary of you; last night was one of their cabal-nights: they have 'em three times a week and meet by turns at one another's apartments, where they come together like the coroner's inquest, to sit upon the murdered reputations of the week.

You and I are excluded, and it was once proposed that all the male sex should be excepted; but somebody moved that to avoid scandal there might be one man of the community, upon which motion Witwoud and Petulant were enrolled members.

MIRABELL

And who may have been the foundress of this sect? My Lady Wishfort, I warrant, who publishes her detestation of mankind, and full of the vigour of fifty-five, declares for a friend and ratafia; and let posterity shift for itself, she'll breed no more.

FAINALL

The discovery of your sham addresses to her, to conceal your love to her niece, has provoked this separation. Had you dissembled better, things might have continued in the state of nature.

MIRABELL

I did as much as man could, with any reasonable conscience; I proceeded to the very last act of flattery with her, and was guilty of a song in her commendation. Nay, I got a friend to put her into a lampoon, and compliment her with the imputation of an affair with a young fellow, which I carried so far, that I told her the malicious town took notice that she was grown fat of a sudden; and when she lay in of a dropsy, persuaded her she was reported to be in labour. The devil's in't, if an old woman is to be flattered further, unless a man should endeavour downright personally to debauch her: and that my virtue forbade me. But for the discovery of this amour, I am indebted to your friend, or your wife's friend, Mrs. Marwood.

FAINALL

What should provoke her to be your enemy, unless she has made you advances which you have slighted? Women do not easily forgive omissions of that nature.

MIRABELL

She was always civil to me, till of late. I confess I am not one of those coxcombs who are apt to interpret a woman's good manners to her prejudice, and think that she who does not refuse 'em everything can refuse 'em nothing.

FAINALL

You are a gallant man, Mirabell; and though you may have cruelty enough not to satisfy a lady's longing, you have too much generosity not to be tender of her honour. Yet you speak with an indifference which seems to be affected, and confesses you are conscious of a negligence.

MIRABELL

You pursue the argument with a distrust that seems to be unaffected, and confesses you are conscious of a concern for which the lady is more indebted to you than is your wife.

FAINALL

Fie, fie, friend, if you grow censorious I must leave you:- I'll look upon the gamesters in the next room.

MIRABELL

Who are they?

FAINALL

Petulant and Witwoud.—Bring me some chocolate.

MIRABELL

Betty, what says your clock?

BETTY

Turned of the last canonical hour, sir.

MIRABELL

How pertinently the jade answers me! Ha! almost one a' clock! [Looking on his watch.] Oh, y'are come!

ACT I

Scene II.

MIRABELL and FOOTMAN.

MIRABELL

Well, is the grand affair over? You have been something tedious.

SERVANT

Sir, there's such coupling at Pancras that they stand behind one another, as 'twere in a country-dance. Ours was the last couple to lead up; and no hopes appearing of dispatch, besides, the parson growing hoarse, we were afraid his lungs would have failed before it came to our turn; so we drove round to Duke's Place, and there they were riveted in a trice.

MIRABELL
So, so; you are sure they are married?
SERVANT
Married and bedded, sir; I am witness.
MIRABELL
Have you the certificate?
SERVANT
Here it is, sir.
MIRABELL
Has the tailor brought Waitwell's clothes home, and the new liveries?
SERVANT
Yes, sir.
MIRABELL
That's well. Do you go home again, d'ye hear, and adjourn the consummation till farther order; bid Waitwell shake his ears, and Dame Partlet rustle up her feathers, and meet me at one a' clock by Rosamond's pond, that I may see her before she returns to her lady. And, as you tender your ears, be secret.

ACT I

Scene III.
MIRABELL, FAINALL, BETTY.
FAINALL
Joy of your success, Mirabell; you look pleased.
MIRABELL
Ay; I have been engaged in a matter of some sort of mirth, which is not yet ripe for discovery. I am glad this is not a cabal-night. I wonder, Fainall, that you who are married, and of consequence should be discreet, will suffer your wife to be of such a party.
FAINALL
Faith, I am not jealous. Besides, most who are engaged are women and relations; and for the men, they are of a kind too contemptible to give scandal.
MIRABELL
I am of another opinion: the greater the coxcomb, always the more the scandal; for a woman who is not a fool can have but one reason for associating with a man who is one.

FAINALL

Are you jealous as often as you see Witwoud entertained by Millamant?

MIRABELL

Of her understanding I am, if not of her person.

FAINALL

You do her wrong; for, to give her her due, she has wit.

MIRABELL

She has beauty enough to make any man think so, and complaisance enough not to contradict him who shall tell her so.

FAINALL

For a passionate lover methinks you are a man somewhat too discerning in the failings of your mistress.

MIRABELL

And for a discerning man somewhat too passionate a lover, for I like her with all her faults; nay, like her for her faults. Her follies are so natural, or so artful, that they become her, and those affectations which in another woman would be odious serve but to make her more agreeable. I'll tell thee, Fainall, she once used me with that insolence that in revenge I took her to pieces, sifted her, and separated her failings: I studied 'em and got 'em by rote. The catalogue was so large that I was not without hopes, one day or other, to hate her heartily. To which end I so used myself to think of 'em, that at length, contrary to my design and expectation, they gave me every hour less and less disturbance, till in a few days it became habitual to me to remember 'em without being displeased. They are now grown as familiar to me as my own frailties, and in all probability in a little time longer I shall like 'em as well.

FAINALL

Marry her, marry her; be half as well acquainted with her charms as you are with her defects, and, my life on't, you are your own man again.

MIRABELL

Say you so?

FAINALL

Ay, ay; I have experience. I have a wife, and so forth.

ACT I

Scene IV.
[To them] MESSENGER.
MESSENGER
Is one Squire Wit would here?
BETTY
Yes; what's your business?
MESSENGER
I have a letter for him, from his brother Sir Wilfull, which I am charged to deliver into his own hands.
BETTY
He's in the next room, friend. That way.

ACT I

Scene V.
MIRABELL, FAINALL, BETTY.
MIRABELL
What, is the chief of that noble family in town, Sir Wilfull Witwoud?
FAINALL
He is expected to-day. Do you know him?
MIRABELL
I have seen him; he promises to be an extraordinary person. I think you have the honour to be related to him.
FAINALL
Yes; he is half-brother to this Witwoud by a former wife, who was sister to my Lady Wishfort, my wife's mother. If you marry Millamant, you must call cousins too.
MIRABELL
I had rather be his relation than his acquaintance.
FAINALL
He comes to town in order to equip himself for travel.
MIRABELL
For travel! Why the man that I mean is above forty.
FAINALL
No matter for that; 'tis for the honour of England that all Europe should know we have blockheads of all ages.
MIRABELL

I wonder there is not an act of parliament to save the credit of the nation and prohibit the exportation of fools.

FAINALL

By no means, 'tis better as 'tis; 'tis better to trade with a little loss, than to be quite eaten up with being overstocked.

MIRABELL

Pray, are the follies of this knight-errant and those of the squire, his brother, anything related?

FAINALL

Not at all: Witwoud grows by the knight like a medlar grafted on a crab. One will melt in your mouth and t'other set your teeth on edge; one is all pulp and the other all core.

MIRABELL

So one will be rotten before he be ripe, and the other will be rotten without ever being ripe at all.

FAINALL

Sir Wilfull is an odd mixture of bashfulness and obstinacy. But when he's drunk, he's as loving as the monster in The Tempest, and much after the same manner. To give bother his due, he has something of good-nature, and does not always want wit.

MIRABELL

Not always: but as often as his memory fails him and his commonplace of comparisons. He is a fool with a good memory and some few scraps of other folks' wit. He is one whose conversation can never be approved, yet it is now and then to be endured. He has indeed one good quality: he is not exceptious, for he so passionately affects the reputation of understanding raillery that he will construe an affront into a jest, and call downright rudeness and ill language satire and fire.

FAINALL

If you have a mind to finish his picture, you have an opportunity to do it at full length. Behold the original.

ACT I

Scene VI.

[To them] WITWOUD.

WITWOUD

Afford me your compassion, my dears; pity me, Fainall, Mirabell, pity me.

MIRABELL

I do from my soul.

FAINALL

Why, what's the matter?

WITWOUD

No letters for me, Betty?

BETTY

Did not a messenger bring you one but now, sir?

WITWOUD

Ay; but no other?

BETTY

No, sir.

WITWOUD

That's hard, that's very hard. A messenger, a mule, a beast of burden, he has brought me a letter from the fool my brother, as heavy as a panegyric in a funeral sermon, or a copy of commendatory verses from one poet to another. And what's worse, 'tis as sure a forerunner of the author as an epistle dedicatory.

MIRABELL

A fool, and your brother, Witwoud?

WITWOUD

Ay, ay, my half-brother. My half-brother he is, no nearer, upon honour.

MIRABELL

Then 'tis possible he may be but half a fool.

WITWOUD

Good, good, Mirabell, LE DROLE! Good, good, hang him, don't let's talk of him.—Fainall, how does your lady? Gad, I say anything in the world to get this fellow out of my head. I beg pardon that I should ask a man of pleasure and the town a question at once so foreign and domestic. But I talk like an old maid at a marriage, I don't know what I say: but she's the best woman in the world.

FAINALL

'Tis well you don't know what you say, or else your commendation would go near to make me either vain or jealous.

WITWOUD

No man in town lives well with a wife but Fainall. Your judgment, Mirabell?

MIRABELL

You had better step and ask his wife, if you would be credibly informed.

WITWOUD

Mirabell!

MIRABELL

Ay.

WITWOUD

My dear, I ask ten thousand pardons. Gad, I have forgot what I was going to say to you.

MIRABELL

I thank you heartily, heartily.

WITWOUD

No, but prithee excuse me:- my memory is such a memory.

MIRABELL

Have a care of such apologies, Witwoud; for I never knew a fool but he affected to complain either of the spleen or his memory.

FAINALL

What have you done with Petulant?

WITWOUD

He's reckoning his money; my money it was: I have no luck to- day.

FAINALL

You may allow him to win of you at play, for you are sure to be too hard for him at repartee: since you monopolise the wit that is between you, the fortune must be his of course.

MIRABELL

I don't find that Petulant confesses the superiority of wit to be your talent, Witwoud.

WITWOUD

Come, come, you are malicious now, and would breed debates. Petulant's my friend, and a very honest fellow, and a very pretty fellow, and has a smattering—faith and troth, a pretty deal of an odd sort of a small wit: nay, I'll do him justice. I'm his friend, I won't wrong him. And if he had any judgment in the world, he would not be altogether contemptible. Come, come, don't detract from the merits of my friend.

FAINALL

You don't take your friend to be over-nicely bred?

WITWOUD

No, no, hang him, the rogue has no manners at all, that I must own; no more breeding than a bum-baily, that I grant you:- 'tis pity; the fellow has fire and life.

MIRABELL

What, courage?

WITWOUD

Hum, faith, I don't know as to that, I can't say as to that. Yes, faith, in a controversy he'll contradict anybody.

MIRABELL

Though 'twere a man whom he feared or a woman whom he loved.

WITWOUD

Well, well, he does not always think before he speaks. We have all our failings; you are too hard upon him, you are, faith. Let me excuse him,—I can defend most of his faults, except one or two; one he has, that's the truth on't,—if he were my brother I could not acquit him—that indeed I could wish were otherwise.

MIRABELL

Ay, marry, what's that, Witwoud?

WITWOUD

Oh, pardon me. Expose the infirmities of my friend? No, my dear, excuse me there.

FAINALL

What, I warrant he's unsincere, or 'tis some such trifle.

WITWOUD

No, no; what if he be? 'Tis no matter for that, his wit will excuse that. A wit should no more be sincere than a woman constant: one argues a decay of parts, as t'other of beauty.

MIRABELL
Maybe you think him too positive?
WITWOUD
No, no; his being positive is an incentive to argument, and keeps up conversation.
FAINALL
Too illiterate?
WITWOUD
That? That's his happiness. His want of learning gives him the more opportunities to show his natural parts.
MIRABELL
He wants words?
WITWOUD
Ay; but I like him for that now: for his want of words gives me the pleasure very often to explain his meaning.
FAINALL
He's impudent?
WITWOUD
No that's not it.
MIRABELL
Vain?
WITWOUD
No.
MIRABELL
What, he speaks unseasonable truths sometimes, because he has not wit enough to invent an evasion?
WITWOUD
Truths? Ha, ha, ha! No, no, since you will have it, I mean he never speaks truth at all, that's all. He will lie like a chambermaid, or a woman of quality's porter. Now that is a fault.

ACT I

Scene VII.
[To them] COACHMAN.
COACHMAN
Is Master Petulant here, mistress?
BETTY

Yes.

COACHMAN

Three gentlewomen in a coach would speak with him.

FAINALL

O brave Petulant! Three!

BETTY

I'll tell him.

COACHMAN

You must bring two dishes of chocolate and a glass of cinnamon water.

ACT I

Scene VIII.

MIRABELL, FAINALL, WITWOUD.

WITWOUD

That should be for two fasting strumpets, and a bawd troubled with wind. Now you may know what the three are.

MIRABELL

You are very free with your friend's acquaintance.

WITWOUD

Ay, ay; friendship without freedom is as dull as love without enjoyment or wine without toasting: but to tell you a secret, these are trulls whom he allows coach-hire, and something more by the week, to call on him once a day at public places.

MIRABELL

How!

WITWOUD

You shall see he won't go to 'em because there's no more company here to take notice of him. Why, this is nothing to what he used to do:- before he found out this way, I have known him call for himself -

FAINALL

Call for himself? What dost thou mean?

WITWOUD

Mean? Why he would slip you out of this chocolate-house, just when you had been talking to him. As soon as your back was turned— whip he was gone; then trip to his lodging, clap on a hood and scarf and a mask, slap into a hackney-coach, and drive hither to the door again in a trice; where he would send in for himself; that I mean, call for himself, wait for himself, nay, and what's more, not finding himself, sometimes leave a letter for himself.

MIRABELL

I confess this is something extraordinary. I believe he waits for himself now, he is so long a coming; oh, I ask his pardon.

ACT I

Scene IX.

PETULANT, MIRABELL, FAINALL, WITWOUD, BETTY.

BETTY

Sir, the coach stays.

PET

Well, well, I come. 'Sbud, a man had as good be a professed midwife as a professed whoremaster, at this rate; to be knocked up and raised at all hours, and in all places. Pox on 'em, I won't come. D'ye hear, tell 'em I won't come. Let 'em snivel and cry their hearts out.

FAINALL

You are very cruel, Petulant.

PETULANT

All's one, let it pass. I have a humour to be cruel.

MIRABELL

I hope they are not persons of condition that you use at this rate.

PETULANT

Condition? Condition's a dried fig, if I am not in humour. By this hand, if they were your—a—a—your what-d'ee-call-'ems themselves, they must wait or rub off, if I want appetite

MIRABELL

What-d'ee-call-'ems! What are they, Witwoud?

WITWOUD

Empresses, my dear. By your what-d'ee-call-'ems he means Sultana Queens.

PETULANT

Ay, Roxolanas.

MIRABELL

Cry you mercy.

FAINALL

Witwoud says they are -

PETULANT

What does he say th'are?

WITWOUD

I? Fine ladies, I say.

PETULANT

Pass on, Witwoud. Harkee, by this light, his relations—two co-heiresses his cousins, and an old aunt, who loves caterwauling better than a conventicle.

WITWOUD

Ha, ha, ha! I had a mind to see how the rogue would come off. Ha, ha, ha! Gad, I can't be angry with him, if he had said they were my mother and my sisters.

MIRABELL

No?

WITWOUD

No; the rogue's wit and readiness of invention charm me, dear Petulant.

BETTY

They are gone, sir, in great anger.

PETULANT

Enough, let 'em trundle. Anger helps complexion, saves paint.

FAINALL

This continence is all dissembled; this is in order to have something to brag of the next time he makes court to Millamant, and swear he has abandoned the whole sex for her sake.

MIRABELL

Have you not left off your impudent pretensions there yet? I shall cut your throat, sometime or other, Petulant, about that business.

PETULANT

Ay, ay, let that pass. There are other throats to be cut.

MIRABELL

Meaning mine, sir?

PETULANT

Not I—I mean nobody—I know nothing. But there are uncles and nephews in the world—and they may be rivals. What then? All's one for that.

MIRABELL

How? Harkee, Petulant, come hither. Explain, or I shall call your interpreter.

PETULANT

Explain? I know nothing. Why, you have an uncle, have you not, lately come to town, and lodges by my Lady Wishfort's?

MIRABELL

True.

PETULANT

Why, that's enough. You and he are not friends; and if he should marry and have a child, yon may be disinherited, ha!

MIRABELL

Where hast thou stumbled upon all this truth?

PETULANT

All's one for that; why, then, say I know something.

MIRABELL

Come, thou art an honest fellow, Petulant, and shalt make love to my mistress, thou shalt, faith. What hast thou heard of my uncle?

PETULANT

I? Nothing, I If throats are to be cut, let swords clash. Snug's the word; I shrug and am silent.

MIRABELL

Oh, raillery, raillery! Come, I know thou art in the women's secrets. What, you're a cabalist; I know you stayed at Millamant's last night after I went. Was there any mention made of my uncle or me? Tell me; if thou hadst but good nature equal to thy wit, Petulant, Tony Witwoud, who is now thy competitor in fame, would show as dim by thee as a dead whiting's eye by a pearl of orient; he would no more be seen by thee than Mercury is by the sun: come, I'm sure thou wo't tell me.

PETULANT

If I do, will you grant me common sense, then, for the future?

MIRABELL

Faith, I'll do what I can for thee, and I'll pray that heav'n may grant it thee in the meantime.

PETULANT

Well, harkee.

FAINALL

Petulant and you both will find Mirabell as warm a rival as a lover.

WITWOUD

Pshaw, pshaw, that she laughs at Petulant is plain. And for my part, but that it is almost a fashion to admire her, I should— harkee—to tell you a secret, but let it go no further between friends, I shall never break my heart for her.

FAINALL

How?

WITWOUD

She's handsome; but she's a sort of an uncertain woman.

FAINALL

I thought you had died for her.

WITWOUD

Umh—no -

FAINALL

She has wit.

WITWOUD

'Tis what she will hardly allow anybody else. Now, demme, I should hate that, if she were as handsome as Cleopatra. Mirabell is not so sure of her as he thinks for.

FAINALL

Why do you think so?

WITWOUD

We stayed pretty late there last night, and heard something of an uncle to Mirabell, who is lately come to town, and is between him and the best part of his estate.

Mirabell and he are at some distance, as my Lady Wishfort has been told; and you know she hates Mirabell worse than a quaker hates a parrot, or than a fishmonger hates a hard frost. Whether this uncle has seen Mrs. Millamant or not, I cannot say; but there were items of such a treaty being in embryo; and if it should come to life, poor Mirabell would be in some sort unfortunately fobbed, i'faith.

FAINALL

'Tis impossible Millamant should hearken to it.

WITWOUD

Faith, my dear, I can't tell; she's a woman and a kind of a humorist.

MIRABELL

And this is the sum of what you could collect last night?

PETULANT

The quintessence. Maybe Witwoud knows more; he stayed longer. Besides, they never mind him; they say anything before him.

MIRABELL

I thought you had been the greatest favourite.

PETULANT

Ay, tete-e-tete; but not in public, because I make remarks.

MIRABELL

You do?

PETULANT

Ay, ay, pox, I'm malicious, man. Now he's soft, you know, they are not in awe of him. The fellow's well bred, he's what you call a—what d'ye-call-'em a fine gentleman, but he's silly withal.

MIRABELL

I thank you, I know as much as my curiosity requires. Fainall, are you for the Mall?

FAINALL

Ay, I'll take a turn before dinner.

WITWOUD

Ay, we'll all walk in the park; the ladies talked of being there.

MIRABELL

I thought you were obliged to watch for your brother Sir Wilfull's arrival.

WITWOUD

No, no, he comes to his aunt's, my Lady Wishfort; pox on him, I shall be troubled with him too; what shall I do with the fool?

PETULANT

Beg him for his estate, that I may beg you afterwards, and so have but one trouble with you both.

WITWOUD

O rare Petulant, thou art as quick as fire in a frosty morning; thou shalt to the Mall with us, and we'll be very severe.

PETULANT

Enough; I'm in a humour to be severe.

MIRABELL

Are you? Pray then walk by yourselves. Let not us be accessory to your putting the ladies out of countenance with your senseless ribaldry, which you roar out aloud as often as they pass by you, and when you have made a handsome woman blush, then you think you have been severe.

PETULANT

What, what? Then let 'em either show their innocence by not understanding what they hear, or else show their discretion by not hearing what they would not be thought to understand.

MIRABELL

But hast not thou then sense enough to know that thou ought'st to be most ashamed thyself when thou hast put another out of countenance?

PETULANT

Not I, by this hand: I always take blushing either for a sign of guilt or ill-breeding.

MIRABELL

I confess you ought to think so. You are in the right, that you may plead the error of your judgment in defence of your practice.

Where modesty's ill manners, 'tis but fit That impudence and malice pass for wit.

ACT II

Scene I.

St. James's Park.

MRS. FAINALL and MRS. MARWOOD.

MRS. FAINALL

Ay, ay, dear Marwood, if we will be happy, we must find the means in ourselves, and among ourselves. Men are ever in extremes; either doting or averse. While they are lovers, if they have fire and sense, their jealousies are insupportable: and when they cease to love (we ought to think at least) they loathe, they look upon us with horror and distaste, they meet us like the ghosts of what we were, and as from such, fly from us.

MRS. MARWOOD

True, 'tis an unhappy circumstance of life that love should ever die before us, and that the man so often should outlive the lover. But say what you will, 'tis better to be left than never to have been loved. To pass our youth in dull indifference, to refuse the sweets of life because they once must leave us, is as preposterous as to wish to have been born old, because we one day must be old. For my part, my youth may wear and waste, but it shall never rust in my possession.

MRS. FAINALL

Then it seems you dissemble an aversion to mankind only in compliance to my mother's humour.

MRS. MARWOOD

Certainly. To be free, I have no taste of those insipid dry discourses with which our sex of force must entertain themselves apart from men. We may affect endearments to each other, profess eternal friendships, and seem to dote like lovers; but 'tis not in our natures long to persevere. Love will resume his empire in our breasts, and every heart, or soon or late, receive and readmit him as its lawful tyrant.

MRS. FAINALL

Bless me, how have I been deceived! Why, you profess a libertine.

MRS. MARWOOD

You see my friendship by my freedom. Come, be as sincere, acknowledge that your sentiments agree with mine.

MRS. FAINALL

Never.

MRS. MARWOOD

You hate mankind?

MRS. FAINALL

Heartily, inveterately.

MRS. MARWOOD

Your husband?

MRS. FAINALL

Most transcendently; ay, though I say it, meritoriously.

MRS. MARWOOD

Give me your hand upon it.

MRS. FAINALL

There.

MRS. MARWOOD

I join with you; what I have said has been to try you.

MRS. FAINALL

Is it possible? Dost thou hate those vipers, men?

MRS. MARWOOD

I have done hating 'em, and am now come to despise 'em; the next thing I have to do is eternally to forget 'em.

MRS. FAINALL

There spoke the spirit of an Amazon, a Penthesilea.

MRS. MARWOOD

And yet I am thinking sometimes to carry my aversion further.

MRS. FAINALL

How?

MRS. MARWOOD

Faith, by marrying; if I could but find one that loved me very well, and would be throughly sensible of ill usage, I think I should do myself the violence of undergoing the ceremony.

MRS. FAINALL

You would not make him a cuckold?

MRS. MARWOOD

No; but I'd make him believe I did, and that's as bad.

MRS. FAINALL

Why had not you as good do it?

MRS. MARWOOD

Oh, if he should ever discover it, he would then know the

worst, and be out of his pain; but I would have him ever to continue upon the rack of fear and jealousy.

MRS. FAINALL

Ingenious mischief! Would thou wert married to Mirabell.

MRS. MARWOOD

Would I were.

MRS. FAINALL

You change colour.

MRS. MARWOOD

Because I hate him.

MRS. FAINALL

So do I; but I can hear him named. But what reason have you to hate him in particular?

MRS. MARWOOD

I never loved him; he is, and always was, insufferably proud.

MRS. FAINALL

By the reason you give for your aversion, one would think it dissembled; for you have laid a fault to his charge, of which his enemies must acquit him.

MRS. MARWOOD

Oh, then it seems you are one of his favourable enemies. Methinks you look a little pale, and now you flush again.

MRS. FAINALL

Do I? I think I am a little sick o' the sudden.

MRS. MARWOOD

What ails you?

MRS. FAINALL

My husband. Don't you see him? He turned short upon me unawares, and has almost overcome me.

ACT II

Scene II.

[To them] FAINALL and MIRABELL.

MRS. MARWOOD

Ha, ha, ha! he comes opportunely for you.

MRS. FAINALL

For you, for he has brought Mirabell with him.

FAINALL

My dear.

MRS. FAINALL

My soul.

FAINALL

You don't look well to-day, child.

MRS. FAINALL

D'ye think so?

MIRABELL

He is the only man that does, madam.

MRS. FAINALL

The only man that would tell me so at least, and the only man from whom I could hear it without mortification.

FAINALL

Oh, my dear, I am satisfied of your tenderness; I know you cannot resent anything from me; especially what is an effect of my concern.

MRS. FAINALL

Mr. Mirabell, my mother interrupted you in a pleasant relation last night: I would fain hear it out.

MIRABELL

The persons concerned in that affair have yet a tolerable reputation. I am afraid Mr. Fainall will be censorious.

MRS. FAINALL

He has a humour more prevailing than his curiosity, and will willingly dispense with the hearing of one scandalous story, to avoid giving an occasion to make another by being seen to walk with his wife. This way, Mr. Mirabell, and I dare promise you will oblige us both.

ACT II

Scene III.

FAINALL, MRS. MARWOOD.

FAINALL

Excellent creature! Well, sure, if I should live to be rid of my wife, I should be a miserable man.

MRS. MARWOOD Ay?

FAINALL

For having only that one hope, the accomplishment of it

of consequence must put an end to all my hopes, and what a wretch is he who must survive his hopes! Nothing remains when that day comes but to sit down and weep like Alexander when he wanted other worlds to conquer.

MRS. MARWOOD

Will you not follow 'em?

FAINALL

Faith, I think not,

MRS. MARWOOD

Pray let us; I have a reason.

FAINALL

You are not jealous?

MRS. MARWOOD

Of whom?

FAINALL

Of Mirabell.

MRS. MARWOOD

If I am, is it inconsistent with my love to you that I am tender of your honour?

FAINALL

You would intimate then, as if there were a fellow-feeling between my wife and him?

MRS. MARWOOD

I think she does not hate him to that degree she would be thought.

FAINALL

But he, I fear, is too insensible.

MRS. MARWOOD

It may be you are deceived.

FAINALL

It may be so. I do not now begin to apprehend it.

MRS. MARWOOD

What?

FAINALL

That I have been deceived, madam, and you are false.

MRS. MARWOOD

That I am false? What mean you?

FAINALL

To let you know I see through all your little arts.—Come, you both love him, and both have equally dissembled your aversion. Your mutual jealousies of one another have made you clash till you have both struck fire. I have seen the warm confession red'ning on your cheeks, and sparkling from your eyes.

MRS. MARWOOD

You do me wrong.

FAINALL

I do not. 'Twas for my ease to oversee and wilfully neglect the gross advances made him by my wife, that by permitting her to be engaged, I might continue unsuspected in my pleasures, and take you oftener to my arms in full security. But could you think, because the nodding husband would not wake, that e'er the watchful lover slept?

MRS. MARWOOD

And wherewithal can you reproach me?

FAINALL

With infidelity, with loving another, with love of Mirabell.

MRS. MARWOOD

'Tis false. I challenge you to show an instance that can confirm your groundless accusation. I hate him.

FAINALL

And wherefore do you hate him? He is insensible, and your resentment follows his neglect. An instance? The injuries you have done him are a proof: your interposing in his love. What cause had you to make discoveries of his pretended passion? To undeceive the credulous aunt, and be the officious obstacle of his match with Millamant?

MRS. MARWOOD

My obligations to my lady urged me: I had professed a friendship to her, and could not see her easy nature so abused by that dissembler.

FAINALL

What, was it conscience then? Professed a friendship! Oh, the pious friendships of the female sex!

MRS. MARWOOD

More tender, more sincere, and more enduring, than all

the vain and empty vows of men, whether professing love to us or mutual faith to one another.

FAINALL

Ha, ha, ha! you are my wife's friend too.

MRS. MARWOOD

Shame and ingratitude! Do you reproach me? You, you upbraid me? Have I been false to her, through strict fidelity to you, and sacrificed my friendship to keep my love inviolate? And have you the baseness to charge me with the guilt, unmindful of the merit? To you it should be meritorious that I have been vicious. And do you reflect that guilt upon me which should lie buried in your bosom?

FAINALL

You misinterpret my reproof. I meant but to remind you of the slight account you once could make of strictest ties when set in competition with your love to me.

MRS. MARWOOD

'Tis false, you urged it with deliberate malice. 'Twas spoke in scorn, and I never will forgive it.

FAINALL

Your guilt, not your resentment, begets your rage. If yet you loved, you could forgive a jealousy: but you are stung to find you are discovered.

MRS. MARWOOD

It shall be all discovered. You too shall be discovered; be sure you shall. I can but be exposed. If I do it myself I shall prevent your baseness.

FAINALL

Why, what will you do?

MRS. MARWOOD

Disclose it to your wife; own what has past between us.

FAINALL

Frenzy!

MRS. MARWOOD

By all my wrongs I'll do't. I'll publish to the world the injuries you have done me, both in my fame and fortune: with both I trusted you, you bankrupt in honour, as indigent of wealth.

FAINALL

Your fame I have preserved. Your fortune has been bestowed as the prodigality of your love would have it, in pleasures which we both have shared. Yet, had not you been false I had e'er this repaid it. 'Tis true—had you permitted Mirabell with Millamant to have stolen their marriage, my lady had been incensed beyond all means of reconcilement: Millamant had forfeited the moiety of her fortune, which then would have descended to my wife. And wherefore did I marry but to make lawful prize of a rich widow's wealth, and squander it on love and you?

MRS. MARWOOD

Deceit and frivolous pretence!

FAINALL

Death, am I not married? What's pretence? Am I not imprisoned, fettered? Have I not a wife? Nay, a wife that was a widow, a young widow, a handsome widow, and would be again a widow, but that I have a heart of proof, and something of a constitution to bustle through the ways of wedlock and this world. Will you yet be reconciled to truth and me?

MRS. MARWOOD

Impossible. Truth and you are inconsistent.—I hate you, and shall for ever.

FAINALL

For loving you?

MRS. MARWOOD

I loathe the name of love after such usage; and next to the guilt with which you would asperse me, I scorn you most. Farewell.

FAINALL

Nay, we must not part thus.

MRS. MARWOOD

Let me go.

FAINALL

Come, I'm sorry.

MRS. MARWOOD

I care not. Let me go. Break my hands, do—I'd leave 'em to get loose.

FAINALL

I would not hurt you for the world. Have I no other hold to keep you here?

MRS. MARWOOD

Well, I have deserved it all.

FAINALL

You know I love you.

MRS. MARWOOD

Poor dissembling! Oh, that—well, it is not yet -

FAINALL

What? What is it not? What is it not yet? It is not yet too late -

MRS. MARWOOD

No, it is not yet too late—I have that comfort.

FAINALL

It is, to love another.

MRS. MARWOOD

But not to loathe, detest, abhor mankind, myself, and the whole treacherous world.

FAINALL

Nay, this is extravagance. Come, I ask your pardon. No tears—I was to blame, I could not love you and be easy in my doubts. Pray forbear—I believe you; I'm convinced I've done you wrong; and any way, every way will make amends: I'll hate my wife yet more, damn her, I'll part with her, rob her of all she's worth, and we'll retire somewhere, anywhere, to another world; I'll marry thee—be pacified.—'Sdeath, they come: hide your face, your tears. You have a mask: wear it a moment. This way, this way: be persuaded.

ACT II

Scene IV.

MIRABELL and MRS. FAINALL.

MRS. FAINALL

They are here yet.

MIRABELL

They are turning into the other walk.

MRS. FAINALL

While I only hated my husband, I could bear to see him;

but since I have despised him, he's too offensive.

MIRABELL

Oh, you should hate with prudence.

MRS. FAINALL

Yes, for I have loved with indiscretion.

MIRABELL

You should have just so much disgust for your husband as may be sufficient to make you relish your lover.

MRS. FAINALL

You have been the cause that I have loved without bounds, and would you set limits to that aversion of which you have been the occasion? Why did you make me marry this man?

MIRABELL

Why do we daily commit disagreeable and dangerous actions? To save that idol, reputation. If the familiarities of our loves had produced that consequence of which you were apprehensive, where could you have fixed a father's name with credit but on a husband? I knew Fainall to be a man lavish of his morals, an interested and professing friend, a false and a designing lover, yet one whose wit and outward fair behaviour have gained a reputation with the town, enough to make that woman stand excused who has suffered herself to be won by his addresses. A better man ought not to have been sacrificed to the occasion; a worse had not answered to the purpose. When you are weary of him you know your remedy.

MRS. FAINALL

I ought to stand in some degree of credit with you, Mirabell.

MIRABELL

In justice to you, I have made you privy to my whole design, and put it in your power to ruin or advance my fortune.

MRS. FAINALL

Whom have you instructed to represent your pretended uncle?

MIRABELL

Waitwell, my servant.

MRS. FAINALL

He is an humble servant to Foible, my mother's woman, and may win her to your interest.

MIRABELL

Care is taken for that. She is won and worn by this time. They were married this morning.

MRS. FAINALL

Who?

MIRABELL

Waitwell and Foible. I would not tempt my servant to betray me by trusting him too far. If your mother, in hopes to ruin me, should consent to marry my pretended uncle, he might, like Mosca in the FOX, stand upon terms; so I made him sure beforehand.

MRS. FAINALL

So, if my poor mother is caught in a contract, you will discover the imposture betimes, and release her by producing a certificate of her gallant's former marriage.

MIRABELL

Yes, upon condition that she consent to my marriage with her niece, and surrender the moiety of her fortune in her possession.

MRS. FAINALL

She talked last night of endeavouring at a match between Millamant and your uncle.

MIRABELL

That was by Foible's direction and my instruction, that she might seem to carry it more privately.

MRS. FAINALL

Well, I have an opinion of your success, for I believe my lady will do anything to get an husband; and when she has this, which you have provided for her, I suppose she will submit to anything to get rid of him.

MIRABELL

Yes, I think the good lady would marry anything that resembled a man, though 'twere no more than what a butler could pinch out of a napkin.

MRS. FAINALL

Female frailty! We must all come to it, if we live to be old, and feel the craving of a false appetite when the true is decayed.

MIRABELL

An old woman's appetite is depraved like that of a girl. 'Tis the green-sickness of a second childhood, and, like the faint offer of a latter spring, serves but to usher in the fall, and withers in an affected bloom.

MRS. FAINALL

Here's your mistress.

ACT II

Scene V.

[To them] MRS. MILLAMANT, WITWOUD, MINCING.

MIRABELL

MRS. FAINALL

I see but one poor empty sculler, and he tows her woman after him.

MIRABELL

You seem to be unattended, madam. You used to have the BEAU MONDE throng after you, and a flock of gay fine perukes hovering round you.

WITWOUD

Like moths about a candle. I had like to have lost my comparison for want of breath.

MILLAMANT

Oh, I have denied myself airs to-day. I have walked as fast through the crowd -

WITWOUD

As a favourite just disgraced, and with as few followers.

MILLAMANT

Dear Mr. Witwoud, truce with your similitudes, for I am as sick of 'em -

WITWOUD

As a physician of a good air. I cannot help it, madam, though 'tis against myself.

MILLAMANT

Yet again! Mincing, stand between me and his wit.

WITWOUD
Do, Mrs. Mincing, like a screen before a great fire. I confess I do blaze to-day; I am too bright.
MRS. FAINALL
But, dear Millamant, why were you so long?
MILLAMANT
Long! Lord, have I not made violent haste? I have asked every living thing I met for you; I have enquired after you, as after a new fashion.
WITWOUD
Madam, truce with your similitudes.—No, you met her husband, and did not ask him for her.
MIRABELL
By your leave, Witwoud, that were like enquiring after an old fashion to ask a husband for his wife.
WITWOUD
Hum, a hit, a hit, a palpable hit; I confess it.
MRS. FAINALL
You were dressed before I came abroad.
MILLAMANT
Ay, that's true. Oh, but then I had—Mincing, what had I? Why was I so long?
MINCING
O mem, your laship stayed to peruse a packet of letters.
MILLAMANT
Oh, ay, letters—I had letters—I am persecuted with letters—I hate letters. Nobody knows how to write letters; and yet one has 'em, one does not know why. They serve one to pin up one's hair.
WITWOUD
Is that the way? Pray, madam, do you pin up your hair with all your letters? I find I must keep copies.
MILLAMANT
Only with those in verse, Mr. Witwoud. I never pin up my hair with prose. I think I tried once, Mincing.
MINCING
O mem, I shall never forget it.
MILLAMANT

Ay, poor Mincing tift and tift all the morning.

MINCING

Till I had the cramp in my fingers, I'll vow, mem. And all to no purpose. But when your laship pins it up with poetry, it fits so pleasant the next day as anything, and is so pure and so crips.

WITWOUD

Indeed, so crips?

MINCING

You're such a critic, Mr. Witwoud.

MILLAMANT

Mirabell, did you take exceptions last night? Oh, ay, and went away. Now I think on't I'm angry—no, now I think on't I'm pleased:- for I believe I gave you some pain.

MIRABELL

Does that please you?

MILLAMANT

Infinitely; I love to give pain.

MIRABELL

You would affect a cruelty which is not in your nature; your true vanity is in the power of pleasing.

MILLAMANT

Oh, I ask your pardon for that. One's cruelty is one's power, and when one parts with one's cruelty one parts with one's power, and when one has parted with that, I fancy one's old and ugly.

MIRABELL

Ay, ay; suffer your cruelty to ruin the object of your power, to destroy your lover—and then how vain, how lost a thing you'll be! Nay, 'tis true; you are no longer handsome when you've lost your lover: your beauty dies upon the instant. For beauty is the lover's gift: 'tis he bestows your charms:- your glass is all a cheat. The ugly and the old, whom the looking-glass mortifies, yet after commendation can be flattered by it, and discover beauties in it. for that reflects our praises rather than your face.

MILLAMANT

Oh, the vanity of these men! Fainall, d'ye hear him? If they did not commend us, we were not handsome! Now you must know they could not commend one if one was not handsome. Beauty the lover's gift! Lord, what is a lover, that it can give? Why, one makes lovers as fast as one pleases, and they live as long as one pleases, and they die as soon as one pleases; and then, if one pleases, one makes more.

WITWOUD

Very pretty. Why, you make no more of making of lovers, madam, than of making so many card-matches.

MILLAMANT

One no more owes one's beauty to a lover than one's wit to an echo. They can but reflect what we look and say: vain empty things if we are silent or unseen, and want a being.

MIRABELL

Yet, to those two vain empty things, you owe two the greatest pleasures of your life.

MILLAMANT

How so?

MIRABELL

To your lover you owe the pleasure of hearing yourselves praised, and to an echo the pleasure of hearing yourselves talk.

WITWOUD

But I know a lady that loves talking so incessantly, she won't give an echo fair play; she has that everlasting rotation of tongue that an echo must wait till she dies before it can catch her last words.

MILLAMANT

Oh, fiction; Fainall, let us leave these men.

MIRABELL

Draw off Witwoud. [Aside to MRS. FAINALL.]

MRS. FAINALL

Immediately; I have a word or two for Mr. Witwoud.

ACT II

Scene VI.

MRS. MILLAMANT, MIRABELL, MINCING.

MIRABELL

I would beg a little private audience too. You had the tyranny to deny me last night, though you knew I came to impart a secret to you that concerned my love.

MILLAMANT

You saw I was engaged.

MIRABELL

Unkind! You had the leisure to entertain a herd of fools: things who visit you from their excessive idleness, bestowing on your easiness that time which is the incumbrance of their lives. How can you find delight in such society? It is impossible they should admire you; they are not capable; or, if they were, it should be to you as a mortification: for, sure, to please a fool is some degree of folly.

MILLAMANT

I please myself.—Besides, sometimes to converse with fools is for my health.

MIRABELL

Your health! Is there a worse disease than the conversation of fools?

MILLAMANT

Yes, the vapours; fools are physic for it, next to assafoetida.

MIRABELL

You are not in a course of fools?

MILLAMANT

Mirabell, if you persist in this offensive freedom you'll displease me. I think I must resolve after all not to have you:- we shan't agree.

MIRABELL

Not in our physic, it may be.

MILLAMANT

And yet our distemper in all likelihood will be the same; for we shall be sick of one another. I shan't endure to be reprimanded nor instructed; 'tis so dull to act always by advice, and so tedious to be told of one's faults, I can't bear it. Well, I won't have you, Mirabell—I'm resolved—I think—you may go—ha, ha, ha! What would you give that you could help loving me?

MIRABELL

I would give something that you did not know I could not help it.

MILLAMANT

Come, don't look grave then. Well, what do you say to me?

MIRABELL

I say that a man may as soon make a friend by his wit, or a fortune by his honesty, as win a woman with plain-dealing and sincerity.

MILLAMANT

Sententious Mirabell! Prithee don't look with that violent and inflexible wise face, like Solomon at the dividing of the child in an old tapestry hanging!

MIRABELL

You are merry, madam, but I would persuade you for a moment to be serious.

MILLAMANT

What, with that face? No, if you keep your countenance, 'tis impossible I should hold mine. Well, after all, there is something very moving in a lovesick face. Ha, ha, ha! Well I won't laugh; don't be peevish. Heigho! Now I'll be melancholy, as melancholy as a watch-light. Well, Mirabell, if ever you will win me, woo me now.—Nay, if you are so tedious, fare you well: I see they are walking away.

MIRABELL

Can you not find in the variety of your disposition one moment -

MILLAMANT

To hear you tell me Foible's married, and your plot like to speed? No.

MIRABELL

But how you came to know it -

MILLAMANT

Without the help of the devil, you can't imagine; unless she should tell me herself. Which of the two it may have been, I will leave you to consider; and when you have done thinking of that, think of me.

ACT II

Scene VII.

MIRABELL alone.

MIRABELL

I have something more.—Gone! Think of you? To think of a whirlwind, though 'twere in a whirlwind, were a case of more steady contemplation, a very tranquillity of mind and mansion. A fellow that lives in a windmill has not a more whimsical dwelling than the heart of a man that is lodged in a woman. There is no point of the compass to which they cannot turn, and by which they are not turned, and by one as well as another; for motion, not method, is their occupation.

To know this, and yet continue to be in love, is to be made wise from the dictates of reason, and yet persevere to play the fool by the force of instinct.—Oh, here come my pair of turtles. What, billing so sweetly? Is not Valentine's day over with you yet?

ACT II

Scene VIII.

[To him] WAITWELL, FOIBLE.

MIRABELL

Sirrah, Waitwell, why, sure, you think you were married for your own recreation and not for my conveniency.

WAITWELL

Your pardon, sir. With submission, we have indeed been solacing in lawful delights; but still with an eye to business, sir. I have instructed her as well as I could. If she can take your directions as readily as my instructions, sir, your affairs are in a prosperous way.

MIRABELL

Give you joy, Mrs. Foible.

FOIBLE

O—las, sir, I'm so ashamed.—I'm afraid my lady has been in a thousand inquietudes for me. But I protest, sir, I made as much haste as I could.

WAITWELL

That she did indeed, sir. It was my fault that she did not make more.

MIRABELL

That I believe.

FOIBLE

But I told my lady as you instructed me, sir, that I had a prospect of seeing Sir Rowland, your uncle, and that I would put her ladyship's picture in my pocket to show him, which I'll be sure to say has made him so enamoured of her beauty, that he burns with impatience to lie at her ladyship's feet and worship the original.

MIRABELL

Excellent Foible! Matrimony has made you eloquent in love.

WAITWELL

I think she has profited, sir. I think so.

FOIBLE

You have seen Madam Millamant, sir?

MIRABELL: Yes.

FOIBLE

I told her, sir, because I did not know that you might find an opportunity; she had so much company last night.

MIRABELL

Your diligence will merit more. In the meantime—[gives money]

FOIBLE

O dear sir, your humble servant.

WAITWELL

Spouse -

MIRABELL

Stand off, sir, not a penny. Go on and prosper, Foible. The lease shall be made good and the farm stocked, if we succeed.

FOIBLE

I don't question your generosity, sir, and you need not doubt of success. If you have no more commands, sir, I'll be gone; I'm sure my lady is at her toilet, and can't dress till I come. Oh dear, I'm sure that [looking out] was Mrs. Marwood that went by in a mask; if she has seen me with you I m sure she'll tell my lady. I'll make haste home and prevent her. Your servant, Sir.—B'w'y, Waitwell.

ACT II

Scene IX.

MIRABELL, WAITWELL.

WAITWELL

Sir Rowland, if you please. The jade's so pert upon her preferment she forgets herself.

MIRABELL

Come, sir, will you endeavour to forget yourself—and transform into Sir Rowland?

WAITWELL

Why, sir, it will be impossible I should remember myself. Married, knighted, and attended all in one day! 'Tis enough to make any man forget himself. The difficulty will be how to recover my acquaintance and familiarity with my former self, and fall from my transformation to a reformation into Waitwell. Nay, I shan't be quite the same Waitwell neither—for now I remember me, I'm married, and can't be my own man again.

Ay, there's my grief; that's the sad change of life: To lose my title, and yet keep my wife.

ACT III

Scene I.

A room in Lady Wishfort's house.

LADY WISHFORT at her toilet, PEG waiting.

LADY

Merciful! No news of Foible yet?

PEG

No, madam.

LADY WISHFORT

I have no more patience. If I have not fretted myself till I am pale again, there's no veracity in me. Fetch me the red the red, do you hear, sweetheart? An errant ash colour, as I'm a person. Look you how this wench stirs! Why dost thou not fetch me a little red? Didst thou not hear me, Mopus?

PEG

The red ratafia, does your ladyship mean, or the cherry brandy?

LADY WISHFORT

Ratafia, fool? No, fool. Not the ratafia, fool—grant me patience!—I mean the Spanish paper, idiot; complexion, darling. Paint, paint, paint, dost thou understand that, changeling, dangling thy hands like bobbins before thee? Why dost thou not stir, puppet? Thou wooden thing upon wires!

PEG

Lord, madam, your ladyship is so impatient.—I cannot come at the paint, madam: Mrs. Foible has locked it up, and carried the key with her.

LADY WISHFORT

A pox take you both.—Fetch me the cherry brandy then.

ACT III

Scene II.

LADY WISHFORT.

I'm as pale and as faint, I look like Mrs. Qualmsick, the curate's wife, that's always breeding. Wench, come, come, wench, what art thou doing? Sipping? Tasting? Save thee, dost thou not know the bottle?

ACT III

Scene III.

LADY WISHFORT, PEG with a bottle and china cup.

PEG

Madam, I was looking for a cup.

LADY WISHFORT

A cup, save thee, and what a cup hast thou brought! Dost thou take me for a fairy, to drink out of an acorn? Why didst thou not bring thy thimble? Hast thou ne'er a brass thimble clinking in thy pocket with a bit of nutmeg? I warrant thee. Come, fill, fill. So, again. See who that is. [One knocks.] Set down the bottle first. Here, here, under the table:- what, wouldst thou go with the bottle in thy hand like a tapster? As I'm a person, this wench has lived in an inn upon the road, before she came to me, like Maritornes the Asturian in Don Quixote. No Foible yet?

PEG

No, madam; Mrs. Marwood.

LADY WISHFORT

Oh, Marwood: let her come in. Come in, good Marwood.

ACT III

Scene IV.

[To them] MRS MARWOOD.

MRS. MARWOOD

I'm surprised to find your ladyship in DESHABILLE at this time of day.

LADY WISHFORT

Foible's a lost thing; has been abroad since morning, and never heard of since.

MRS. MARWOOD

I saw her but now, as I came masked through the park, in conference with Mirabell.

LADY WISHFORT

With Mirabell? You call my blood into my face with mentioning that traitor. She durst not have the confidence. I sent her to negotiate an affair, in which if I'm detected I'm undone. If that wheedling villain has wrought upon Foible to detect me, I'm ruined. O my dear friend, I'm a wretch of wretches if I'm detected.

MRS. MARWOOD

O madam, you cannot suspect Mrs. Foible's integrity.

LADY WISHFORT

Oh, he carries poison in his tongue that would corrupt integrity itself. If she has given him an opportunity, she has as good as put her integrity into his hands. Ah, dear Marwood, what's integrity to an opportunity? Hark! I hear her. Dear friend, retire into my closet, that I may examine her with more in reedom— you'll pardon me, dear friend, I can make bold with you there are books over the chimney—Quarles and Pryn, and the SHORT VIEW OF THE STAGE, with Bunyan's works to entertain you.—Go, you thing, and send her in. [To PEG.]

ACT III

Scene V.

LADY WISHFORT, FOIBLE.

LADY WISHFORT

O Foible, where hast thou been? What hast thou been doing?

FOIBLE

Madam, I have seen the party.

LADY WISHFORT

But what hast thou done?

FOIBLE

Nay, 'tis your ladyship has done, and are to do; I have only promised. But a man so enamoured—so transported! Well, if worshipping of pictures be a sin—poor Sir Rowland, I say.

LADY WISHFORT

The miniature has been counted like. But hast thou not betrayed me, Foible? Hast thou not detected me to that faithless Mirabell? What hast thou to do with him in the park? Answer me, has he got nothing out of thee?

FOIBLE

So, the devil has been beforehand with me; what shall I say?- -Alas, madam, could I help it, if I met that confident thing? Was I in fault? If you had heard how he used me, and all upon your ladyship's account, I'm sure you would not suspect my fidelity. Nay, if that had been the worst I could have borne: but he had a fling at your ladyship too, and then I could not hold; but, i'faith I gave him his own.

LADY WISHFORT

Me? What did the filthy fellow say?

FOIBLE

O madam, 'tis a shame to say what he said, with his taunts and his fleers, tossing up his nose. Humh, says he, what, you are a-hatching some plot, says he, you are so early abroad, or catering, says he, ferreting for some disbanded officer, I warrant. Half pay is but thin subsistence, says he. Well, what pension does your lady propose? Let me see, says he, what, she must come down pretty deep now, she's superannuated, says he, and -

LADY WISHFORT

Ods my life, I'll have him—I'll have him murdered. I'll have him poisoned. Where does he eat? I'll marry a drawer to have him poisoned in his wine. I'll send for Robin from Locket's— immediately.

FOIBLE

Poison him? Poisoning's too good for him. Starve him, madam, starve him; marry Sir Rowland, and get him disinherited. Oh, you would bless yourself to hear what he said.

LADY WISHFORT

A villain; superannuated?

FOIBLE

Humh, says he, I hear you are laying designs against me too, says he, and Mrs. Millamant is to marry my uncle (he does not suspect a word of your ladyship); but, says he, I'll fit you for that, I warrant you, says he, I'll hamper you for that, says he, you and your old frippery too, says he, I'll handle you -

LADY WISHFORT

Audacious villain! Handle me? Would he durst? Frippery? Old frippery? Was there ever such a foul-mouthed fellow? I'll be married to-morrow, I'll be contracted to-night.

FOIBLE

The sooner the better, madam.

LADY WISHFORT

Will Sir Rowland be here, say'st thou? When, Foible?

FOIBLE

Incontinently, madam. No new sheriff's wife expects the return of her husband after knighthood with that impatience in which Sir Rowland burns for the dear hour of kissing your ladyship's hand after dinner.

LADY WISHFORT

Frippery? Superannuated frippery? I'll frippery the villain; I'll reduce him to frippery and rags, a tatterdemalion!—I hope to see him hung with tatters, like a Long Lane penthouse, or a gibbet thief. A slander-mouthed railer! I warrant the spendthrift prodigal's in debt as much as the million lottery, or the whole court upon a birthday. I'll spoil his credit with his tailor. Yes, he shall have my niece with her fortune, he shall.

FOIBLE

He? I hope to see him lodge in Ludgate first, and angle into Blackfriars for brass farthings with an old mitten.

LADY WISHFORT

Ay, dear Foible; thank thee for that, dear Foible. He has put me out of all patience. I shall never recompose my features to receive Sir Rowland with any economy of face. This wretch has fretted me that I am absolutely decayed. Look, Foible.

FOIBLE

Your ladyship has frowned a little too rashly, indeed, madam. There are some cracks discernible in the white vernish.

LADY WISHFORT

Let me see the glass. Cracks, say'st thou? Why, I am arrantly flayed: I look like an old peeled wall. Thou must repair me, Foible, before Sir Rowland comes, or I shall never keep up to my picture.

FOIBLE

I warrant you, madam: a little art once made your picture like you, and now a little of the same art must make you like your picture. Your picture must sit for you, madam.

LADY WISHFORT

But art thou sure Sir Rowland will not fail to come? Or will a not fail when he does come? Will he be importunate, Foible, and push? For if he should not be importunate I shall never break decorums. I shall die with confusion if I am forced to advance—oh no, I can never advance; I shall swoon if he should expect advances. No, I hope Sir Rowland is better bred than to put a lady to the necessity of breaking her forms. I won't be too coy neither—I won't give him despair. But a little disdain is not amiss; a little scorn is alluring.

FOIBLE

A little scorn becomes your ladyship.

LADY WISHFORT

Yes, but tenderness becomes me best a sort of a dyingness. You see that picture has a sort of a—ha, Foible? A swimmingness in the eyes. Yes, I'll look so. My niece affects it; but she wants features. Is Sir Rowland handsome? Let my toilet be removed—I'll dress above. I'll receive Sir Rowland here. Is he handsome? Don't answer me. I won't know; I'll be surprised. I'll be taken by surprise.

FOIBLE

By storm, madam. Sir Rowland's a brisk man.

LADY WISHFORT

Is he? Oh, then, he'll importune, if he's a brisk man. I shall save decorums if Sir Rowland importunes. I have a mortal terror at the apprehension of offending against decorums. Oh, I'm glad he's a brisk man. Let my things be removed, good Foible.

ACT III

Scene VI.

MRS. FAINALL, FOIBLE.

MRS. FAINALL

O Foible, I have been in a fright, lest I should come too late. That devil, Marwood, saw you in the park with Mirabell, and I'm afraid will discover it to my lady.

FOIBLE

Discover what, madam?

MRS. FAINALL

Nay, nay, put not on that strange face. I am privy to the whole design, and know that Waitwell, to whom thou wert this morning married, is to personate Mirabell's uncle, and, as such winning my lady, to involve her in those difficulties from which Mirabell only must release her, by his making his conditions to have my cousin and her fortune left to her own disposal.

FOIBLE

O dear madam, I beg your pardon. It was not my confidence in your ladyship that was deficient; but I thought the former good correspondence between your ladyship and Mr. Mirabell might have hindered his communicating this secret.

MRS. FAINALL

Dear Foible, forget that.

FOIBLE

O dear madam, Mr. Mirabell is such a sweet winning

gentleman. But your ladyship is the pattern of generosity. Sweet lady, to be so good! Mr. Mirabell cannot choose but be grateful. I find your ladyship has his heart still. Now, madam, I can safely tell your ladyship our success: Mrs. Marwood had told my lady, but I warrant I managed myself. I turned it all for the better. I told my lady that Mr. Mirabell railed at her. I laid horrid things to his charge, I'll vow; and my lady is so incensed that she'll be contracted to Sir Rowland to-night, she says; I warrant I worked her up that he may have her for asking for, as they say of a Welsh maidenhead.

MRS. FAINALL

O rare Foible!

FOIBLE

Madam, I beg your ladyship to acquaint Mr. Mirabell of his success. I would be seen as little as possible to speak to him— besides, I believe Madam Marwood watches me. She has a month's mind; but I know Mr. Mirabell can't abide her. [Calls.] John, remove my lady's toilet. Madam, your servant. My lady is so impatient, I fear she'll come for me, if I stay.

MRS. FAINALL

I'll go with you up the back stairs, lest I should meet her.

ACT III

Scene VII.

MRS. MARWOOD alone.

MRS. MARWOOD

Indeed, Mrs. Engine, is it thus with you? Are you become a go-between of this importance? Yes, I shall watch you. Why this wench is the PASSE-PARTOUT, a very master-key to everybody's strong box. My friend Fainall, have you carried it so swimmingly? I thought there was something in it; but it seems it's over with you. Your loathing is not from a want of appetite then, but from a surfeit. Else you could never be so cool to fall from a principal to be an assistant, to procure for him! A pattern of generosity, that I confess. Well, Mr. Fainall, you have met with your match.—O man, man! Woman, woman! The devil's an ass:

if I were a painter, I would draw him like an idiot, a

driveller with a bib and bells. Man should have his head and horns, and woman the rest of him. Poor, simple fiend! 'Madam Marwood has a month's mind, but he can't abide her.' 'Twere better for him you had not been his confessor in that affair, without you could have kept his counsel closer. I shall not prove another pattern of generosity; he has not obliged me to that with those excesses of himself, and now I'll have none of him. Here comes the good lady, panting ripe, with a heart full of hope, and a head full of care, like any chymist upon the day of projection.

ACT III

Scene VIII.

[To her] LADY WISHFORT.

LADY WISHFORT

O dear Marwood, what shall I say for this rude forgetfulness? But my dear friend is all goodness.

MRS. MARWOOD

No apologies, dear madam. I have been very well entertained.

LADY WISHFORT

As I'm a person, I am in a very chaos to think I should so forget myself. But I have such an olio of affairs, really I know not what to do. [Calls.] Foible!—I expect my nephew Sir Wilfull ev'ry moment too.—Why, Foible!—He means to travel for improvement.

MRS. MARWOOD

Methinks Sir Wilfull should rather think of marrying than travelling at his years. I hear he is turned of forty.

LADY WISHFORT

Oh, he's in less danger of being spoiled by his travels. I am against my nephew's marrying too young. It will be time enough when he comes back, and has acquired discretion to choose for himself.

MRS. MARWOOD

Methinks Mrs. Millamant and he would make a very fit match. He may travel afterwards. 'Tis a thing very usual with young gentlemen.

LADY WISHFORT

I promise you I have thought on't—and since 'tis your judgment, I'll think on't again. I assure you I will; I value your judgment extremely. On my word, I'll propose it.

ACT III

Scene IX.

[To them] FOIBLE.

LADY WISHFORT

Come, come, Foible—I had forgot my nephew will be here before dinner—I must make haste.

FOIBLE

Mr. Witwoud and Mr. Petulant are come to dine with your ladyship.

LADY WISHFORT

Oh dear, I can't appear till I am dressed. Dear Marwood, shall I be free with you again, and beg you to entertain em? I'll make all imaginable haste. Dear friend, excuse me.

ACT III

Scene X.

MRS. MARWOOD, MRS. MILLAMANT, MINCING.

MILLAMANT

Sure, never anything was so unbred as that odious man. Marwood, your servant.

MRS. MARWOOD : You have a colour; what's the matter?

MILLAMANT

That horrid fellow Petulant has provoked me into a flame—I have broke my fan—Mincing, lend me yours.—Is not all the powder out of my hair?

MRS. MARWOOD

No. What has he done?

MILLAMANT

Nay, he has done nothing; he has only talked. Nay, he has said nothing neither; but he has contradicted everything that has been said. For my part, I thought Witwoud and he would have quarrelled.

MINCING

I vow, mem, I thought once they would have fit.

MILLAMANT

Well, 'tis a lamentable thing, I swear, that one has not the liberty of choosing one's acquaintance as one does one's clothes.

MRS. MARWOOD

If we had that liberty, we should be as weary of one set of acquaintance, though never so good, as we are of one suit, though never so fine. A fool and a doily stuff would now and then find days of grace, and be worn for variety.

MILLAMANT

I could consent to wear 'em, if they would wear alike; but fools never wear out. They are such DRAP DE BERRI things! Without one could give 'em to one's chambermaid after a day or two.

MRS. MARWOOD

'Twere better so indeed. Or what think you of the playhouse? A fine gay glossy fool should be given there, like a new masking habit, after the masquerade is over, and we have done with the disguise. For a fool's visit is always a disguise, and never admitted by a woman of wit, but to blind her affair with a lover of sense.

If you would but appear barefaced now, and own Mirabell, you might as easily put off Petulant and Witwoud as your hood and scarf. And indeed 'tis time, for the town has found it, the secret is grown too big for the pretence. 'Tis like Mrs. Primly's great belly: she may lace it down before, but it burnishes on her hips. Indeed, Millamant, you can no more conceal it than my Lady Strammel can her face, that goodly face, which in defiance of her Rhenish-wine tea will not be comprehended in a mask.

MILLAMANT

I'll take my death, Marwood, you are more censorious than a decayed beauty, or a discarded toast:- Mincing, tell the men they may come up. My aunt is not dressing here; their folly is less provoking than your malice.

ACT III

Scene XI.

MRS. MILLAMANT, MRS. MARWOOD.

MILLAMANT

The town has found it? What has it found? That Mirabell loves me is no more a secret than it is a secret that you discovered it to my aunt, or than the reason why you discovered it is a secret.

MRS. MARWOOD: You are nettled.

MILLAMANT: You're mistaken. Ridiculous!

MRS. MARWOOD

Indeed, my dear, you'll tear another fan, if you don't mitigate those violent airs.

MILLAMANT

O silly! Ha, ha, ha! I could laugh immoderately. Poor Mirabell! His constancy to me has quite destroyed his complaisance for all the world beside. I swear I never enjoined it him to be so coy. If I had the vanity to think he would obey me, I would command him to show more gallantry: 'tis hardly well-bred to be so particular on one hand and so insensible on the other. But I despair to prevail, and so let him follow his own way. Ha, ha, ha! Pardon me, dear creature, I must laugh; ha, ha, ha! Though I grant you 'tis a little barbarous; ha, ha, ha!

MRS. MARWOOD

What pity 'tis so much fine raillery, and delivered with so significant gesture, should be so unhappily directed to miscarry.

MILLAMANT

Heh? Dear creature, I ask your pardon. I swear I did not mind you.

MRS. MARWOOD

Mr. Mirabell and you both may think it a thing impossible, when I shall tell him by telling you -

MILLAMANT

Oh dear, what? For it is the same thing, if I hear it. Ha, ha, ha!

MRS. MARWOOD

That I detest him, hate him, madam.

MILLAMANT

O madam, why, so do I And yet the creature loves me, ha, ha, ha! How can one forbear laughing to think of it? I am a sibyl if I am not amazed to think what he can see in me. I'll take my death, I think you are handsomer, and within a year or two as young. If you could but stay for me, I should overtake you—but that cannot be. Well, that thought makes me melancholic.—Now I'll be sad.

MRS. MARWOOD

Your merry note may be changed sooner than you think.

MILLAMANT

D'ye say so? Then I'm resolved I'll have a song to keep up my spirits.

ACT III

Scene XII.

[To them] MINCING.

MINCING

The gentlemen stay but to comb, madam, and will wait on you.

MILLAMANT

Desire Mrs.—that is in the next room, to sing the song I would have learnt yesterday. You shall hear it, madam. Not that there's any great matter in it—but 'tis agreeable to my humour.

SONG.

Set by Mr. John Eccles.

I

Love's but the frailty of the mind
When 'tis not with ambition joined;
A sickly flame, which if not fed expires,
And feeding, wastes in self-consuming fires.

II

'Tis not to wound a wanton boy
Or am'rous youth, that gives the joy;
But 'tis the glory to have pierced a swain
For whom inferior beauties sighed in vain.

III

Then I alone the conquest prize,

When I insult a rival's eyes;
If there's delight in love, 'tis when I see
That heart, which others bleed for, bleed for me.

ACT III

Scene XIII.

[To them] PETULANT, WITWOUD.

MILLAMANT

Is your animosity composed, gentlemen?

WITWOUD

Raillery, raillery, madam; we have no animosity. We hit off a little wit now and then, but no animosity. The falling out of wits is like the falling out of lovers:- we agree in the main, like treble and bass. Ha, Petulant?

PETULANT

Ay, in the main. But when I have a humour to contradict

WITWOUD

Ay, when he has a humour to contradict, then I contradict too. What, I know my cue. Then we contradict one another like two battledores; for contradictions beget one another like Jews.

PETULANT

If he says black's black—if I have a humour to say 'tis blue--let that pass—all's one for that. If I have a humour to prove it, it must be granted.

WITWOUD

Not positively must. But it may; it may.

PETULANT

Yes, it positively must, upon proof positive.

WITWOUD

Ay, upon proof positive it must; but upon proof presumptive it only may. That's a logical distinction now, madam.

MRS. MARWOOD

I perceive your debates are of importance, and very learnedly handled.

PETULANT

Importance is one thing and learning's another; but a debate's a debate, that I assert.

WITWOUD

Petulant's an enemy to learning; he relies altogether on his parts.

PETULANT

No, I'm no enemy to learning; it hurts not me.

MRS. MARWOOD

That's a sign, indeed, it's no enemy to you.

PETULANT

No, no, it's no enemy to anybody but them that have it.

MILLAMANT

Well, an illiterate man's my aversion; I wonder at the impudence of any illiterate man to offer to make love.

WITWOUD

That I confess I wonder at, too.

MILLAMANT

Ah, to marry an ignorant that can hardly read or write!

PETULANT

Why should a man be any further from being married, though he can't read, than he is from being hanged? The ordinary's paid for setting the psalm, and the parish priest for reading the ceremony. And for the rest which is to follow in both cases, a man may do it without book. So all's one for that.

MILLAMANT

D'ye hear the creature? Lord, here's company; I'll begone.

ACT III

Scene XIV.

SIR WILFULL WITWOUD in a riding dress, MRS. MARWOOD, PETULANT, WITWOUD, FOOTMAN.

WITWOUD

In the name of Bartlemew and his Fair, what have we here?

MRS. MARWOOD

'Tis your brother, I fancy. Don't you know him?

WITWOUD

Not I:- yes, I think it is he. I've almost forgot him; I have not seen him since the revolution.

FOOTMAN

Sir, my lady's dressing. Here's company, if you please to walk in, in the meantime.

SIR WILFULL WITWOUD

Dressing! What, it's but morning here, I warrant, with you in London; we should count it towards afternoon in our parts down in Shropshire:- why, then, belike my aunt han't dined yet. Ha, friend?

FOOTMAN

Your aunt, sir?

SIR WILFULL WITWOUD

My aunt, sir? Yes my aunt, sir, and your lady, sir; your lady is my aunt, sir. Why, what dost thou not know me, friend? Why, then, send somebody hither that does. How long hast thou lived with thy lady, fellow, ha?

FOOTMAN

A week, sir; longer than anybody in the house, except my lady's woman.

SIR WILFULL WITWOUD

Why, then, belike thou dost not know thy lady, if thou seest her. Ha, friend?

FOOTMAN

Why, truly, sir, I cannot safely swear to her face in a morning, before she is dressed. 'Tis like I may give a shrewd guess at her by this time.

SIR WILFULL WITWOUD

Well, prithee try what thou canst do; if thou canst not guess, enquire her out, dost hear, fellow? And tell her her nephew, Sir Wilfull Witwoud, is in the house.

FOOTMAN

I shall, sir.

SIR WILFULL WITWOUD

Hold ye, hear me, friend, a word with you in your ear: prithee who are these gallants?

FOOTMAN

Really, sir, I can't tell; here come so many here, 'tis hard to know 'em all.

ACT III

Scene XV.

SIR WILFULL WITWOUD, PETULANT, WITWOUD, MRS. MARWOOD.

SIR WILFULL WITWOUD
Oons, this fellow knows less than a starling: I don't think a knows his own name.

MRS. MARWOOD
Mr. Witwoud, your brother is not behindhand in forgetfulness. I fancy he has forgot you too.

WITWOUD
I hope so. The devil take him that remembers first, I say.

SIR WILFULL WITWOUD
Save you, gentlemen and lady.

MRS. MARWOOD
For shame, Mr. Witwoud; why won't you speak to him?— And you, sir.

WITWOUD
Petulant, speak.

PETULANT
And you, sir.

SIR WILFULL WITWOUD
No offence, I hope? [Salutes MARWOOD.]

MRS. MARWOOD
No, sure, sir.

WITWOUD
This is a vile dog, I see that already. No offence? Ha, ha, ha. To him, to him, Petulant, smoke him.

PETULANT
It seems as if you had come a journey, sir; hem, hem. [Surveying him round.]

SIR WILFULL WITWOUD
Very likely, sir, that it may seem so.

PETULANT
No offence, I hope, sir?

WITWOUD
Smoke the boots, the boots, Petulant, the boots; ha, ha, ha!

SIR WILL
Maybe not, sir; thereafter as 'tis meant, sir.

PETULANT

Sir, I presume upon the information of your boots.

SIR WILFULL WITWOUD

Why, 'tis like you may, sir: if you are not satisfied with the information of my boots, sir, if you will step to the stable, you may enquire further of my horse, sir.

PETULANT

Your horse, sir! Your horse is an ass, sir!

SIR WILFULL WITWOUD

Do you speak by way of offence, sir?

MRS. MARWOOD

The gentleman's merry, that's all, sir. 'Slife, we shall have a quarrel betwixt an horse and an ass, before they find one another out.—You must not take anything amiss from your friends, sir. You are among your friends here, though it—may be you don't know it. If I am not mistaken, you are Sir Wilfull Witwoud?

SIR WILFULL WITWOUD

Right, lady; I am Sir Wilfull Witwoud, so I write myself; no offence to anybody, I hope? and nephew to the Lady Wishfort of this mansion.

MRS. MARWOOD

Don't you know this gentleman, sir?

SIR WILFULL WITWOUD

Hum! What, sure 'tis not—yea by'r lady but 'tis— 'sheart, I know not whether 'tis or no. Yea, but 'tis, by the Wrekin. Brother Antony! What, Tony, i'faith! What, dost thou not know me? By'r lady, nor I thee, thou art so becravated and so beperiwigged. 'Sheart, why dost not speak? Art thou o'erjoyed?

WITWOUD

Odso, brother, is it you? Your servant, brother.

SIR WILFULL WITWOUD

Your servant? Why, yours, sir. Your servant again—'sheart, and your friend and servant to that—and a—[puff] and a flap-dragon for your service, sir, and a hare's foot and a hare's scut for your service, sir, an you be so cold and so courtly!

WITWOUD

No offence, I hope, brother?

SIR WILFULL WITWOUD

'Sheart, sir, but there is, and much offence. A pox, is this your inns o' court breeding, not to know your friends and your relations, your elders, and your betters?

WITWOUD

Why, brother Wilfull of Salop, you may be as short as a Shrewsbury cake, if you please. But I tell you 'tis not modish to know relations in town. You think you're in the country, where great lubberly brothers slabber and kiss one another when they meet, like a call of sergeants. 'Tis not the fashion here; 'tis not, indeed, dear brother.

SIR WILFULL WITWOUD

The fashion's a fool and you're a fop, dear brother. 'Sheart, I've suspected this—by'r lady I conjectured you were a fop, since you began to change the style of your letters, and write in a scrap of paper gilt round the edges, no bigger than a subpoena. I might expect this when you left off 'Honoured brother,' and 'Hoping you are in good health,' and so forth, to begin with a 'Rat me, knight, I'm so sick of a last night's debauch.' Ods heart, and then tell a familiar tale of a cock and a bull, and a whore and a bottle, and so conclude. You could write news before you were out of your time, when you lived with honest Pumple-Nose, the attorney of Furnival's Inn. You could intreat to be remembered then to your friends round the Wrekin. We could have Gazettes then, and Dawks's Letter, and the Weekly Bill, till of late days.

PETULANT

'Slife, Witwoud, were you ever an attorney's clerk? Of the family of the Furnivals? Ha, ha, ha!

WITWOUD

Ay, ay, but that was but for a while. Not long, not long; pshaw, I was not in my own power then. An orphan, and this fellow was my guardian; ay, ay, I was glad to consent to that man to come to London. He had the disposal of me then. If I had not agreed to that, I might have been bound prentice to a feltmaker in Shrewsbury: this fellow would have bound me to a maker of felts.

SIR WILFULL WITWOUD

'Sheart, and better than to be bound to a maker of fops, where, I suppose, you have served your time, and now you may set up for yourself.

MRS. MARWOOD

You intend to travel, sir, as I'm informed?

SIR WILFULL WITWOUD

Belike I may, madam. I may chance to sail upon the salt seas, if my mind hold.

PETULANT: And the wind serve.

SIR WILFULL WITWOUD

Serve or not serve, I shan't ask license of you, sir, nor the weathercock your companion. I direct my discourse to the lady, sir. 'Tis like my aunt may have told you, madam? Yes, I have settled my concerns, I may say now, and am minded to see foreign parts. If an how that the peace holds, whereby, that is, taxes abate.

MRS. MARWOOD

I thought you had designed for France at all adventures.

SIR WILFULL WITWOUD

I can't tell that; 'tis like I may, and 'tis like I may not. I am somewhat dainty in making a resolution, because when I make it I keep it. I don't stand shill I, shall I, then; if I say't, I'll do't. But I have thoughts to tarry a small matter in town, to learn somewhat of your lingo first, before I cross the seas. I'd gladly have a spice of your French as they say, whereby to hold discourse in foreign countries.

MRS. MARWOOD

Here's an academy in town for that use.

SIR WILFULL WITWOUD

There is? 'Tis like there may.

MRS. MARWOOD

No doubt you will return very much improved.

WITWOUD

Yes, refined like a Dutch skipper from a whale-fishing.

ACT III

Scene XVI.

[To them] LADY WISHFORT and FAINALL.

LADY WISHFORT

Nephew, you are welcome.

SIR WILFULL WITWOUD

Aunt, your servant.

FAINALL

Sir Wilfull, your most faithful servant.

SIR WILFULL WITWOUD

Cousin Fainall, give me your hand.

LADY WISHFORT

Cousin Witwoud, your servant; Mr. Petulant, your servant. Nephew, you are welcome again. Will you drink anything after your journey, nephew, before you eat? Dinner's almost ready.

SIR WILFULL WITWOUD

I'm very well, I thank you, aunt. However, I thank you for your courteous offer. 'Sheart, I was afraid you would have been in the fashion too, and have remembered to have forgot your relations. Here's your cousin Tony, belike, I mayn't call him brother for fear of offence.

LADY WISHFORT

Oh, he's a rallier, nephew. My cousin's a wit: and your great wits always rally their best friends to choose. When you have been abroad, nephew, you'll understand raillery better. [FAINALL and MRS. MARWOOD talk apart.]

SIR WILFULL WITWOUD

Why, then, let him hold his tongue in the meantime, and rail when that day comes.

ACT III

Scene XVII.

[To them] MINCING.

MINCING

Mem, I come to acquaint your laship that dinner is impatient.

SIR WILFULL WITWOUD

Impatient? Why, then, belike it won't stay till I pull off my boots. Sweetheart, can you help me to a pair of slippers? My man's with his horses, I warrant.

LADY WISHFORT

Fie, fie, nephew, you would not pull off your boots here? Go down into the hall:- dinner shall stay for you. My nephew's a little unbred: you'll pardon him, madam. Gentlemen, will you walk? Marwood?

MRS. MARWOOD

I'll follow you, madam,—before Sir Wilfull is ready.

ACT III

Scene XVIII.

MRS. MARWOOD, FAINALL.

FAINALL

Why, then, Foible's a bawd, an errant, rank match-making bawd. And I, it seems, am a husband, a rank husband, and my wife a very errant, rank wife,—all in the way of the world. 'Sdeath, to be a cuckold by anticipation, a cuckold in embryo! Sure I was born with budding antlers like a young satyr, or a citizen's child, 'sdeath, to be out-witted, to be out-jilted, out-matrimonied. If I had kept my speed like a stag, 'twere somewhat, but to crawl after, with my horns like a snail, and be outstripped by my wife—'tis scurvy wedlock.

MRS. MARWOOD

Then shake it off: you have often wished for an opportunity to part, and now you have it. But first prevent their plot:- the half of Millamant's fortune is too considerable to be parted with to a foe, to Mirabell.

FAINALL

Damn him, that had been mine—had you not made that fond discovery. That had been forfeited, had they been married. My wife had added lustre to my horns by that increase of fortune: I could have worn 'em tipt with gold, though my forehead had been furnished like a deputy-lieutenant's hall.

MRS. MARWOOD

They may prove a cap of maintenance to you still, if you can away with your wife. And she's no worse than when you had her:- I dare swear she had given up her game before she was married.

FAINALL

Hum! That may be -

MRS. MARWOOD

You married her to keep you; and if you can contrive to have her keep you better than you expected, why should you not keep her longer than you intended?

FAINALL

The means, the means?

MRS. MARWOOD

Discover to my lady your wife's conduct; threaten to part with her. My lady loves her, and will come to any composition to save her reputation. Take the opportunity of breaking it just upon the discovery of this imposture. My lady will be enraged beyond bounds, and sacrifice niece, and fortune and all at that conjuncture. And let me alone to keep her warm: if she should flag in her part, I will not fail to prompt her.

FAINALL

Faith, this has an appearance.

MRS. MARWOOD

I'm sorry I hinted to my lady to endeavour a match between Millamant and Sir Wilfull; that may be an obstacle.

FAINALL

Oh, for that matter, leave me to manage him; I'll disable him for that, he will drink like a Dane. After dinner I'll set his hand in.

MRS. MARWOOD

Well, how do you stand affected towards your lady?

FAINALL

Why, faith, I'm thinking of it. Let me see. I am married already; so that's over. My wife has played the jade with me; well, that's over too. I never loved her, or if I had, why that would have been over too by this time. Jealous of her I cannot be, for I am certain; so there's an end of jealousy. Weary of her I am and shall be. No, there's no end of that; no, no, that were too much to hope. Thus far concerning my repose. Now for my reputation: as to my own, I married not for it; so that's out of the question. And as to my part in my wife's—why, she had parted with hers before; so, bringing none to me, she can take none from me: 'tis against all rule of play that I should lose to one who has not wherewithal to stake.

MRS. MARWOOD

Besides you forget, marriage is honourable.

FAINALL

Hum! Faith, and that's well thought on: marriage is honourable, as you say; and if so, wherefore should cuckoldom be a discredit, being derived from so honourable a root?

MRS. MARWOOD

Nay, I know not; if the root be honourable, why not the branches?

FAINALL

So, so; why this point's clear. Well, how do we proceed?

MRS. MARWOOD

I will contrive a letter which shall be delivered to my lady at the time when that rascal who is to act Sir Rowland is with her. It shall come as from an unknown hand—for the less I appear to know of the truth the better I can play the incendiary. Besides, I would not have Foible provoked if I could help it, because, you know, she knows some passages. Nay, I expect all will come out. But let the mine be sprung first, and then I care not if I am discovered.

FAINALL

If the worst come to the worst, I'll turn my wife to grass. I have already a deed of settlement of the best part of her estate, which I wheedled out of her, and that you shall partake at least.

MRS. MARWOOD

I hope you are convinced that I hate Mirabell now? You'll be no more jealous?

FAINALL

Jealous? No, by this kiss. Let husbands be jealous, but let the lover still believe: or if he doubt, let it be only to endear his pleasure, and prepare the joy that follows, when he proves his mistress true. But let husbands' doubts convert to endless jealousy; or if they have belief, let it corrupt to superstition and blind credulity. I am single and will herd no more with 'em. True, I wear the badge, but I'll disown the order. And since I take my leave of 'em, I care not if I leave 'em a common motto to their common crest.

All husbands must or pain or shame endure; The wise too jealous are, fools too secure.

ACT IV

Scene I.

Scene Continues.

LADY WISHFORT and FOIBLE.

LADY WISHFORT

Is Sir Rowland coming, say'st thou, Foible? And are things in order?

FOIBLE

Yes, madam. I have put wax-lights in the sconces, and placed the footmen in a row in the hall, in their best liveries, with the coachman and postillion to fill up the equipage.

LADY WISHFORT

Have you pulvilled the coachman and postillion, that they may not stink of the stable when Sir Rowland comes by?

FOIBLE

Yes, madam.

LADY WISHFORT

And are the dancers and the music ready, that he may be entertained in all points with correspondence to his passion?

FOIBLE

All is ready, madam.

LADY WISHFORT

And—well—and how do I look, Foible?

FOIBLE

Most killing well, madam.

LADY WISHFORT

Well, and how shall I receive him? In what figure shall I give his heart the first impression? There is a great deal in the first impression. Shall I sit? No, I won't sit, I'll walk,—ay, I'll walk from the door upon his entrance, and then turn full upon him. No, that will be too sudden. I'll lie,—ay, I'll lie down. I'll receive him in my little dressing-room; there's a couch—yes, yes, I'll give the first impression on a couch. I won't lie neither, but loll and lean upon one elbow, wi h one foot a little dangling off, jogging in a thoughtful way. Y :s; and then as soon as he appears, start, ay, start and be surprised, and rise to meet him in a pretty disorder.

Yes; oh, nothing is more alluring than a levee from a couch in some confusion. It shows the foot to advantage, and furnishes with blushes and re-composing airs beyond comparison. Hark! There's a coach.

FOIBLE

'Tis he, madam.

LADY WISHFORT

Oh dear, has my nephew made his addresses to Millamant? I ordered him.

FOIBLE

Sir Wilfull is set in to drinking, madam, in the parlour.

LADY WISHFORT

Ods my life, I'll send him to her. Call her down, Foible; bring her hither. I'll send him as I go. When they are together, then come to me, Foible, that I may not be too long alone with Sir Rowland.

ACT IV

Scene II.

MRS. MILLAMANT, MRS. FAINALL, FOIBLE.

FOIBLE

Madam, I stayed here to tell your ladyship that Mr. Mirabell has waited this half hour for an opportunity to talk with you; though my lady's orders were to leave you and Sir Wilfull together. Shall I tell Mr. Mirabell that you are at leisure?

MILLAMANT

No. What would the dear man have? I am thoughtful and would amuse myself; bid him come another time.

There never yet was woman made, Nor shall, but to be cursed. [Repeating and walking about.]

That's hard!

MRS. FAINALL

You are very fond of Sir John Suckling to-day, Millamant, and the poets.

MILLAMANT

He? Ay, and filthy verses. So I am.

FOIBLE

Sir Wilfull is coming, madam. Shall I send Mr. Mirabell away?

MILLAMANT

Ay, if you please, Foible, send him away, or send him hither, just as you will, dear Foible. I think I'll see him. Shall I? Ay, let the wretch come.

Thyrsis, a youth of the inspired train. [Repeating]

Dear Fainall, entertain Sir Wilfull:- thou hast philosophy to undergo a fool; thou art married and hast patience. I would confer with my own thoughts.

MRS. FAINALL

I am obliged to you that you would make me your proxy in this affair, but I have business of my own.

ACT IV

Scene III.

[To them] SIR WILFULL.

MRS. FAINALL

O Sir Wilfull, you are come at the critical instant. There's your mistress up to the ears in love and contemplation; pursue your point, now or never.

SIR WILFULL WITWOUD

Yes, my aunt will have it so. I would gladly have been encouraged with a bottle or two, because I'm somewhat wary at first, before I am acquainted. [This while MILLAMANT walks about repeating to herself.] But I hope, after a time, I shall break my mind—that is, upon further acquaintance.—So for the present, cousin, I'll take my leave. If so be you'll be so kind to make my excuse, I'll return to my company -

MRS. FAINALL

Oh, fie, Sir Wilfull! What, you must not be daunted.

SIR WILFULL WITWOUD

Daunted? No, that's not it; it is not so much for that— for

if so be that I set on't I'll do't. But only for the present, 'tis sufficient till further acquaintance, that's all—your servant.

MRS. FAINALL

Nay, I'll swear you shall never lose so favourable an opportunity, if I can help it. I'll leave you together and lock the door.

ACT IV

Scene IV.

SIR WILFULL, MILLAMANT.

SIR WILFULL WITWOUD

Nay, nay, cousin. I have forgot my gloves. What d'ye do? 'Sheart, a has locked the door indeed, I think.—Nay, cousin Fainall, open the door. Pshaw, what a vixen trick is this? Nay, now a has seen me too.—Cousin, I made bold to pass through as it were—I think this door's enchanted.

MILLAMANT

[repeating]:-

I prithee spare me, gentle boy, Press me no more for that slight toy.

SIR WILFULL WITWOUD

Anan? Cousin, your servant.

MILLAMANT

That foolish trifle of a heart-Sir Wilfull!

SIR WILFULL WITWOUD

Yes—your servant. No offence, I hope, cousin?

MILLAMANT

[repeating]:-

I swear it will not do its part, Though thou dost thine, employ'st thy power and art.

Natural, easy Suckling!

SIR WILFULL WITWOUD

Anan? Suckling? No such suckling neither, cousin, nor stripling: I thank heaven I'm no minor.

MILLAMANT

Ah, rustic, ruder than Gothic.

SIR WILFULL WITWOUD

Well, well, I shall understand your lingo one of these days, cousin; in the meanwhile I must answer in plain English.

MILLAMANT

Have you any business with me, Sir Wilfull?

SIR WILFULL WITWOUD

Not at present, cousin. Yes, I made bold to see, to come and know if that how you were disposed to fetch a walk this evening; if so be that I might not be troublesome, I would have sought a walk with you.

MILLAMANT

A walk? What then?

SIR WILFULL WITWOUD

Nay, nothing. Only for the walk's sake, that's all.

MILLAMANT

I nauseate walking: 'tis a country diversion; I loathe the country and everything that relates to it.

SIR WILFULL WITWOUD

Indeed! Hah! Look ye, look ye, you do? Nay, 'tis like you may. Here are choice of pastimes here in town, as plays and the like, that must be confessed indeed -

MILLAMANT

Ah, L'ETOURDI! I hate the town too.

SIR WILFULL WITWOUD

Dear heart, that's much. Hah! that you should hate 'em both! Hah! 'tis like you may! There are some can't relish the town, and others can't away with the country, 'tis like you may be one of those, cousin.

MILLAMANT

Ha, ha, ha! Yes, 'tis like I may. You have nothing further to say to me?

SIR WILFULL WITWOUD

Not at present, cousin. 'Tis like when I have an opportunity to be more private—I may break my mind in some measure- -I conjecture you partly guess. However, that's as time shall try. But spare to speak and spare to speed, as they say.

MILLAMANT

If it is of no great importance, Sir Wilfull, you will oblige me to leave me: I have just now a little business.

SIR WILFULL WITWOUD

Enough, enough, cousin. Yes, yes, all a case. When you're disposed, when you're disposed. Now's as well as another time; and another time as well as now. All's one for that. Yes, yes; if your concerns call you, there's no haste: it will keep cold as they say. Cousin, your servant. I think this door's locked.

MILLAMANT

You may go this way, sir.

SIR WILFULL WITWOUD

Your servant; then with your leave I'll return to my company.

MILLAMANT

Ay, ay; ha, ha, ha!

Like Phoebus sung the no less am'rous boy.

ACT IV

Scene V.

MRS. MILLAMANT, MIRABELL.

MIRABELL

Like Daphne she, as lovely and as coy.

Do you lock yourself up from me, to make my search more curious? Or is this pretty artifice contrived, to signify that here the chase must end, and my pursuit be crowned, for you can fly no further?

MILLAMANT

Vanity! No—I'll fly and be followed to the last moment; though I am upon the very verge of matrimony, I expect you should solicit me as much as if I were wavering at the grate of a monastery, with one foot over the threshold. I'll be solicited to the very last; nay, and afterwards.

MIRABELL

What, after the last?

MILLAMANT

Oh, I should think I was poor and had nothing to bestow if I were reduced to an inglorious ease, and freed from the agreeable fatigues of solicitation.

MIRABELL

But do not you know that when favours are conferred

upon instant and tedious solicitation, that they diminish in their value, and that both the giver loses the grace, and the receiver lessens his pleasure?

MILLAMANT

It may be in things of common application, but never, sure, in love. Oh, I hate a lover that can dare to think he draws a moment's air independent on the bounty of his mistress. There is not so impudent a thing in nature as the saucy look of an assured man confident of success: the pedantic arrogance of a very husband has not so pragmatical an air. Ah, I'll never marry, unless I am first made sure of my will and pleasure.

MIRABELL

Would you have 'em both before marriage? Or will you be contented with the first now, and stay for the other till after grace?

MILLAMANT

Ah, don't be impertinent. My dear liberty, shall I leave thee? My faithful solitude, my darling contemplation, must I bid you then adieu? Ay-h, adieu. My morning thoughts, agreeable wakings, indolent slumbers, all ye DOUCEURS, ye SOMMEILS DU MATIN, adieu. I can't do't, 'tis more than impossible—positively, Mirabell, I'll lie a-bed in a morning as long as I please.

MIRABELL

Then I'll get up in a morning as early as I please.

MILLAMANT

Ah! Idle creature, get up when you will. And d'ye hear, I won't be called names after I'm married; positively I won't be called names.

MIRABELL

Names?

MILLAMANT

Ay, as wife, spouse, my dear, joy, jewel, love, sweet-heart, and the rest of that nauseous cant, in which men and their wives are so fulsomely familiar—I shall never bear that. Good Mirabell, don't let us be familiar or fond, nor kiss before folks, like my Lady Fadler and Sir Francis; nor go to Hyde Park together the first Sunday in a new chariot, to provoke eyes and whispers, and then never be seen there together again, as if we were proud of one another the first week, and ashamed of one another ever after. Let us never visit together, nor go to a play together, but let us be very strange and well-bred. Let us be as strange as if we had been married a great while, and as well-bred as if we were not married at all.

MIRABELL

Have you any more conditions to offer? Hitherto your demands are pretty reasonable.

MILLAMANT

Trifles; as liberty to pay and receive visits to and from whom I please; to write and receive letters, without interrogatories or wry faces on your part; to wear what I please, and choose conversation with regard only to my own taste; to have no obligation upon me to converse with wits that I don't like, because they are your acquaintance, or to be intimate with fools, because they may be your relations. Come to dinner when I please, dine in my dressing- room when I'm out of humour, without giving a reason. To have my closet inviolate; to be sole empress of my tea-table, which you must never presume to approach without first asking leave. And lastly, wherever I am, you shall always knock at the door before you come in. These articles subscribed, if I continue to endure you a little longer, I may by degrees dwindle into a wife.

MIRABELL

Your bill of fare is something advanced in this latter account. Well, have I liberty to offer conditions:- that when you are dwindled into a wife, I may not be beyond measure enlarged into a husband?

MILLAMANT

You have free leave: propose your utmost, speak and spare not.

MIRABELL

I thank you. IMPRIMIS, then, I covenant that your acquaintance be general; that you admit no sworn confidant or intimate of your own sex; no she friend to screen her affairs under your countenance, and tempt you to make trial of a mutual secrecy. No decoy-duck to wheedle you a FOP-

SCRAMBLING to the play in a mask, then bring you home in a pretended fright, when you think you shall be found out, and rail at me for missing the play, and disappointing the frolic which you had to pick me up and prove my constancy.

MILLAMANT

Detestable IMPRIMIS! I go to the play in a mask!

MIRABELL

ITEM, I article, that you continue to like your own face as long as I shall, and while it passes current with me, that you endeavour not to new coin it. To which end, together with all vizards for the day, I prohibit all masks for the night, made of oiled skins and I know not what—hog's bones, hare's gall, pig water, and the marrow of a roasted cat. In short, I forbid all commerce with the gentlewomen in what-d'ye-call-it court. ITEM, I shut my doors against all bawds with baskets, and pennyworths of muslin, china, fans, atlases, etc. ITEM, when you shall be breeding -

MILLAMANT

Ah, name it not!

MIRABELL

Which may be presumed, with a blessing on our endeavours -

MILLAMANT

Odious endeavours!

MIRABELL

I denounce against all strait lacing, squeezing for a shape, till you mould my boy's head like a sugar-loaf, and instead of a man-child, make me father to a crooked billet. Lastly, to the dominion of the tea-table I submit; but with proviso, that you exceed not in your province, but restrain yourself to native and simple tea-table drinks, as tea, chocolate, and coffee. As likewise to genuine and authorised tea-table talk, such as mending of fashions, spoiling reputations, railing at absent friends, and so forth.

But that on no account you encroach upon the men's prerogative, and presume to drink healths, or toast fellows; for prevention of which, I banish all foreign forces, all auxiliaries to the tea-table, as orange-brandy, all aniseed, cinnamon, citron, and Barbadoes waters, together with ratafia and the most noble spirit of clary. But for cowslip-wine, poppy-water, and all dormitives, those I allow. These provisos admitted, in other things I may prove a tractable and complying husband.

MILLAMANT

Oh, horrid provisos! Filthy strong waters! I toast fellows, odious men! I hate your odious provisos.

MIRABELL

Then we're agreed. Shall I kiss your hand upon the contract? And here comes one to be a witness to the sealing of the deed.

ACT IV

Scene VI.

[To them] MRS. FAINALL.

MILLAMANT

Fainall, what shall I do? Shall I have him? I think I must have him.

MRS. FAINALL

Ay, ay, take him, take him, what should you do?

MILLAMANT

Well then—I'll take my death I'm in a horrid fright—Fainall, I shall never say it. Well—I think—I'll endure you.

MRS. FAINALL

Fie, fie, have him, and tell him so in plain terms: for I am sure you have a mind to him.

MILLAMANT

Are you? I think I have; and the horrid man looks as if he thought so too. Well, you ridiculous thing you, I'll have you. I won't be kissed, nor I won't be thanked.—Here, kiss my hand though, so hold your tongue now; don't say a word.

MRS. FAINALL

Mirabell, there's a necessity for your obedience: you have neither time to talk nor stay. My mother is coming; and in my conscience if she should see you, would fall into fits, and maybe not recover time enough to return to Sir Rowland, who, as Foible tells me, is in a fair way to succeed. Therefore spare your ecstasies for another occasion, and slip down the back stairs, where Foible waits to consult you.

MILLAMANT

Ay, go, go. In the meantime I suppose you have said something to please me.

MIRABELL

I am all obedience.

ACT IV

Scene VII.

MRS. MILLAMANT, MRS. FAINALL.

MRS. FAINALL

Yonder Sir Wilfull's drunk, and so noisy that my mother has been forced to leave Sir Rowland to appease him; but he answers her only with singing and drinking. What they may have done by this time I know not, but Petulant and he were upon quarrelling as I came by.

MILLAMANT

Well, if Mirabell should not make a good husband, I am a lost thing: for I find I love him violently.

MRS. FAINALL

So it seems; for you mind not what's said to you. If you doubt him, you had best take up with Sir Wilfull.

MILLAMANT

How can you name that superannuated lubber? foh!

ACT IV

Scene VIII.

[To them] WITWOUD from drinking.

MRS. FAINALL

So, is the fray made up that you have left 'em?

WITWOUD

Left 'em? I could stay no longer. I have laughed like ten Christ'nings. I am tipsy with laughing—if I had stayed any longer I should have burst,—I must have been let out and pieced in the sides like an unsized camlet. Yes, yes, the fray is composed; my lady came in like a NOLI PROSEQUI, and stopt the proceedings.

MILLAMANT
What was the dispute?
WITWOUD
That's the jest: there was no dispute. They could neither of 'em speak for rage; and so fell a sputt'ring at one another like two roasting apples.

ACT IV

Scene IX.
[To them] PETULANT drunk.
WITWOUD
Now, Petulant? All's over, all's well? Gad, my head begins to whim it about. Why dost thou not speak? Thou art both as drunk and as mute as a fish.
PETULANT
Look you, Mrs. Millamant, if you can love me, dear Nymph, say it, and that's the conclusion—pass on, or pass off—that's all.
WITWOUD
Thou hast uttered volumes, folios, in less than decimo sexto, my dear Lacedemonian. Sirrah, Petulant, thou art an epitomiser of words.
PETULANT
Witwoud,—you are an annihilator of sense.
WITWOUD
Thou art a retailer of phrases, and dost deal in remnants of remnants, like a maker of pincushions; thou art in truth (metaphorically speaking) a speaker of shorthand.
PETULANT
Thou art (without a figure) just one half of an ass, and Baldwin yonder, thy half-brother, is the rest. A Gemini of asses split would make just four of you.
WITWOUD
Thou dost bite, my dear mustard-seed; kiss me for that.
PETULANT
Stand off—I'll kiss no more males—I have kissed your Twin yonder in a humour of reconciliation till he [hiccup] rises upon my stomach like a radish.

MILLAMANT
Eh! filthy creature; what was the quarrel?
PETULANT
There was no quarrel; there might have been a quarrel.
WITWOUD
If there had been words enow between 'em to have expressed provocation, they had gone together by the ears like a pair of castanets.
PETULANT
You were the quarrel.
MILLAMANT Me?
PETULANT
If I have a humour to quarrel, I can make less matters conclude premises. If you are not handsome, what then? If I have a humour to prove it? If I shall have my reward, say so; if not, fight for your face the next time yourself—I'll go sleep.
WITWOUD
Do, wrap thyself up like a woodlouse, and dream revenge. And, hear me, if thou canst learn to write by to-morrow morning, pen me a challenge. I'll carry it for thee.
PETULANT
Carry your mistress's monkey a spider; go flea dogs and read romances. I'll go to bed to my maid.
MRS. FAINALL
He's horridly drunk—how came you all in this pickle?
WITWOUD
A plot, a plot, to get rid of the knight—your husband's advice; but he sneaked off.

ACT IV

Scene X.
SIR WILFULL, drunk, LADY WISHFORT, WITWOUD, MRS. MILLAMANT, MRS. FAINALL.
LADY WISHFORT
Out upon't, out upon't, at years of discretion, and comport yourself at this rantipole rate!
SIR WILFULL WITWOUD
No offence, aunt.

LADY WISHFORT

Offence? As I'm a person, I'm ashamed of you. Fogh! How you stink of wine! D'ye think my niece will ever endure such a Borachio? You're an absolute Borachio.

SIR WILFULL WITWOUD

Borachio?

LADY WISHFORT

At a time when you should commence an amour, and put your best foot foremost -

SIR WILFULL WITWOUD

'Sheart, an you grutch me your liquor, make a bill.—Give me more drink, and take my purse. [Sings]:-

Prithee fill me the glass,
Till it laugh in my face,
With ale that is potent and mellow;
He that whines for a lass
Is an ignorant ass,
For a bumper has not its fellow.

But if you would have me marry my cousin, say the word, and I'll do't. Wilfull will do't, that's the word. Wilfull will do't, that's my crest,—my motto I have forgot.

LADY WISHFORT

My nephew's a little overtaken, cousin, but 'tis drinking your health. O' my word, you are obliged to him -

SIR WILFULL WITWOUD

IN VINO VERITAS, aunt. If I drunk your health to-day, cousin,—I am a Borachio.—But if you have a mind to be married, say the word and send for the piper; Wilfull will do't. If not, dust it away, and let's have t'other round. Tony—ods-heart, where's Tony?- -Tony's an honest fellow, but he spits after a bumper, and that's a fault.

We'll drink and we'll never ha' done, boys,
Put the glass then around with the sun, boys,
Let Apollo's example invite us;
For he's drunk every night,
And that makes him so bright,
That he's able next morning to light us.

The sun's a good pimple, an honest soaker, he has a cellar

at your antipodes. If I travel, aunt, I touch at your antipodes—your antipodes are a good rascally sort of topsy-turvy fellows. If I had a bumper I'd stand upon my head and drink a health to 'em. A match or no match, cousin with the hard name; aunt, Wilfull will do't. If she has her maidenhead let her look to 't; if she has not, let her keep her own counsel in the meantime, and cry out at the nine months' end.

MILLAMANT

Your pardon, madam, I can stay no longer. Sir Wilfull grows very powerful. Egh! how he smells! I shall be overcome if I stay. Come, cousin.

ACT IV

Scene XI.

LADY WISHFORT, SIR WILFULL WITWOUD, MR. WITWOUD, FOIBLE; LADY WISHFORT

Smells? He would poison a tallow-chandler and his family. Beastly creature, I know not what to do with him. Travel, quotha; ay, travel, travel, get thee gone, get thee but far enough, to the Saracens, or the Tartars, or the Turks—for thou art not fit to live in a Christian commonwealth, thou beastly pagan.

SIR WILFULL WITWOUD

Turks? No; no Turks, aunt. Your Turks are infidels, and believe not in the grape. Your Mahometan, your Mussulman is a dry stinkard. No offence, aunt. My map says that your Turk is not so honest a man as your Christian—I cannot find by the map that your Mufti is orthodox, whereby it is a plain case that orthodox is a hard word, aunt, and [hiccup] Greek for claret. [Sings]:-

To drink is a Christian diversion,
Unknown to the Turk or the Persian.
Let Mahometan fools
Live by heathenish rules,
And be damned over tea-cups and coffee.
But let British lads sing,
Crown a health to the King,
And a fig for your Sultan and Sophy.

Ah, Tony! [FOIBLE whispers LADY W.]

LADY WISHFORT

Sir Rowland impatient? Good lack! what shall I do with this beastly tumbril? Go lie down and sleep, you sot, or as I'm a person, I'll have you bastinadoed with broomsticks. Call up the wenches with broomsticks.

SIR WILFULL WITWOUD

Ahey! Wenches? Where are the wenches?

LADY WISHFORT

Dear Cousin Witwoud, get him away, and you will bind me to you inviolably. I have an affair of moment that invades me with some precipitation.—You will oblige me to all futurity.

WITWOUD

Come, knight. Pox on him, I don't know what to say to him. Will you go to a cock-match?

SIR WILFULL WITWOUD

With a wench, Tony? Is she a shake-bag, sirrah? Let me bite your cheek for that.

WITWOUD

Horrible! He has a breath like a bagpipe. Ay, ay; come, will you march, my Salopian?

SIR WILFULL WITWOUD

Lead on, little Tony. I'll follow thee, my Anthony, my Tantony. Sirrah, thou shalt be my Tantony, and I'll be thy pig.

And a fig for your Sultan and Sophy.

LADY WISHFORT

This will never do. It will never make a match,—at least before he has been abroad.

ACT IV

Scene XII.

LADY WISHFORT, WAITWELL disguised as for SIR ROWLAND.

LADY WISHFORT

Dear Sir Rowland, I am confounded with confusion at the retrospection of my own rudeness,—I have more pardons to ask than the pope distributes in the year of jubilee. But I hope where there is likely to be so near an alliance, we may unbend the severity of decorum, and dispense with a little ceremony.

WAITWELL

My impatience, madam, is the effect of my transport; and till I have the possession of your adorable person, I am tantalised on the rack, and do but hang, madam, on the tenter of expectation.

LADY WISHFORT

You have excess of gallantry, Sir Rowland, and press things to a conclusion with a most prevailing vehemence. But a day or two for decency of marriage -

WAITWELL

For decency of funeral, madam! The delay will break my heart—or if that should fail, I shall be poisoned. My nephew will get an inkling of my designs and poison me—and I would willingly starve him before I die—I would gladly go out of the world with that satisfaction. That would be some comfort to me, if I could but live so long as to be revenged on that unnatural viper.

LADY WISHFORT

Is he so unnatural, say you? Truly I would contribute much both to the saving of your life and the accomplishment of your revenge. Not that I respect myself; though he has been a perfidious wretch to me.

WAITWELL

Perfidious to you?

LADY WISHFORT

O Sir Rowland, the hours that he has died away at my feet, the tears that he has shed, the oaths that he has sworn, the palpitations that he has felt, the trances and the tremblings, the ardours and the ecstasies, the kneelings and the risings, the heart- heavings and the hand-gripings, the pangs and the pathetic regards of his protesting eyes!—Oh, no memory can register.

WAITWELL

What, my rival? Is the rebel my rival? A dies.

LADY WISHFORT

No, don't kill him at once, Sir Rowland: starve him gradually, inch by inch.

WAITWELL

I'll do't. In three weeks he shall be barefoot; in a month out at knees with begging an alms; he shall starve upward and upward, 'till he has nothing living but his head, and then go out in a stink like a candle's end upon a save-all.

LADY WISHFORT

Well, Sir Rowland, you have the way,—you are no novice in the labyrinth of love,—you have the clue. But as I am a person, Sir Rowland, you must not attribute my yielding to any sinister appetite or indigestion of widowhood; nor impute my complacency to any lethargy of continence. I hope you do not think me prone to any iteration of nuptials?

WAITWELL

Far be it from me -

LADY WISHFORT

If you do, I protest I must recede, or think that I have made a prostitution of decorums, but in the vehemence of compassion, and to save the life of a person of so much importance -

WAITWELL

I esteem it so -

LADY WISHFORT

Or else you wrong my condescension -

WAITWELL

I do not, I do not -

LADY WISHFORT

Indeed you do.

WAITWELL

I do not, fair shrine of virtue.

LADY WISHFORT

If you think the least scruple of causality was an ingredient

WAITWELL

Dear madam, no. You are all camphire and frankincense, all chastity and odour.

LADY WISHFORT

Or that -

ACT IV

Scene XIII.

[To them] FOIBLE.

FOIBLE

Madam, the dancers are ready, and there's one with a letter, who must deliver it into your own hands.

LADY WISHFORT

Sir Rowland, will you give me leave? Think favourably, judge candidly, and conclude you have found a person who would suffer racks in honour's cause, dear Sir Rowland, and will wait on you incessantly.

ACT IV

Scene XIV.

WAITWELL, FOIBLE.

WAITWELL

Fie, fie! What a slavery have I undergone; spouse, hast thou any cordial? I want spirits.

FOIBLE

What a washy rogue art thou, to pant thus for a quarter of an hour's lying and swearing to a fine lady?

WAITWELL

Oh, she is the antidote to desire. Spouse, thou wilt fare the worse for't. I shall have no appetite to iteration of nuptials- -this eight-and-forty hours. By this hand I'd rather be a chairman in the dog-days than act Sir Rowland till this time to-morrow.

ACT IV

Scene XV.

[To them] LADY with a letter.

LADY WISHFORT

Call in the dancers; Sir Rowland, we'll sit, if you please, and see the entertainment. [Dance.] Now, with your permission, Sir Rowland, I will peruse my letter. I would open it in your presence, because I would not make you uneasy. If it should make you uneasy, I would burn it—speak if it does—but you may see, the superscription is like a woman's hand.

FOIBLE

By heaven! Mrs. Marwood's, I know it,—my heart aches—get it from her! [To him.]

WAITWELL

A woman's hand? No madam, that's no woman's hand: I see that already. That's somebody whose throat must be cut.

LADY WISHFORT

Nay, Sir Rowland, since you give me a proof of your passion by your jealousy, I promise you I'll make a return by a frank communication. You shall see it—we'll open it together. Look you here. [Reads.] madam, though unknown to you (look you there, 'tis from nobody that i know.) i have that honour for your character, that i think myself obliged to let you know you are abused he who pretends to be sir rowland is a cheat and a rascal o heavens! What's this?

FOIBLE

Unfortunate; all's ruined.

WAITWELL

How, how, let me see, let me see. [Reading.] a rascal, and disguised and suborned for that imposture—o villainy! O villainy!— by the contrivance of -

LADY WISHFORT

I shall faint, I shall die. Oh!

FOIBLE

Say 'tis your nephew's hand. Quickly, his plot, swear, swear it! [To him.]

WAITWELL

Here's a villain! Madam, don't you perceive it? Don't you see it?

LADY WISHFORT

Too well, too well. I have seen too much.

WAITWELL

I told you at first I knew the hand. A woman's hand? The rascal writes a sort of a large hand: your Roman hand.—I saw there was a throat to be cut presently. If he were my son, as he is my nephew, I'd pistol him.

FOIBLE

O treachery! But are you sure, Sir Rowland, it is his writing?

WAITWELL

Sure? Am I here? Do I live? Do I love this pearl of India? I have twenty letters in my pocket from him in the same character.

LADY WISHFORT

How?

FOIBLE

Oh, what luck it is, Sir Rowland, that you were present at this juncture! This was the business that brought Mr. Mirabell disguised to Madam Millamant this afternoon. I thought something was contriving, when he stole by me and would have hid his face.

LADY WISHFORT

How, how? I heard the villain was in the house indeed; and now I remember, my niece went away abruptly when Sir Wilfull was to have made his addresses.

FOIBLE

Then, then, madam, Mr. Mirabell waited for her in her chamber; but I would not tell your ladyship to discompose you when you were to receive Sir Rowland.

WAITWELL

Enough, his date is short.

FOIBLE

No, good Sir Rowland, don't incur the law.

WAITWELL

Law? I care not for law. I can but die, and 'tis in a good cause. My lady shall be satisfied of my truth and innocence, though it cost me my life.

LADY WISHFORT

No, dear Sir Rowland, don't fight: if you should be killed I must never show my face; or hanged,—oh, consider my reputation, Sir Rowland. No, you shan't fight: I'll go in and examine my niece; I'll make her confess. I conjure you, Sir Rowland, by all your love not to fight.

WAITWELL

I am charmed, madam; I obey. But some proof you must

let me give you: I'll go for a black box, which contains the writings of my whole estate, and deliver that into your hands.

LADY WISHFORT

Ay, dear Sir Rowland, that will be some comfort; bring the black box.

WAITWELL

And may I presume to bring a contract to be signed this night? May I hope so far?

LADY WISHFORT

Bring what you will; but come alive, pray come alive. Oh, this is a happy discovery.

WAITWELL

Dead or alive I'll come—and married we will be in spite of treachery; ay, and get an heir that shall defeat the last remaining glimpse of hope in my abandoned nephew. Come, my buxom widow:

E'er long you shall substantial proof receive That I'm an arrant knight -

FOIBLE

Or arrant knave.

ACT V

Scene I.

Scene continues.

LADY WISHFORT and FOIBLE.

LADY WISHFORT

Out of my house, out of my house, thou viper, thou serpent that I have fostered, thou bosom traitress that I raised from nothing! Begone, begone, begone, go, go; that I took from washing of old gauze and weaving of dead hair, with a bleak blue nose, over a chafing-dish of starved embers, and dining behind a traver's rag, in a shop no bigger than a bird-cage. Go, go, starve again, do, do!

FOIBLE

Dear madam, I'll beg pardon on my knees.

LADY WISHFORT

Away, out, out, go set up for yourself again, do; drive a trade, do, with your threepennyworth of small ware, flaunting upon a packthread, under a brandy-seller's bulk, or against a dead wall by a balladmonger. Go, hang out an old frisoneer-gorget, with a yard of yellow colberteen again, do; an old gnawed mask, two rows of pins, and a child's fiddle; a glass necklace with the beads broken, and a quilted night-cap with one ear. Go, go, drive a trade. These were your commodities, you treacherous trull; this was the merchandise you dealt in, when I took you into my house, placed you next myself, and made you governant of my whole family. You have forgot this, have you, now you have feathered your nest?

FOIBLE

No, no, dear madam. Do but hear me, have but a moment's patience—I'll confess all. Mr. Mirabell seduced me; I am not the first that he has wheedled with his dissembling tongue. Your ladyship's own wisdom has been deluded by him; then how should I, a poor ignorant, defend myself? O madam, if you knew but what he promised me, and how he assured me your ladyship should come to no damage, or else the wealth of the Indies should not have bribed me to conspire against so good, so sweet, so kind a lady as you have been to me.

LADY WISHFORT

No damage? What, to betray me, to marry me to a cast serving-man; to make me a receptacle, an hospital for a decayed pimp? No damage? O thou frontless impudence, more than a big- bellied actress!

FOIBLE

Pray do but hear me, madam; he could not marry your ladyship, madam. No indeed, his marriage was to have been void in law; for he was married to me first, to secure your ladyship. He could not have bedded your ladyship, for if he had consummated with your ladyship, he must have run the risk of the law, and been put upon his clergy. Yes indeed, I enquired of the law in that case before I would meddle or make.

LADY WISHFORT

What? Then I have been your property, have I? I have been convenient to you, it seems, while you were catering for

Mirabell; I have been broker for you? What, have you made a passive bawd of me? This exceeds all precedent. I am brought to fine uses, to become a botcher of second-hand marriages between Abigails and Andrews! I'll couple you. Yes, I'll baste you together, you and your Philander. I'll Duke's Place you, as I'm a person. Your turtle is in custody already. You shall coo in the same cage, if there be constable or warrant in the parish.

FOIBLE

Oh, that ever I was born! Oh, that I was ever married! A bride? Ay, I shall be a Bridewell bride. Oh!

ACT V

Scene II.

MRS. FAINALL, FOIBLE.

MRS. FAINALL

Poor Foible, what's the matter?

FOIBLE

O madam, my lady's gone for a constable; I shall be had to a justice, and put to Bridewell to beat hemp. Poor Waitwell's gone to prison already.

MRS. FAINALL

Have a good heart, Foible: Mirabell's gone to give security for him. This is all Marwood's and my husband's doing.

FOIBLE

Yes, yes; I know it, madam: she was in my lady's closet, and overheard all that you said to me before dinner. She sent the letter to my lady, and that missing effect, Mr. Fainall laid this plot to arrest Waitwell, when he pretended to go for the papers; and in the meantime Mrs. Marwood declared all to my lady.

MRS. FAINALL

Was there no mention made of me in the letter? My mother does not suspect my being in the confederacy? I fancy Marwood has not told her, though she has told my husband.

FOIBLE

Yes, madam; but my lady did not see that part. We stifled the letter before she read so far. Has that mischievous devil told Mr. Fainall of your ladyship then?

MRS. FAINALL

Ay, all's out: my affair with Mirabell, everything discovered. This is the last day of our living together; that's my comfort.

FOIBLE

Indeed, madam, and so 'tis a comfort, if you knew all. He has been even with your ladyship; which I could have told you long enough since, but I love to keep peace and quietness by my good will. I had rather bring friends together than set 'em at distance. But Mrs. Marwood and he are nearer related than ever their parents thought for.

MRS. FAINALL

Say'st thou so, Foible? Canst thou prove this?

FOIBLE

I can take my oath of it, madam; so can Mrs. Mincing. We have had many a fair word from Madam Marwood to conceal something that passed in our chamber one evening when you were at Hyde Park, and we were thought to have gone a-walking. But we went up unawares—though we were sworn to secrecy too: Madam Marwood took a book and swore us upon it: but it was but a book of poems. So long as it was not a bible oath, we may break it with a safe conscience.

MRS. FAINALL

This discovery is the most opportune thing I could wish. Now, Mincing?

ACT V

Scene III.

[To them] MINCING.

MINCING

My lady would speak with Mrs. Foible, mem. Mr. Mirabell is with her; he has set your spouse at liberty, Mrs. Foible, and would have you hide yourself in my lady's closet till my old lady's anger is abated. Oh, my old lady is in a perilous passion at something Mr. Fainall has said; he swears, and my old lady cries. There's a fearful hurricane, I vow. He says, mem, how that he'll have my lady's fortune made over to him, or he'll be divorced.

MRS. FAINALL

Does your lady or Mirabell know that?

MINCING

Yes mem; they have sent me to see if Sir Wilfull be sober, and to bring him to them. My lady is resolved to have him, I think, rather than lose such a vast sum as six thousand pound. Oh, come, Mrs. Foible, I hear my old lady.

MRS. FAINALL

Foible, you must tell Mincing that she must prepare to vouch when I call her.

FOIBLE

Yes, yes, madam.

MINCING

Oh, yes mem, I'll vouch anything for your ladyship's service, be what it will.

ACT V

Scene IV.

MRS. FAINALL, LADY WISHFORT, MRS. MARWOOD.

LADY WISHFORT

O my dear friend, how can I enumerate the benefits that I have received from your goodness? To you I owe the timely discovery of the false vows of Mirabell; to you I owe the detection of the impostor Sir Rowland. And now you are become an intercessor with my son-in-law, to save the honour of my house and compound for the frailties of my daughter. Well, friend, you are enough to reconcile me to the bad world, or else I would retire to deserts and solitudes, and feed harmless sheep by groves and purling streams. Dear Marwood, let us leave the world, and retire by ourselves and be shepherdesses.

MRS. MARWOOD

Let us first dispatch the affair in hand, madam. We shall have leisure to think of retirement afterwards. Here is one who is concerned in the treaty.

LADY WISHFORT

O daughter, daughter, is it possible thou shouldst be my child, bone of my bone, and flesh of my flesh, and as I may say, another me, and yet transgress the most minute particle of severe virtue? Is it possible you should lean aside to iniquity, who have been cast in the direct mould of virtue? I have not only been a mould but a pattern for you, and a model for you, after you were brought into the world.

MRS. FAINALL

I don't understand your ladyship.

LADY WISHFORT

Not understand? Why, have you not been naught? Have you not been sophisticated? Not understand? Here I am ruined to compound for your caprices and your cuckoldoms. I must pawn my plate and my jewels, and ruin my niece, and all little enough -

MRS. FAINALL

I am wronged and abused, and so are you. 'Tis a false accusation, as false as hell, as false as your friend there; ay, or your friend's friend, my false husband.

MRS. MARWOOD

My friend, Mrs. Fainall? Your husband my friend, what do you mean?

MRS. FAINALL

I know what I mean, madam, and so do you; and so shall the world at a time convenient.

MRS. MARWOOD

I am sorry to see you so passionate, madam. More temper would look more like innocence. But I have done. I am sorry my zeal to serve your ladyship and family should admit of misconstruction, or make me liable to affronts. You will pardon me, madam, if I meddle no more with an affair in which I am not personally concerned.

LADY WISHFORT

O dear friend, I am so ashamed that you should meet with such returns. You ought to ask pardon on your knees, ungrateful creature; she deserves more from you than all your life can accomplish. Oh, don't leave me destitute in this perplexity! No, stick to me, my good genius.

MRS. FAINALL

I tell you, madam, you're abused. Stick to you? Ay, like a

leech, to suck your best blood; she'll drop off when she's full. Madam, you shan't pawn a bodkin, nor part with a brass counter, in composition for me. I defy 'em all. Let 'em prove their aspersions: I know my own innocence, and dare stand a trial.

ACT V

Scene V.

LADY WISHFORT, MRS. MARWOOD.

LADY WISHFORT

Why, if she should be innocent, if she should be wronged after all, ha? I don't know what to think, and I promise you, her education has been unexceptionable. I may say it, for I chiefly made it my own care to initiate her very infancy in the rudiments of virtue, and to impress upon her tender years a young odium and aversion to the very sight of men; ay, friend, she would ha' shrieked if she had but seen a man till she was in her teens. As I'm a person, 'tis true. She was never suffered to play with a male child, though but in coats. Nay, her very babies were of the feminine gender. Oh, she never looked a man in the face but her own father or the chaplain, and him we made a shift to put upon her for a woman, by the help of his long garments, and his sleek face, till she was going in her fifteen.

MRS. MARWOOD

'Twas much she should be deceived so long.

LADY WISHFORT

I warrant you, or she would never have borne to have been catechised by him, and have heard his long lectures against singing and dancing and such debaucheries, and going to filthy plays, and profane music meetings, where the lewd trebles squeak nothing but bawdy, and the basses roar blasphemy.

Oh, she would have swooned at the sight or name of an obscene play-book—and can I think after all this that my daughter can be naught? What, a whore? And thought it excommunication to set her foot within the door of a playhouse. O dear friend, I can't believe it. No, no; as she says, let him prove it, let him prove it.

MRS. MARWOOD

Prove it, madam? What, and have your name prostituted in a public court; yours and your daughter's reputation worried at the bar by a pack of bawling lawyers? To be ushered in with an OH YES of scandal, and have your case opened by an old fumbling leacher in a quoif like a man midwife; to bring your daughter's infamy to light; to be a theme for legal punsters and quibblers by the statute; and become a jest, against a rule of court, where there is no precedent for a jest in any record, not even in Doomsday Book. To discompose the gravity of the bench, and provoke naughty interrogatories in more naughty law Latin; while the good judge, tickled with the proceeding, simpers under a grey beard, and fidges off and on his cushion as if he had swallowed cantharides, or sate upon cow-itch.

LADY WISHFORT

Oh, 'tis very hard!

MRS. MARWOOD

And then to have my young revellers of the Temple take notes, like prentices at a conventicle; and after talk it over again in Commons, or before drawers in an eating-house.

LADY WISHFORT

Worse and worse.

MRS. MARWOOD

Nay, this is nothing; if it would end here 'twere well. But it must after this be consigned by the shorthand writers to the public press; and from thence be transferred to the hands, nay, into the throats and lungs, of hawkers, with voices more licentious than the loud flounder-man's. And this you must hear till you are stunned; nay, you must hear nothing else for some days.

LADY WISHFORT

Oh 'tis insupportable. No, no, dear friend, make it up, make it up; ay, ay, I'll compound. I'll give up all, myself and my all, my niece and her all, anything, everything, for composition.

MRS. MARWOOD

Nay, madam, I advise nothing, I only lay before you, as a friend, the inconveniences which perhaps you have overseen.

Here comes Mr. Fainall; if he will be satisfied to huddle up all in silence, I shall be glad. You must think I would rather congratulate than condole with you.

ACT V

Scene VI.

FAINALL, LADY WISHFORT, MRS. MARWOOD.

LADY WISHFORT

Ay, ay, I do not doubt it, dear Marwood. No, no, I do not doubt it.

FAINALL

Well, madam, I have suffered myself to be overcome by the importunity of this lady, your friend, and am content you shall enjoy your own proper estate during life, on condition you oblige yourself never to marry, under such penalty as I think convenient.

LADY WISHFORT

Never to marry?

FAINALL

No more Sir Rowlands, the next imposture may not be so timely detected.

MRS. MARWOOD

That condition, I dare answer, my lady will consent to, without difficulty; she has already but too much experienced the perfidiousness of men. Besides, madam, when we retire to our pastoral solitude, we shall bid adieu to all other thoughts.

LADY WISHFORT

Ay, that's true; but in case of necessity, as of health, or some such emergency -

FAINALL

Oh, if you are prescribed marriage, you shall be considered; I will only reserve to myself the power to choose for you. If your physic be wholesome, it matters not who is your apothecary. Next, my wife shall settle on me the remainder of her fortune, not made over already; and for her maintenance depend entirely on my discretion.

LADY WISHFORT

This is most inhumanly savage: exceeding the barbarity of a Muscovite husband.

FAINALL

I learned it from his Czarish Majesty's retinue, in a winter evening's conference over brandy and pepper, amongst other secrets of matrimony and policy, as they are at present practised in the northern hemisphere. But this must be agreed unto, and that positively.

Lastly, I will be endowed, in right of my wife, with that six thousand pound, which is the moiety of Mrs. Millamant's fortune in your possession, and which she has forfeited (as will appear by the last will and testament of your deceased husband, Sir Jonathan Wishfort) by her disobedience in contracting herself against your consent or knowledge, and by refusing the offered match with Sir Wilfull Witwoud, which you, like a careful aunt, had provided for her.

LADY WISHFORT

My nephew was NON COMPOS, and could not make his addresses.

FAINALL

I come to make demands—I'll hear no objections.

LADY WISHFORT

You will grant me time to consider?

FAINALL

Yes, while the instrument is drawing, to which you must set your hand till more sufficient deeds can be perfected: which I will take care shall be done with all possible speed. In the meanwhile I will go for the said instrument, and till my return you may balance this matter in your own discretion.

ACT V

Scene VII.

LADY WISHFORT, MRS. MARWOOD.

LADY WISHFORT

This insolence is beyond all precedent, all parallel. Must I be subject to this merciless villain?

MRS. MARWOOD

'Tis severe indeed, madam, that you should smart for your daughter's wantonness.

LADY WISHFORT

'Twas against my consent that she married this barbarian, but she would have him, though her year was not out. Ah! her first husband, my son Languish, would not have carried it thus. Well, that was my choice, this is hers; she is matched now with a witness- -I shall be mad, dear friend; is there no comfort for me? Must I live to be confiscated at this rebel-rate? Here come two more of my Egyptian plagues too.

ACT V

Scene VIII.

[To them] MRS. MILLAMANT, SIR WILFULL.

SIR WILFULL WITWOUD

Aunt, your servant.

LADY WISHFORT

Out, caterpillar, call not me aunt; I know thee not.

SIR WILFULL WITWOUD

I confess I have been a little in disguise, as they say. 'Sheart! and I'm sorry for't. What would you have? I hope I committed no offence, aunt—and if I did I am willing to make satisfaction; and what can a man say fairer? If I have broke anything I'll pay for't, an it cost a pound. And so let that content for what's past, and make no more words. For what's to come, to pleasure you I'm willing to marry my cousin. So, pray, let's all be friends, she and I are agreed upon the matter before a witness.

LADY WISHFORT

How's this, dear niece? Have I any comfort? Can this be true?

MILLAMANT

I am content to be a sacrifice to your repose, madam, and to convince you that I had no hand in the plot, as you were misinformed. I have laid my commands on Mirabell to come in person, and be a witness that I give my hand to this flower of knighthood; and for the contract that passed between Mirabell and me, I have obliged him to make a resignation of it in your ladyship's presence. He is without and waits your leave for admittance.

LADY WISHFORT

Well, I'll swear I am something revived at this testimony of your obedience; but I cannot admit that traitor,—I fear I cannot fortify myself to support his appearance. He is as terrible to me as a Gorgon: if I see him I swear I shall turn to stone, petrify incessantly.

MILLAMANT

If you disoblige him he may resent your refusal, and insist upon the contract still. Then 'tis the last time he will be offensive to you.

LADY WISHFORT

Are you sure it will be the last time? If I were sure of that—shall I never see him again?

MILLAMANT

Sir Wilfull, you and he are to travel together, are you not?

SIR WILFULL WITWOUD

'Sheart, the gentleman's a civil gentleman, aunt, let him come in; why, we are sworn brothers and fellow-travellers. We are to be Pylades and Orestes, he and I He is to be my interpreter in foreign parts. He has been overseas once already; and with proviso that I marry my cousin, will cross 'em once again, only to bear me company. 'Sheart, I'll call him in,—an I set on't once, he shall come in; and see who'll hinder him. [Goes to the door and hems.]

MRS. MARWOOD

This is precious fooling, if it would pass; but I'll know the bottom of it.

LADY WISHFORT

O dear Marwood, you are not going?

MRS. MARWOOD

Not far, madam; I'll return immediately.

ACT V

Scene IX.

LADY WISHFORT, MRS. MILLAMANT, SIR WILFULL, MIRABELL.

SIR WILFULL WITWOUD

Look up, man, I'll stand by you; 'sbud, an she do frown,

she can't kill you. Besides—harkee, she dare not frown desperately, because her face is none of her own. 'Sheart, an she should, her forehead would wrinkle like the coat of a cream cheese; but mum for that, fellow-traveller.

MIRABELL

If a deep sense of the many injuries I have offered to so good a lady, with a sincere remorse and a hearty contrition, can but obtain the least glance of compassion. I am too happy. Ah, madam, there was a time—but let it be forgotten. I confess I have deservedly forfeited the high place I once held, of sighing at your feet; nay, kill me not by turning from me in disdain, I come not to plead for favour. Nay, not for pardon: I am a suppliant only for pity:- I am going where I never shall behold you more.

SIR WILFULL WITWOUD

How, fellow-traveller? You shall go by yourself then.

MIRABELL

Let me be pitied first, and afterwards forgotten. I ask no more.

SIR WILFULL WITWOUD

By'r lady, a very reasonable request, and will cost you nothing, aunt. Come, come, forgive and forget, aunt. Why you must an you are a Christian.

MIRABELL

Consider, madam; in reality you could not receive much prejudice: it was an innocent device, though I confess it had a face of guiltiness—it was at most an artifice which love contrived- -and errors which love produces have ever been accounted venial. At least think it is punishment enough that I have lost what in my heart I hold most dear, that to your cruel indignation I have offered up this beauty, and with her my peace and quiet; nay, all my hopes of future comfort.

SIR WILFULL WITWOUD

An he does not move me, would I may never be o' the quorum. An it were not as good a deed as to drink, to give her to him again, I would I might never take shipping. Aunt, if you don't forgive quickly, I shall melt, I can tell you that. My contract went no farther than a little mouth-glue, and that's hardly dry; one doleful sigh more from my fellow-traveller and 'tis dissolved.

LADY WISHFORT

Well, nephew, upon your account. Ah, he has a false insinuating tongue. Well, sir, I will stifle my just resentment at my nephew's request. I will endeavour what I can to forget, but on proviso that you resign the contract with my niece immediately.

MIRABELL

It is in writing and with papers of concern; but I have sent my servant for it, and will deliver it to you, with all acknowledgments for your transcendent goodness.

LADY WISHFORT

Oh, he has witchcraft in his eyes and tongue; when I did not see him I could have bribed a villain to his assassination; but his appearance rakes the embers which haveso long lain smothered in my breast. [Aside.]

ACT V

Scene X.

[To them] FAINALL, MRS. MARWOOD.

FAINALL

Your date of deliberation, madam, is expired. Here is the instrument; are you prepared to sign?

LADY WISHFORT

If I were prepared, I am not impowered. My niece exerts a lawful claim, having matched herself by my direction to Sir Wilfull.

FAINALL

That sham is too gross to pass on me, though 'tis imposed on you, madam.

MILLAMANT

Sir, I have given my consent.

MIRABELL: And, sir, I have resigned my pretensions.

SIR WILFULL WITWOUD

And, sir, I assert my right; and will maintain it in defiance of you, sir, and of your instrument. 'Sheart, an you talk of an instrument sir, I have an old fox by my thigh shall hack your instrument of ram vellum to shreds, sir. It shall not be sufficient for a Mittimus or a tailor's measure; therefore withdraw your instrument, sir, or, by'r lady, I shall draw mine.

LADY WISHFORT

Hold, nephew, hold.

MILLAMANT

Good Sir Wilfull, respite your valour.

FAINALL

Indeed? Are you provided of your guard, with your single beef-eater there? But I'm prepared for you, and insist upon my first proposal. You shall submit your own estate to my management, and absolutely make over my wife's to my sole use, as pursuant to the purport and tenor of this other covenant. I suppose, madam, your consent is not requisite in this case; nor, Mr. Mirabell, your resignation; nor, Sir Wilfull, your right. You may draw your fox if you please, sir, and make a bear-garden flourish somewhere else; for here it will not avail. This, my Lady Wishfort, must be subscribed, or your darling daughter's turned adrift, like a leaky hulk to sink or swim, as she and the current of this lewd town can agree.

LADY WISHFORT

Is there no means, no remedy, to stop my ruin? Ungrateful wretch! Dost thou not owe thy being, thy subsistance, to my daughter's fortune?

FAINALL

I'll answer you when I have the rest of it in my possession.

MIRABELL

But that you would not accept of a remedy from my hands—I own I have not deserved you should owe any obligation to me; or else, perhaps, I could devise -

LADY WISHFORT

Oh, what? what? To save me and my child from ruin, from want, I'll forgive all that's past; nay, I'll consent to anything to come, to be delivered from this tyranny.

MIRABELL

Ay, madam; but that is too late, my reward is intercepted. You have disposed of her who only could have made me a compensation for all my services. But be it as it may, I am resolved I'll serve you; you shall not be wronged in this savage manner.

LADY WISHFORT

How? Dear Mr. Mirabell, can you be so generous at last? But it is not possible. Harkee, I'll break my nephew's match; you shall have my niece yet, and all her fortune, if you can but save me from this imminent danger.

MIRABELL

Will you? I take you at your word. I ask no more. I must have leave for two criminals to appear.

LADY WISHFORT

Ay, ay, anybody, anybody.

MIRABELL

Foible is one, and a penitent.

ACT V

Scene XI.

[To them] MRS. FAINALL, FOIBLE, MINCING.

MRS. MARWOOD

O my shame! [MIRABELL and LADY go to MRS. FAINALL and FOIBLE.] These currupt things are brought hither to expose me. [To FAINALL.]

FAINALL

If it must all come out, why let 'em know it, 'tis but the way of the world. That shall not urge me to relinquish or abate one tittle of my terms; no, I will insist the more.

FOIBLE

Yes, indeed, madam; I'll take my bible-oath of it.

MINCING

And so will I, mem.

LADY WISHFORT

O Marwood, Marwood, art thou false? My friend deceive me? Hast thou been a wicked accomplice with that profligate man?

MRS. MARWOOD

Have you so much ingratitude and injustice to give credit, against your friend, to the aspersions of two such mercenary trulls?

MINCING

Mercenary, mem? I scorn your words. 'Tis true we found you and Mr. Fainall in the blue garret; by the same token, you swore us to secrecy upon Messalinas's poems. Mercenary? No, if we would have been mercenary, we should have held our tongues; you would have bribed us sufficiently.

FAINALL

Go, you are an insignificant thing. Well, what are you the better for this? Is this Mr. Mirabell's expedient? I'll be put off no longer. You, thing, that was a wife, shall smart for this. I will not leave thee wherewithal to hide thy shame: your body shall be naked as your reputation.

MRS. FAINALL

I despise you and defy your malice. You have aspersed me wrongfully—I have proved your falsehood. Go, you and your treacherous—I will not name it, but starve together. Perish.

FAINALL

Not while you are worth a groat, indeed, my dear. Madam, I'll be fooled no longer.

LADY WISHFORT

Ah, Mr. Mirabell, this is small comfort, the detection of this affair.

MIRABELL

Oh, in good time. Your leave for the other offender and penitent to appear, madam.

ACT V

Scene XII.

[To them] WAITWELL with a box of writings.

LADY WISHFORT

O Sir Rowland! Well, rascal?

WAITWELL

What your ladyship pleases. I have brought the black box at last, madam.

MIRABELL

Give it me. Madam, you remember your promise.

LADY WISHFORT

Ay, dear sir.

MIRABELL

Where are the gentlemen?

WAITWELL

At hand, sir, rubbing their eyes,—just risen from sleep.

FAINALL

'Sdeath, what's this to me? I'll not wait your private concerns.

ACT V

Scene XIII.

[To them] PETULANT, WITWOUD.

PETULANT

How now? What's the matter? Whose hand's out?

WITWOUD

Hey day! What, are you all got together, like players at the end of the last act?

MIRABELL

You may remember, gentlemen, I once requested your hands as witnesses to a certain parchment.

WITWOUD

Ay, I do, my hand I remember—Petulant set his mark.

MIRABELL

You wrong him; his name is fairly written, as shall appear. You do not remember, gentlemen, anything of what that parchment contained? [Undoing the box.]

WITWOUD

No.

PETULANT

Not I I writ; I read nothing.

MIRABELL

Very well, now you shall know. Madam, your promise.

LADY WISHFORT

Ay, ay, sir, upon my honour.

MIRABELL

Mr. Fainall, it is now time that you should know that your lady, while she was at her own disposal, and before you had by your insinuations wheedled her out of a pretended settlement of the greatest part of her fortune -

FAINALL

Sir! Pretended?

MIRABELL

Yes, sir. I say that this lady, while a widow, having, it seems, received some cautions respecting your inconstancy and tyranny of temper, which from her own partial opinion and fondness of you she could never have suspected—she did, I say, by the wholesome advice of friends and of sages learned in the laws of this land, deliver this same as her act and deed to me in trust, and to the uses within mentioned. You may read if you please [holding out the parchment], though perhaps what is written on the back may serve your occasions.

Fainall

Very likely, sir. What's here? Damnation! [Reads] a deed of conveyance of the whole estate real of arabella languish, widow, in trust to edward mirabell confusion!

MIRABELL

Even so, sir: 'tis the way of the world, sir; of the widows of the world. I suppose this deed may bear an elder date than what you have obtained from your lady.

FAINALL

Perfidious fiend! Then thus I'll be revenged. [Offers to run at MRS. FAINALL.]

SIR WILFULL WITWOUD

Hold, sir; now you may make your bear-garden flourish somewhere else, sir.

FAINALL

Mirabell, you shall hear of this, sir; be sure you shall. Let me pass, oaf.

MRS. FAINALL

Madam, you seem to stifle your resentment. You had better give it vent.

MRS. MARWOOD

Yes, it shall have vent, and to your confusion, or I'll perish in the attempt.

ACT V

Scene the Last.

Lady wishfort, mrs. Millamant, mirabell, mrs. Fainall, sir wilfull, petulant, witwoud, foible, mincing, waitwell.

LADY WISHFORT

O daughter, daughter, 'tis plain thou hast inherited thy mother's prudence.

MRS. FAINALL

Thank Mr. Mirabell, a cautious friend, to whose advice all is owing.

LADY WISHFORT

Well, Mr. Mirabell, you have kept your promise, and I must perform mine. First, I pardon for your sake Sir Rowland there and Foible. The next thing is to break the matter to my nephew, and how to do that -

MIRABELL

For that, madam, give yourself no trouble; let me have your consent. Sir Wilfull is my friend: he has had compassion upon lovers, and generously engaged a volunteer in this action, for our service, and now designs to prosecute his travels.

SIR WILFULL WITWOUD

'Sheart, aunt, I have no mind to marry. My cousin's a fine lady, and the gentleman loves her and she loves him, and they deserve one another; my resolution is to see foreign parts. I have set on't, and when I'm set on't I must do't. And if these two gentlemen would travel too, I think they may be spared.

PETULANT

For my part, I say little. I think things are best off or on.

WITWOUD

I'gad, I understand nothing of the matter: I'm in a maze yet, like a dog in a dancing school.

LADY WISHFORT

Well, sir, take her, and with her all the joy I can give you.

MILLAMANT

Why does not the man take me? Would you have me give myself to you over again?

MIRABELL

Ay, and over and over again. [Kisses her hand.] I would have you as often as possibly I can. Well, heav'n grant I love you not too well; that's all my fear.

SIR WILFULL WITWOUD

'Sheart, you'll have time enough to toy after you're married, or, if you will toy now, let us have a dance in the meantime; that we who are not lovers may have some other employment besides looking on.

MIRABELL

With all my heart, dear Sir Wilfull. What shall we do for music?

FOIBLE

Oh, sir, some that were provided for Sir Rowland's entertainment are yet within call. [A dance.]

LADY WISHFORT

As I am a person, I can hold out no longer: I have wasted my spirits so to-day already that I am ready to sink under the fatigue; and I cannot but have some fears upon me yet, that my son Fainall will pursue some desperate course.

MIRABELL

Madam, disquiet not yourself on that account: to my knowledge his circumstances are such he must of force comply. For my part I will contribute all that in me lies to a reunion. In the meantime, madam [to MRS. FAINALL], let me before these witnesses restore to you this deed of trust: it may be a means, well managed, to make you live easily together.

From hence let those be warned, who mean to wed,
Lest mutual falsehood stain the bridal-bed:
For each deceiver to his cost may find
That marriage frauds too oft are paid in kind.

Chapter 16

Study Questions

Q. Critically comment on William Congreve's "The Way of the World"

Or

Q. Discuss the actwise summary of "The Way of the world"

The Prologue

The prologue tells the audience that writers are fools who gamble that their audiences will like their offerings, and Congreve throws himself on the mercy of his audience. He tells them not to expect a satire, since they are already perfect.

Act 1

The first act is set in a chocolate house, a men's club where men go to talk, read the paper, drink, catch up on business, gossip and gamble. It introduces the male characters in person, and piques our interest about the women, as we are introduced to them through the men's discussion.

Mirabell is losing at cards to his friend, Fainall. Mirabell tells Fainall that Mrs. Millamant rebuffed him in public the night before. (As a courtesy, women were addressed as "Mrs." whether or not they were married.)

We learn that Millamant is heiress to a fortune, but half of it depends on whether her aunt Lady Wishfort approves of her marriage. Mirabell had pretended to love Lady Wishfort in order to get closer to Millamant, but Millamant's friend Mrs. Marwood revealed Mirabell's deception. Lady Wishfort, naturally humiliated, now hates Mirabell and will obviously not approve of his marrying her niece. The major conflict of the play is established. We learn that another character, Waitwell, is married "and bedded." Mirabell says he is working on "a Matter of some sort of Mirth" but can't say anything about it yet.

Mirabell, who seems obsessed with Millamant, tells Fainall that she puts up with fools around her (Witwoud and Petulant, two coxcombs, or conceited fools) and then confesses that he likes her in spite of her faults—perhaps even because of them.

A letter arrives from Sir Wilfull Witwoud to his half-brother Witwoud, who is playing cards at the club. Sir Wilfull has come to prepare to travel abroad for the first time, looking for adventure at his advanced age of 40.

Witwoud enters and lives up to his name, describing his friend Petulant's faults as virtues, and understanding as jokes the insults that Fainall and Mirabell poke at him.

The plot advances as Mirabell learns that Lady Wishfort has a plan to marry her niece, Millamant, to Mirabell's uncle, Sir Rowland, who is coming to London hoping to disinherit Mirabell. (Money is important in this society.)

The men decide to go walk in the Mall where they know they will meet the ladies, and Mirabell asks the two fops to go on their own, as he is embarrassed by Petulant's rude catcalls to women in the park.

As the act closes, Mirabell comments in rhyme that behaviour like Petulant's is not wit but ignorance.

Act 2

This act is set in St James' Park, a favourite society walk. Mrs. Fainall (Lady Wishfort's daughter and Fainall's wife) and Mrs. Marwood discuss the nastiness of men, but show us, however, that each is attracted to Mirabell. Fainall and Mirabell meet the ladies, and they all split up. In the next scene we learn that Fainall and Mrs. Marwood are lovers, and that Mirabell and Mrs. Fainall once had an affair. Mrs. Marwood and Fainall quarrel, and she covers her tearful face with a mask as Mirabell and Mrs. Fainall enter. Mrs. Fainall tells Mirabell that she despises her husband, and once loved Mirabell "without bounds." She married Fainall only to preserve her reputation. Mirabell tells her the details of the intrigue he has under way (the "Matter of some sort of Mirth" he alluded to in the first act): Mirabell's servant, Waitwell, has married Lady Wishfort's maid, Foible. Waitwell will pretend to be Mirabell's uncle, Sir Rowland, and woo Lady Wishfort. When she discovers his true identity she will be so embarrassed she will allow Millamant to rescue her and marry Mirabell, to save her reputation.

Millamant arrives, in full sail, and we finally see the would-be lovers together. Mirabell demands to know why Millamant snubbed him. The scene shows us the conventions of the time: pretense, cruelty, secrets, jokes. When they are alone he asks her why she spends time with fools, and she says he is tiresome and walks away, saying she knows of his plot. Mirabell wonders about the "whirlwind" of love.

At the end of this act we meet the newly-married servants, Foible and Waitwell. Foible, a willing conspirator in Mirabell's plot, tells him that she has claimed to show Lady Wishfort's picture to Sir Rowland to inflame his desire for her, and is planning to report his impatience to Lady Wishfort. As Mirabell gives her some money, Foible panics as she sees Mrs. Marwood go by, masked, afraid she will tell her mistress that she saw Foible with Mirabell. She runs home, and Mirabell tells Waitwell to transform into Sir Rowland.

Act 3

This act takes place in Lady Wishfort's home. Lady Wishfort is anxiously bidding her servant Peg to make up her face. Mrs. Marwood arrives and tells Lady Wishfort that she saw Foible with Mirabell. Lady Wishfort asks her to hide in the closet while she questions Foible.

Foible does a masterful job of lying. She says that Mirabell insulted Lady Wishfort again by calling her old ("superannuated"), and says that Sir Rowland will arrive soon. Lady Wishfort is flustered, in need of her makeup, anxious that she not have to make advances to Sir Rowland and "break decorums." She is desperate for a husband but unwilling to make the first move. Her fears are calmed when Foible tells her that the lusty Sir Rowland will take her by storm, and leaves.

Mrs. Fainall enters and tells Foible she knows of the plot against Lady Wishfort. Foible tells Mrs. Fainall that she is worried about Mrs. Marwood, who watches her, and that Mrs. Marwood likes Mirabell, who can't "abide her." They are unaware that Mrs. Marwood in the closet is overhearing everything. When they leave Mrs. Marwood resolves to ruin everything for Mirabell. She suggests to Lady Wishfort that she marry Millamant to Wilfull Witwoud. Lady Wishfort likes the idea, and Lady Wishfort and Foible leave to change for dinner.

The next to enter is Millamant, with her maid, Mincing. Marwood cruelly tells Millamant that her love is known and there is no need for pretense. They accuse each other, and then both say they hate Mirabell. Marwood warns Millamant that her happiness may be changed sooner than she thinks; Millamant calls for a song (a convention of Restoration theatre) that says only ambitious love is worthwhile, and Petulant and Witwoud arrive to join in the fun.

When Millamant and Mincing exit, Sir Wilfull enters to meet his half-brother Witwoud. In this scene Witwoud affects to not know his country brother, and he and Petulant make fun of Sir Wilfull for his rough manners. He is no weakling though. "You're a fop, dear brother," he says, and castigates Witwoud for leaving his attorney's job to be a dandy. He says he will stay in London for a while to learn "your lingo."

After everyone else leaves for dinner, Mrs. Marwood tells Fainall of Mirabell's plot. Fainall is outraged and upset that his wife was previously involved with Mirabell and that she has outwitted him now. Mrs. Marwood, determined to prevent Mirabell from getting Millamant's fortune, suggests a plot of her own: if they tell Lady Wishfort of her daughter's dalliance with Mirabell, she will be so enraged she will do anything to save Mrs. Fainall's reputation. Mrs. Marwood worries that the idea she proposed to Lady Wishfort of having Millamant marry Sir Wilfull may be bad, because Millamant will claim her fortune, but Fainall promises to make Sir Wilfull so drunk he will not able to win Millamant. Mrs. Marwood plans to write a letter to Lady Wishfort, revealing all, and Fainall says that at least he has most of his wife's money because he "wheadl'd a deed of Settlement out of her." The act ends with a couplet by the nefarious Fainall, telling husbands they must endure and not be too wise or too foolish or they will suffer.

Act 4

In a very funny scene, Lady Wishfort works out the best pose for the moment Sir Rowland sees her. Foible tells Lady Wishfort that Wilfull is getting drunk, and Lady Wishfort sends her to bring Millamant so she won't be left long alone with Sir Rowland.

Mirabell agrees to see Millamant, who is waiting for him. A severely intoxicated and extremely reluctant Wilfull enters, intercepted by Mrs. Fainall, who urges him to woo Millamant and locks him in the room. He is unable to match wits with Millamant who sends him away as Mirabell enters.

The next scene is the famous "Proviso" scene, in which Millamant and Mirabell set conditions for their marriage in the first pre-nuptial contract ever staged. Each is anxious to preserve their independence. Millamant fears that she will "by degrees dwindle into a wife," and Mirabell wants to make sure that Millamant will not be a slave to silly fashion or be involved in scandals, before he is "enlarg'd into a Husband." The two eventually agree on their contract. Mrs. Fainall is happy for them, but hurries Mirabell out as Lady Wishfort enters. Millamant says she loves Mirabell.

Rowdiness comes next, as we learn that Lady Wishfort has broken up a fight between Petulant and Wilfull. An intoxicated Petulant enters and rudely proposes to Millamant. He and Witwoud insult each other; Petulant, who has defended Millamant's beauty, tells her to "fight for your Face the next time yourself," and leaves. Witwoud explains that all the fuss is due to Fainall's plan to get rid of Sir Wilfull by getting him drunk. Next Lady Wishfort and Sir Wilfull enter. He is amenable, loud and drunk, agreeing to marry Millamant, singing and discussing travel plans. He smells so terrible that Millamant and Fainall leave. Witwoud takes him away at Lady Wishfort's behest. Then Waitwell enters as Sir Rowland. He pretends to be madly in love with Lady Wishfort and she quickly agrees to marry him, after making sure that he does not believe any sexual appetite of hers, with a concomitant loss of honour, is involved in her desire to marry!

Foible tells Lady Wishfort a letter has come for her and she goes to get it. When she returns, Waitwell reads the letter with her, and the plot is uncovered, to Lady Wishfort's horror. Waitwell, thinking fast, says it is another trick of Mirabell's and promises to prove his veracity by bringing her the black box containing all the dealings of his estate. Lady Wishfort agrees, and the scene ends with a couplet by Waitwell, finished by Foible.

Act 5

Still in Lady Wishfort's house, the dénouement unfolds. As the act begins, Lady Wishfort is raging at Foible, threatening her with jail, where her husband is. She leaves and Mrs. Fainall tells Foible that Mirabell has freed Waitwell. Foible tells Mrs. Fainall that Mrs. Marwood and Fainall have been having an affair. She and Mincing were forced to swear to secrecy after catching them. Mrs. Fainall is surprised, but sees an opportunity to use the information to her advantage.

Mincing enters, to tell Foible to hide in the closet until Lady Wishfort has calmed down. Fainall has demanded her fortune, threatening divorce. Millamant is ready to marry Sir Wilfull to save her fortune. They leave.

Lady Wishfort and Mrs. Marwood enter next. Lady Wishfort thanks Mrs. Marwood for uncovering the plots, then attacks her for her bad behaviour, finding it all the worse since she herself has always been a model of virtue. Mrs. Fainall says they were both wronged, and says she will prove Mrs. Marwood's illicit relationship with Fainall. Over Mrs. Marwood's denials she warns her mother that Marwood is a "leach" who will "drop off when she is full of her [mother's] blood."

As Lady Wishfort rails that she brought up her daughter to hate all men, she realizes that Fainall must be wrong in his accusations and agrees he must prove his assertions against his wife. However, Mrs. Marwood horrifies her with a description of the possible court scene and its social ramifications, and she changes her mind.

Fainall now enters, as the absolute villain that he has shown himself to be, and tells Lady Wishfort what she must do: she may not marry without his approval; Mrs. Fainall must settle her whole fortune on him; and Millamant must give him 6,000 pounds which she has "forfeited by her disobedience." He leaves after giving Lady Wishfort time to draw up the necessary papers, and Lady Wishfort turns for comfort to Mrs. Marwood, calling Fainall a "barbarian" compared to her daughter's first husband, Languish.

Millamant and Wilfull enter, saying they will marry. Mirabell waits outside. Lady Wishfort is happy to hear the news of Millamant's marriage, and finally agrees to see Mirabell after Millamant says he is going to travel with Wilfull and never bother her again. Wilfull confirms that this is true, and Mrs. Marwood leaves, sensing trouble. When Mirabell enters, Lady Wishfort agrees to give up her anger if Mirabell gives up his contract with Millamant. Mirabell says he has already done so. Lady Wishfort in an aside tells us that she is still attracted to him.

The schemers Mrs. Marwood and Fainall enter, Fainall flourishing papers for Lady Wishfort to sign, and disbelieving the sham of Millamant marrying Wilfull. He warns that he will set Mrs. Fainall adrift "like a leaky hulk, to sink or swim." Distraught, Lady Wishfort accepts Mirabell's help. He asks for Millamant "in compensation" but says he will help Lady Wishfort regardless, and Lady Wishfort agrees that he can have Millamant if he saves them all from Fainall.

Mrs. Fainall, Foible and Mincing enter and tell of the affair between Mrs. Marwood and Fainall. In a supreme example of double standards, Fainall continues to threaten to expose his wife's shame in having loved Mirabell, and says he will still "ruin" her.

Waitwell arrives with the promised black box. Inside is Mrs. Fainall's settlement, signed in trust to Mirabell before she married Fainall to prevent the kind of treachery that is now occurring. Fainall realizes the settlement he has made his wife sign is false. Astonishingly, he tries to run at her with his sword, but is stopped by Sir Wilfull. Fainall leaves, vowing revenge. Mrs. Fainall confronts Mrs. Marwood, who also promises revenge, and leaves.

The lovers come together, and Mirabell tells Lady Wishfort not to worry about Fainall, as he needs his wife's marriage in order to survive. He says he will be the mediator of peace. He gives back the deed of trust to Mrs. Fainall suggesting she can use it to "live Easily together"—i.e., to have some power, finally, in her marriage. The act ends with a quatrain against the evils of adultery.

Epilogue

The closing lines are addressed to the drama critics in the audience, making sure that they all know no single person is the butt of the play, but that it is *the times* that have been satirized.

Q. Discuss Congreve, Dryden, Jonson and the drama of theatrical succession.

Or

Q. Comment on Congreve as a playwright.

In Self-crowned Laureates, Richard Helgerson asserts that "when the writer first appears before his audience, the pressure on self-presentation is greatest. To some extent, each beginning-beginnings of individual works as well as beginnings of careers-brings a renewal of self-presentational pressures."' Helgerson is surely correct to emphasize the self-presentational weight on that moment when authors first formally introduce themselves to their audience, inaugurating a relationship fraught with personal, cultural, and economic implications.

Yet Helgerson's concern with the origins of early modern conceptions of authorial identity-his general focus on beginnings"-explains his inattention to how "endings" may also define moments when "the pressure on self-presentation is greatest." Taking leave of one's audience, imagining the end of one's career, involves a writer in a host of literary and emotional issues that are invariably charged with and transformed by the recognition of the writer's individual mortality, that moment when self-presentational pressures may indeed be said to be greatest," when all must render their accounts before God.

In this essay I will examine an unusual "moment" when the "beginning" of one writer's career takes place in conjunction with the "ending" of another's, when authorial introduction and farewell are conjoined in a self-conscious attempt to create an important drama of cultural succession. William Congreve was not an unpublished author when the first editions of his first two plays, The Old Batchelour and The Double-Dealer, appeared in March and December of 1693, within weeks of each play's premiere. But Incognita had been published anonymously early in 1692, and the poems and translations also published in that year in Charles Gildon's Miscellany of Original Poems and John Dryden's Satires of Juvenal and Persius represent occasional efforts rather than the beginning of a career.

The two play quartos of 1693, however, reveal Congreve's desire to present himself to fin de siecle London as a dramatist, and to imagine his literary career within the precincts and traditions of the English theatre. It is not only the plays themselves, and particularly their prologues and epilogues, which articulate Congreve's authorial identity, but the two dedications and sundry commendatory verses that herald his arrival on the literary scene.

Although we must take care in reading such highly conventional forms of writing, which employ familiar tropes and obey specific rhetorical rules, the careful fabrication of each quarto, and the quite evident links between them, suggest that Congreve thought of these two slender volumes as far more than the simple publication of dramatic texts that provided the opportunity to exploit economically one very successful and one less successful play.2 They represent rather a determined attempt to formulate a history of the seventeenth-century English theatre and to position the fledgling playwright as the fulfillment of its most important traditions.

At the centre of this strategy are not the plays themselves, but Dryden's "To my Dear Friend Mr. Congreve, On His Comedy, call'd The Double-Dealer," in which the elderly literary lion formally pronounces Congreve his poetic successor. Dryden rehearsed his retirement from the stage in other forums as well, most notably in the 1694 production of his final play, Love Triumphant, where the prologue announces that "He Dies, at least to us, and to the Stage," while the epilogue even imagines that "the Poet's dead."

But in the verses prefixed to Congreve's play Dryden clearly desires to create a cultural moment of great literary significance, one that attempts to encompass the past development of English drama and to enforce a particular vision of the theatrical present. The aged eminence, like his younger counterpart, expresses his concern for his place in history and his determination to formulate that history in ways that can legitimate his art and career.

In examining these two quartos I want to revise a conventional narrative of the dramatist's relationship to the stage that Jonas Barish, for instance, employs in The Antitheatrical Prejudice when he places Ben Jonson "among a galaxy of talented playwrights who at a given moment in their careers have seen their whole enterprise as hollow, and proceeded to renounce it, or else reform it. When applied to the career of William Congreve, this narrative seizes on the reputed failure of his acknowledged masterpiece, The Way of the World, as the decisive "moment" when the artist formally recognizes the unworthiness of his audience-fools and knaves all-and retires in high dudgeon from a vile commercial theatre that has failed to properly appreciate, and even threatened to pollute his genius.

In this essay I want to suggest the inappropriateness of this narrative to Congreve's career, for the first editions of Congreve's first two plays don't simply anticipate Congreve's later rejection of the theatre, but inscribe it in his very assumption of the dramatist's mantle. The playwright's alienation from the spectator is a foundational trope in Congreve's construction of a theatrical identity. The commencement of Congreve's dramatic career reveals that Congreve does not gradually come to despair of his audience, but rejects them from the very first in order to legitimate himself as the heir of the aging Dryden, who himself organizes his theatrical farewell around the repudiation of an audience that had attended and applauded his plays for thirty years.

Dryden's distrust of the theatre expresses itself most famously in his 1685 ode to Anne Killigrew, where he laments a lubric and adult'rate age" by denouncing "the steaming ordures of the stage." But his participation in Congreve's debut allows Dryden to authorize his moral disdain for a corrupt theatrical enterprise by linking it to a pattern of literary and generational succession. In fashioning a distinguished genealogy of poetic genius, Congreve and Dryden reinforce their mutual distance from and contempt for a loathed stage and its unworthy auditors. These two first editions enact a drama of poetic succession that occurs alongside of, but separate from, the comedies that ostensibly provide the reason for their being. Congreve enforces this separation through a fascinating act of self-presentation in which the role he assumes on stage is carefully distinguished from and even repudiated by the identity he orchestrates in the dedications and poetic tributes that accompany his two plays.

If, as Harry Berger suggests, "the theatre process involves a double mode of representation.... Representation in the presence of an audience is thus at the same time representation of that audience,"4 Congreve plays to and privileges a literate readership above a despised playhouse audience by distinguishing between the fledgling playwright and the heir to Dryden's poetic estate. Such a strategy illuminates what Jocelyn Powell has termed the Janus-faced" nature of Restoration theatre, which looks "one way towards the glamorous patronage of the Court and another towards its own independent development as a commercial institution. The drama of the later seventeenth century is best understood as a playing out of the tensions implicit in such a position." Although these tensions manifest themselves in different ways throughout the century, they characterize not only the Restoration theatre but the entire development of English theatre in the seventeenth century. Congreve's determined effort to undermine and scapegoat his theatrical audience, which emerges from such a process as a despicable other whose alienation from the playwright defines one of the conditions of his success, represents one resolution of these tensions; and it marks the last decade of the century as a pivotal moment in the evolution of the theatre in England.

The audience attending the initial fourteen performances of The Old Batchelour would have been cheerfully unaware of anything unusual in its relationship to a new and extraordinarily successful dramatist. In both the prologue and epilogue to the play Congreve flatters his first audiences by presenting himself in the utterly conventional guise of the theatrical novice whose immaturity and uncertainty prove his own virginity while testifying to the experience and sophistication of his auditors. Indeed, the prologue-delivered by the young and notoriously chaste Mrs. Bracegirdle, who herself specialized in virginal heroines-insists that in doing so Congreve recalls a "former" age, an unfallen dramatic past when "Poets beg'd a Blessing" and acted "like Suppliants" before an audience kindly imagined as Guests.Such days," however, are past, for playwrights now make war against their former guests and "threaten you who do for Judges sit, / To save our plays, or else we damn your Pit".

The prologue never attempts to identify this former time, and we should remember, as Leo Hughes notes, that "pitting the past against the present or the present against the past" is a conventional rhetorical device in prologues and epilogues.1 But its nostalgic evocation as a vague mythic golden age is precisely what allows Congreve to condemn explicitly the adversarial relationship between playwright and audience that characterizes a vile [contemporary] World." Congreve, this prologue insists, returns us to that former glory, promising an unproblematic relationship between author and audience:

But for your Comfort, it falls out to day,
We've a young Author and his first born Play;
So, standing only on his good Behaviour,

He's very civil, and entreats your Favour. Congreve here plays the "bashful Poet," and Bracegirdle mimics his uncertainty by pretending to forget her lines, running from the stage in what might be described as a "pretty confusion."

The epilogue presents similar sentiments, though the more experienced, knowing, and sexually compromised Mrs. Barry-who played Laetitia Fondlewife-places them in an entirely different erotic register. She begins by cynically emphasizing the playwright's sexual vulnerability, comparing him to "a rash Girl, who will all Hazards run, / And be enjoy'd, tho' sure to be undone". "Our Poet," like the ruined miss, would now "repent" and recover her lost Toy," but he too has irrevocably lost his "Reputation."

Fearful, undone, dejected, the poet has asked his presenter "humbly to petition" his audience's favour, though she concludes by again insisting on the identity that yokes the sexually compromised female and the artistically vulnerable dramatist: "Women and Wits are used e'en much at one: / You gain your End, and damn 'em when you've done." This language of theatrical eroticism even appears in the prologue—unperformed but nonetheless included in the printed edition of the play-composed by Antony Carey, fifth viscount Falkland, who imagines the anxious dramatist, a "pert Beginner," as the overawed bridegroom of a sexually experienced and voracious widow.

Though the concluding couplet of this prologue vindicates its playwright, who emerges as "a Man of Might" when he "holds out to please you the third Night," it reveals, as does Congreve's own prologue and epilogue, the fragile and uncertain relationship between Restoration playwrights and their notoriously unruly audiences that was conventionally characterized in terms of sexual prowess, vulnerability, and exploitation. The erotic nature of Restoration prologues and epilogues may originally stem from a desire on the part of male playwrights and theatrical companies to exploit the novel and titillating presence of women on the stage. It may testify as well to the intimate relationship, particularly in the 1660s and 1670s, between the theatres and a libertine court.9 The sexual vocabulary of Congreve's first quartos, however, discloses both the uncertainty of the fledgling playwright, as well as his aggression. In her examination of eighteenth-century players, Kristina Straub argues that "as men who make spectacles of themselves-and their sexuality-for a living, actors are placed by popular discourse in a feminine' relation to self-display."10 Congreve seems to have feared that such feminization threatened playwrights as well, for while he gracefully exploits the implications of his conventional pose as the virgin dramatist in order to woo his theatre audience, he embeds in his own prologue an assurance that he "has Malice" and will "out grow" his current timidity.

Such a promise insists that Congreve will abandon the role he now plays so well and transform the comfortable relationship with his audience that he now assumes; his maturation as a dramatist will inevitably put him at odds with his audience. In fact, the first of the verses that accompany his publication of The Old Batchelour explicitly rejects the image of the sexually compromised playwright. Indeed, Thomas Southerne's "To Mr. Congreve," the first of the three poems interpolated between Congreve's dedication and Carey's prologue, portrays him not as a vulnerable virgin but as a rapist:

Nature so coy, so hardly to be Woo'd
Flies, like a Mistress, but to be pursu'd.
O CONGREVE! boldly follow on the Chase;
She looks behind, and wants thy strong Embrace:
She yields, she yields, surrenders all her Charms,
Do you but force her gently to your Arms:
Such Nerves, such Graces, in your Lines appear,
As you were made to be her Ravisher.

If the Shakespearean theater imagined itself in terms of a mirror held up to nature, the Restoration dramatist in Southerne's lines assumes a much more active and sexually potent role in forcing nature to yield her secrets. Southerne's transforms Congreve from erotic innocent to sexual aggressor, the oxymoronic formulation of "gentle force" the only check on his overmastering masculine and class power.

This transformation, moreover, immediately leads to the issue of succession, for the word "Ravisher" is followed by the name of Dryden and the depiction of "his Command, / By Right-divine, quite through the Muses Land, / Absolute Lord." These lines may very well allude to the opening stanza of Dryden's Macflecknoe-where Flecknoe "was own'd without dispute / Through all the realms of Nonsense, absolute"-and in doing so they clearly rewrite that earlier poem's parody of succession. Southerne's poem presents the true succession, not the ludicrous line of Shadwell and Flecknoe, but the passage of the "undoubted Crown" from Apollo to Dryden to Congreve. Wycherley, Etherege, Lee, and Otway all have a place in such a genealogy, but the first in "wise Retreat," the second in "wild Pleasures tost,"—Etherege had in fact died in 1691-the last two dead, cede their position to Congreve, "The Darling, and last Comfort of [Dryden's] Years."

Congreve chose with great care those contemporaries who would accompany and adorn his formal introduction to the public. He dedicated the play itself to Charles Boyle, Lord Clifford of Lanesborough, the eldest son of the powerful noble-the second earl of Cork and Burlington—to whom Congreve's family owed many obligations. Antony Carey was an important member of the government who had a position on the Queen's privy Council and was made First Lord of the Admiralty shortly before his death in 1694; he was as well a friend of Dryden's who had helped secure permission for the production of Cleomenes in 1692.

Jerry March and Bevil Higgons, whose verses follow Southerne's, possessed important and influential family connections; the former was the son of the Archbishop of Dublin—and was himself to become Dean of Kilmore—while the latter, an historian and poet, belonged to a family prominent for its Stuart sympathies. Higgons's uncle, Dean Denis Granville, had accompanied James to France, and Higgons himself was briefly imprisoned in 1696 because of his knowledge concerning a conspiracy against William ill. While these men secured Congreve's diverse political connections—essential for a writer hoping to attract patronage-it is Southerne who most importantly places Congreve among his theatrical contemporaries, and who first introduces the theme of succession that constitutes the primary focus of the two quartos. In 1693 Southerne was near the height of his fame, one of the more successful dramatists on the contemporary scene.

His approbation would of itself have been sufficient to launch a new playwright, but Southerne determinedly obscures his own presence behind the powerful figure of Dryden, who dominates the theatrical history that Southerne rehearses. Indeed, Dryden's eminence constitutes a considerable problem in the poem, for Southerne has difficulty imagining not only a future dramatic landscape bereft of its "great Master," but a theatrical past that can explain or locate his genius: Dryden, the poem assures us, holds now from none / But great Apollo, his undoubted Crown." Southerne, of course, pays Dryden an elaborate compliment here by erasing theatrical history in favour of divine election; at the same time, he acknowledges, in the force of now," Dryden's longevity, which has effectively buried all those who preceded him.

Southerne voices the concerns of a dramatic community that fears the imminent loss of the commanding figure who has constituted the single most important influence on recent theatrical history, who has placed his unmistakable stamp on comic and tragic form, as well as heroic drama. But in obscuring Dryden's theatrical origins, Southerne also registers the dilemma of a commercial enterprise uncertain about its own past, marked by the enforced closure of the theatres that to an important extent severed Restoration playwrights from their forebears. Dryden's verses to Congreve, I argue below, confront this extraordinary eighteen-year disruption of theatrical history as well, its powerful effects felt not only during the 1660s, when commercial theatres had to reinvent themselves, but thirty years later, when the most successful playwright of the era was widely perceived to be reaching the end of his career. Dryden had reigned so long that in 1693 Southerne can hardly imagine a role for Dryden's successor:

(That Empire settled, and grown old in Pow'r) Can wish for nothing, but a Successor: Not to enlarge his Limits, but maintain Those Provinces, which he alone could gain. By the end of his poem, Southerne will turn the proper compliment to Congreve's power by assuring him that as the "natural Successor of his Mind) / Then may'st thou finish what he has begun." But the earlier lines suggest that Southerne remains uncertain about just what Congreve must finish." The "Limits" of dramatic empire have long since been forged by Dryden, mere maintenance the legacy he leaves his heir. The uncertainties of Southerne's contribution to The Old Batchelour find little echo in Congreve's self-assured dedication, which presents an author very much at odds with the "bashful Poet" of Congreve's prologue.

Indeed, the lines from Horace's Epistle II.i. that Congreve appended to the title-page reveal a self-possession and critical awareness of the nature of a literary career that belie the naivety and timidity of the prologue and epilogue. These lines insist that the poet must despise "the wind of praise" that governs "Fame's mad voyage," for the "breath [that] revives" the poet can easily become the "breath [that] o'erthrows." The tactic of citing Horace to distance an author from his audience echoes Jonson's decision in 1616 to adorn the first folio edition of a collected works by an English dramatist with Horace's "I do not work so that I will be admired by the crowd, but am content with a few readers". Congreve begins his dramatic career with a Jonsonian gesture that reveals a critical and even cynical apprehension of an author's endeavors, and which possessed particular resonance for a dramatist aware of the tension between the demands of popular entertainment and the pretensions of high art.

In order to protect himself from these fickle winds of an audience's favour, Congreve attempts to fashion himself in the dedications to his first two plays as perfectly self-contained, attentive to the taste and approbation of those whose patronage he seeks—Charles Boyle in the first play, and

Charles Montague in the second—but otherwise above the vulgar critics who might judge his art. Indeed, the dedication to The Old Batchelour includes a brief literary autobiography in which Congreve betrays an uneasiness about acknowledging a poetic childhood or apprenticeship:

It [his play] is the first Offence I have committed in this kind, or indeed, in any kind of Poetry, tho' not the first made publick; and, therefore, I hope will the more easily be pardoned: But had it been Acted, when it was first written, more might have been said in its behalf; Ignorance of the Town and Stage, would then, have been excuses in a young Writer, which now, almost four Years experience, will scarce allow of. Congreve here desires his readers to recognize that this play is the offspring of a virgin muse, "the first Offence I have committed... in any kind of Poetry."

At the same time, he wants us to know that he has already published other works—"tho' not the first made publick"—and so is not, in fact, "a young Writer." The passage thus manages to ask "pardon" for the first fruits of the writer's pen, while at the same time insisting that he desires no special consideration from his audience, for his "first Offence" becomes the product of "four Years experience." Congreve isn't quite suggesting that he has sprung fullblown from the head of Zeus, but he does reveal, in the tortured logic and prose of this passage, a considerable discomfort with the role of the "young Writer" and the vulnerability that such an identity might betray. The acknowledgement of authorial inexperience is a conventional part of such dedications, but Congreve's unusual anxiety and edginess is striking when compared, for instance, to the ease and grace with which Southerne, in the dedication to his first play, The Loyal Brother (1682), offers to the duke of Richmond "the first fruits of my Muse," happy to lay "my Maiden-head at your Door.

While grudgingly confessing his authorial youthfulness, Congreve asks for no favors on that account, and he goes on to make clear that he will grant none either. To his critics he has "nothing to say," for whether they make "just Exceptions... [orl find fault in the wrong place," "I think there are no Faults in it, but what I do know." I find this a remarkable claim, the perfect antithesis to the "bashful Poet" who speaks through Anne Bracegirdle in the prologue. Congreve presents himself in the dedication as complete in himself, mature and all knowing. He doesn't, of course, deny that his first play has faults, or even that some critics have discovered them. What he does claim, however, is that he has no need of critics, for he already possesses an ideal knowledge of his play, one that needs no amendment from outside.

Congreve has already imagined himself in terms of Dryden's tribute to his next play, for "Genius must be born; and never can be taught." Congreve's self-presentation participates in what Richard Helgerson has described as "the laureate self a virtuous, centered, serious self, characterized by its knowledge of and fidelity to itself and the governing ethos of the age." In the last decade of the seventeenth century, such a figure—perfect, whole, and entire in himself—needs no audience at all, as Congreve's elaboration and enlargement of this identity makes clear in the dedication to his second play, where the audience generates tremendous scorn in the slighted playwright. The "lavish" applause that greeted his first play here becomes a sign of the audience's lack of discrimination, for their failure to applaud equally Congreve's superior second offering suggests that "they are to be treated cheaply, and I have been at an unnecessary expense."

Congreve here inverts the real economic exchange that marks the theatre, appropriating the complaints of a dissatisfied audience demanding its money back. In fact, Congreve insists that for him the theatrical audience represents an unnecessary presence, for "this Play in relation to my concern for its Reputation, succeeded before It was Acted, for thro' your [Charles Montague's] early Patronage it had an audience of several Persons of the first Rank both in Wit and Quality." This is a "fit audience though few" with a vengeance, the entire theatrical exchange between a paying audience and the commercial playwright rendered superfluous by Congreve's refusal to participate in the dramatic economy of the public theatre. Although dedications possessed well established rhetorical conventions, which include the elevation of the respected patron above the vulgar audience, even Congreve recognized that this dedication betrayed an excessive and therefore too revealing disdain for "Illiterate Criticks" and an ignorant "Town." In all subsequent editions of the play Congreve took care not to reprint the second paragraph of the dedication.

Yet Congreve's contempt is hardly restricted to this one paragraph, for he elsewhere repeats the gestures of self-containment and inviolability that characterized the first dedication: I was Conscious where a true Critick might have put me upon my defence. I was prepared for their Attack; and am pretty confident I could have vindicated some parts, and excused others; and where there were any plain Miscarriages, I would most ingenuously have confess'd 'em. But I have not heard any thing said sufficient to provoke an Answer.

Again, Congreve has nothing to say to his critics, for a "true Critick" simply doesn't exist in his theatrical world. Again, Congreve assures us that his play possesses faults, but that he alone recognizes them. Again, Congreve thwarts any exchange between audience and playwright, "the Ignorance and Malice of the greater part of the Audience" making a dialogue or interchange impossible.

Congreve here participates in what Peter Stallybrass and Allon white have described as a process of cultural cleansing that stretches from Ben Jonson in the early seventeenth century to Wordsworth in the early nineteenth." Congreve's construction of his laureate self depends on both his vulgarization of the theatrical audience and a pattern of literary filiation that subtends and authorizes his estrangement from that audience. Congreve and Southerne generate a myth of literary succession and dramatic vulgarity as an alternate body for themselves, one that uses the fixity of print and a body of type as a defence against the bodily uncontrol and self-exposure that is a necessary condition of entertainment in a popular and commercial theatre.

It is left to Dryden—whose "To my Dear Friend, Mr. Congreve" is the singular adornment of the quarto of The

Double-Dealer aside from Congreve's own dedication—to perfect the image of the laureate author prepared by Congreve and Southerne. Dryden's poem deploys and develops both the topos of dramatic vulgarity and that of literary succession in ways that inevitably for a modern reader recall Macflecknoe. Dryden here stands in the place of Flecknoe, grown old and "subject to decay," inspired by his closeness to death to vatic pronouncements in a "prophetic mood." A basso counterpoint to the shrill tenor of the earlier poem, the verses to Congreve attempt to justify and valorize Dryden's career by providing the authorized history of seventeenth-century English theatre. Congreve provides the occasion for Dryden's poem, but Dryden is its subject.

The poem claims prophetic, even apocalyptic speech in its first lines, which announce the coming of "the promis'd hour" when "The present Age of Wit obscures the past." Congreve's succession from Dryden completes a cycle of history, representing the triumph of contemporary poetry over its own past. This competition with the past marks Dryden, as Walter Jackson Bate noted years ago, as one of the first English poets to suffer from a sense of his own belatedness, to experience his literary past as a burden and source of anxiety.

"The Gyant Race, before the Flood" that oppresses Dryden's literary imagination does so not simply because of its strength and outsized accomplishments, its "Gyant" stature, but because it came "before the Flood," preceding the cataclysmic events that tragically divide present from past, one age from the next. The almost twenty years of civil upheaval, which encompass the Civil War, execution of Charles I, elevation of Cromwell, and closing of the theatres, dominate Dryden's understanding of both political and literary history, dividing him from his past and disrupting the orderly progression of generations.

The reestablishment of proper order and stability, as always for Dryden, defends on Charles's Restoration, which inaugurates "Our Age." Early in Dryden's career, in Astraea Redux, Charles's healing power is represented in the figure of Augustus: "Oh, happy age! Oh, times like those alone / By fate reserv'd for great Augustus' throne." In the verses to Congreve, however, a more profound experience of temporal dislocation forces Dryden to employ the legendary first king of Italy, Janus, who the stubborn Soil manur'd,

With Rules of Husbandry the rankness cur'd:
Tam'd us to manners, when the Stage was rude;
And boistrous English Wit, with Art indu'd.

The transition from republican to imperial Rome represented by Augustus fails to register the epic temporality that Dryden seeks in the opening to his poem on Congreve. That passage, after all, defines an historical event, while the flood and establishment of agriculture are mythic, prehistoric, originary. Dryden and "Our Age" stand at an immense distance from an early-seventeenth-century theatre that here can be imagined only in terms of legend, prehistory, and biblical mythology: "Our Builders were, with want of Genius, curst; / The second Temple was not like the first."

The burden of Dryden's poem is precisely to fashion a second temple that can eclipse the first, not simply to recover a theatrical past but to surpass it. The enormous temporal scale constructed early in the poem can be pressed into service in this regard, for in effectively transforming the thirty-three years of Restoration history into centuries, Dryden can repeatedly emphasize the slow and inexorable progress of history: "the promis'd hour is come at last"; "Our Age was cultivated thus at length"; "till You, the best Vitruvius, come at length."

Dryden's progressive history, imaged in terms of foundational arts like agriculture and architecture, appears to unfold languidly over millennia, the brief history of Restoration drama describing a long, stately, and finally overpowering flowering of poetic virtues, as Congreve inherits both the "Tallents" of "their Age" and "all Beauties of this Age." The narrative voice of this long first stanza is determinedly collective; although certain dramatists like Etherege, Southerne, and "Witcherly" are singled out for praise, Dryden himself speaks only through the collective pronouns "we" and "our." The slow cultivation of "our

Beauties" and "our strength," the careful assembly and joining of "Dorique Pillars" and "Fair Corinthian Crowns," defines a seamless, linear, collective progression from the early "rankness" of the "rude" Restoration stage to the present felicity of Congreve's elevation, which seems in this first stanza to promise the fulfillment of history.

The second stanza, however, rudely interrupts this pleasant illusion, revealing that for Dryden time remains hopelessly out of joint. Dryden himself remains always too late, sundered both from the mythic past of "the Gyant Race" and even from his own history:

Oh that your Brows my Lawrel had sustain'd,
Well had I been Depos'd, if You had reign'd!
The Father had descended for the son;
For only You are lineal to the Throne.

However ironic and nasty his portrait of Flecknoe, Dryden had granted that "aged Prince" a dignity denied Dryden himself: the power to "settle the succession of the state." In his verses to Congreve, however, Dryden can assume his own identity, can claim the power of the narrative "I," can anoint a successor only after he has already been deposed. Dryden certainly claims the power to determine the succession in these verses, but that power is now purely symbolic, for he has been stripped of his "Lawrel" crown by others. Dryden can here assume his monarchical identity only as the Edward II of poets, laureateship imagined as an experience of defeat, deposition, imprisonment, and eventual murder.

Dryden does attempt to rewrite defeat as victory: his identity as Edward II allows him to pay Congreve, who becomes the "Greater" Edward III, an elaborate compliment, while a return to a collective understanding of history qualifies the burden of Dryden's individual defeat. Reassuming a prophetic voice, Dryden can even foresee the triumph of history with which the poem began: "Yet this I Prophecy; Thou shalt be seen, / (Tho' with some short Parenthesis between:) / High on the Throne of Wit." But this "short Parenthesis" and its imitative line jar against the epic history that Dryden worked so hard to establish in the opening stanza. Poetic history has not found its promised fulfillment, "For Tom the Second reigns like Tom the first." The "Gyant Race" remains securely beyond the reach of Restoration aspirations, satire and not panegyric the result of Dryden's attempt to surpass his forebears and rivals.

Like the Stuarts whose political star he followed, Dryden becomes a monarch in exile, a pretender to the throne that he should "rightfully" occupy. The final stanza presents an extraordinary contrast to the hopeful accents of the poem's opening, for the experience of defeat in the second stanza leads to a succession marked by bitterness, despair, and contempt:

Maintain your Post: That's all the Fame You need;
For 'tis impossible you shou'd proceed.
Already I am worn with Cares and Age;
And just abandoning th'Ungrateful Stage.

The curious use of the term "Post"—which hardly suggests that Congreve occupies the "Throne of Wit" of stanza two—calls into question the dynamics of succession, suggesting instead that Congreve must be content, in these degenerate times, with a martyred fame. Dryden imagines here, I think, not Southerne's uncertainty about how a successor might extend Dryden's realm, but a laureate dramatist in opposition, in exile, defined by his refusal to accept a position within a corrupt government that has "curs'd" the empire of poetry.

The poem's conclusion attempts to return to the expected language of compliment when Dryden assures his heir that Congreve is "to better Fortune born," that his "Lawrels" will "descend to You." Here Dryden perhaps suggests the political differences that in the early 1690s radically separated the still anonymous young poet on the make from the aged public figure whose religious and political beliefs had cost him his patronage and figuratively exiled him.

Congreve certainly possessed friends among the Jacobites, but in Antony Carey and Charles Montague he links himself to two very powerful and influential figures within the government from which Dryden is alienated. Though political preferment was to come slowly—Congreve's first appointment as one of five commissioners for licensing hackney coaches only came in 1695, and a more lucrative though still minor post as commissioner for wines did not follow until 1705—Congreve eventually secured a comfortable income when appointed Secretary to jamaica in 1714. Congreve, unlike Dryden, was not to suffer in a losing cause. The bitterness of Dryden's autobiography as he contemplates his lost patronage, his sense of weariness, isolation, and betrayal, deny the conventional accents of panegyrical celebration that Congreve's future successes might occasion. Congreve's ambiguous "Post" heralds not a glorious future, but the mere defence of his predecessor's memory, which must be protected from the vandals of the new age.

In this final stanza Dryden doesn't take his leave of the stage, but abandons it, turning his back on a dramatic realm unworthy of his talents. The most successful dramatist of the age, the playwright who best exploited the financial potential of the Restoration stage, constructs a theatrical history that elides his years of prosperity, presenting himself, in fact, as abandoned by the very institution that most contributed to his economic prosperity. Dryden and his heir emerge not as the masters of a new theatrical history, but as those left behind by a theatrical public unworthy of its legitimate rulers. The bitterness of Dryden's autobiography as he contemplates his lost patronage, his sense of weariness, isolation, and betrayal, deny the conventional accents of panegyrical celebration that Congreve's future successes might occasion.

Congreve's ambiguous "Post" heralds not a glorious future, but the mere defence of his predecessor's memory, which must be protected from the vandals of the new age. In this final stanza Dryden doesn't take his leave of the stage, but abandons it, turning his back on a dramatic realm unworthy of his talents. The most successful dramatist of the age, the playwright who best exploited the financial potential of the Restoration stage, constructs a theatrical history that elides his years of prosperity, presenting himself, in fact, as abandoned by the very institution that most contributed to his economic prosperity. Dryden and his heir emerge not as the masters of a new theatrical history, but as those left behind by a theatrical public unworthy of its legitimate rulers. During the course of his long and varied dramatic career, Dryden's assessment of his theatrical public had not always been quite so dismissive as it was in 1693. As Leo Hughes suggests in his survey of Dryden's changeable appraisal of "the taste of the day," the poet, moving between the poles of "courtier" and "professional writer," expresses contradictory sentiments regarding his relationship to the audience for whom he wrote: "In every case, care must be taken to ascertain the point of view, the role of the moment."

Although the composition and nature of Restoration theatrical audiences remains a contentious issue among scholars, most would now agree that by or during the 1690s playwrights, players, and theatre managers had to adapt to a changing, and radically different body of spectators. Indeed, Robert D. Hume insists that in the 1690s "the principal problem for the theatres... seems to have been finding and holding an audience.". If we return to Jocelyn Powell's formulation of a theatre world poised between court patronage and commercial demands, the triumph of the latter marks the theatre's evolution in the years between 1660 and 1700. According to Elizabeth Howe, "What did disappear, however, as the century wore on, wasthe direct patronage and support of the monarchy so evidentat the start.

While James II shared his brother's fondness forthe theatre the troubled years of his reign from 1685 to 1689saw a general reduction in theatrical activity. Under Williamand Mary court support for the theatre dwindled still further:their interest in drama was minimal, as was that of theirsuccessor, Queen Anne. This lack of court supportrendered the stage more vulnerable to attacks by moralists,which strengthened during the 1690s. Contemporary evidence for this change can be difficult to assess, but John Dennis's A Large Account of the Taste in Poetry, and the Causes of the Degeneracy of It in 1702 and James Wright's Historia Histrionica in 1699 both insist that the absence of the court, "the more Civilized Part of the Town" in Wright's words, had severely compromised the integrity of the audience during the last decade of the century they who were not qualified to judge in King Charles hisReign, were influenced by the authority of those who were;and that is of the Court, which always in a peculiar mannerinfluences the pleasures of the Gentry.... But the Court ofEngland at present has other things to mind than to take careof Comedy.

Whereas of late, the Play-houses are so extreamly pestered with Vizard-masks and their Trade, (occasioning continual-quarrels and Abuses) that many of the more Civilized Part of the Town are uneasy in the Company, and shun the Theater as they would a House of Scandal.the present Plays with all that shew, can hardly draw an Audience, unless there be the additional Invitation of a Signior Fideli, a Monsieur L'Abbe, or some such Foreign Regale expresst in the bottom of the Bill. Wright's contemptuous final reference to the development of the "Whole Show" that was to dominate the eighteenth-century theatre reveals the same prejudices that Dryden and Congreve express for the changing composition of the audience in the 1690s and the new demands it placed on a playwright contemplating a professional career.

Not all playwrights, of course, set themselves against the triumph of a more popular as opposed to elite theatre. Southerne's dedications, for instance, demonstrate a very different attitude towards the reception of his plays and even suggest an identification with his audience. His dedication to Sir Anthony Love insists that he is "gratefully sensible of the general good Nature of the Town, to me, which you must give me leave to value my self upon." And even when his plays were not successful, as with The Wives' Excuse, Southerne could maintain that he refused to be "mortifi'd into a despair of pleasing the more reasonable part of Mankind."

Another of Congreve's contemporaries, George Farquhar, provides an even more powerful contrast to Congreve, for while the latter prides himself in his dedication to The Double-Dealer on his decision to "preserve the Three Unities of the Drama," Farquhar dismisses such "Rules" in his attempt to satisfy a diverse and demanding audience: "How must this secret of pleasing so many different Tastes be discovered? Not by tumbling over Volumes of the Ancients, but by studying the Humour of the Modems: The Rules of English Comedy don't lie in the Compass of Aristotle, or his Followers, but in the Pit, Box, and Galleries."

I began this essay by evoking Ben Jonson and wish to conclude by returning to jonson, not only because he represented one of "the Gyant Race, before the Flood" who so oppressed Dryden's theatrical imagination, but because aspects of Jonson's vocation served as a model for some of the ways in which Dryden and Congreve understood their own relation to the theatre. In his book Jonson and the Psychology of Public Theater, John Gordon Sweeney surveys Jonson's theatrical output as "a fascinating record of an artist's struggle to define himself through, and against, his audience": "The idea that meaning, like value, is something negotiated between the parties of the stage and gallery lies at the heart of Jonson's sense of theater."

The striking difference between Jonson and Congreve lies not simply in the loss of any balance between "through, and against" in Congreve's brief career, but in the absence of any apparent struggle to arrive at such a position. Jonson committed himself to the conception of theater as negotiation in spite of his powerfully ambivalent attitude toward his audience; Congreve I argue rejected this model from the very start. Jonson's long and varied career bears witness to the productive tension between playwright and spectator that animates his engagement with the public theater. As he in turn berates, cajoles, dismisses, and dupes his audience, Jonson reveals the excitement and novelty of working within commercial and artistic structures that were hardly a quarter-century old when he first began to write for the stage.

Jonson also displays the tremendous frustration and rage engendered by those structures, his choleric response to the failure of one of his last plays, The New Inne (first performed in 1629), the centre of a notorious public controversy. The unusual title-page to the 1631 edition of the play explicitly damns both the actors who performed and the audience that attended the original production: "As it was neuer acted, but most negligently play'd, by some, the Kings Seruants. And more squeamishly beheld, and censured by others, the Kings Subiects. 1629. Now, at last, set at liberty to the Readers, his Ma[sup.ties], Seruants, and Subiects, to be judg'd. 1631. By the Author, B. Ionson."

In its insistence on the difference between production and publication, these lines suggest how Jonson's relationship to the stage had become a bondage, "liberty" now represented by a print industry far more responsive to the authority of the "Author, B. Ionson" than a promiscuous and negligent rout of actors and spectators. This title-page moreover merely hints at the depths of Jonson's anger, for hostile responses to The New Inne even occasioned Jonson's "Ode to himselfe"—written in 1629 after the failure of his play and appended to its 1631 publication—which opens with the famous command to "Come leaue the lothed stage, / And the more lothsome age," and includes, in its earliest version, a parodic succession that defines for the resentful dramatist the futility of working for the commercial theater:

Broomes sweepings doe as well
Thear as his Masters Meale.
For, who the relish of these ghests will fit
Needs set them, but, the almes-basket Of Wit.

Richard Brome, both Jonson's servant and protege, enjoyed a tremendous success in 1629 with The Love-sick Maid, the contrast between his triumph and Jonson's bitter failure highlighting for the aging poet the absurdity of writing for those "Whose appetites are dead!"

In the polemics occasioned by Jonson's denunciation of the theatrical public for its failure to receive properly The New Inne, we can glimpse the genesis of the role of martyred playwright that Congreve and Dryden were later to assume, as well as the resistance to that role and the pretensions it was thought to exemplify. Owen Felltham's answer to Jonson's "Ode" advises the playwright that "To rail men into approbation / Is new, is yours alone, / And prospers not," while Thomas Carew's poem occasioned by the "Ode" assures Jonson that he is right to R. Goodwin counsels Jonson to

"Staine not that Well-gaind Honour, with the Crude, / or the rash Censure, of a Multitude," anticipating the glorification of failure that Congreve and Dryden later articulate when he promises the dramatist that "Their dislike is thine Honour."

Let others glut on the extorted praise
Of vulgar breath, trust thou to after dayes:
Thy labour'd workes shall live, when Time devoures
Th'abortive off-spring of their hastie houres.

For Sir John Suckling, on the other hand, Jonson's appalling arrogance, which makes him the first to demand the laurel from Apollo in "A Session of the Poets," is best displayed in Jonson's decision to call his "works, where others were but plays," and in his posturing over The New Inne: "And therefore Apollo call'd him back again, / And made him mine host of his own New Inn."

By the time Congreve began his theatrical career, Jonson's contempt for his audience had become an integral part of his reputation as a dramatist. In John Oldham's 1678 ode "Upon the Works of Ben. Johnson," this defines an essential feature of Jonson's genius, a mark of the elite dramatist who transcends the "empty vapour," the "common breath," the "popular Air":

Let meaner Spirits stoop to low precarious fame,
Content on gross and coarse Applause to live,
And what the dull and sensless Rabble give,
Thou didst it still with noble scorn contemn.

In such a formulation, Jonson's dismissal of his audience becomes one of the proofs of his merit. As Thomas Randolph had written years earlier in his response to Jonson's "Ode," "Their hiss is thy applause."

Published only two years before Congreve's theatrical debut, Gerard Langbaine's An Account of the English Dramatick Poets provided a recapitulation of the debate over Jonson's relationship to his audience that centered around The New Inne. Langbaine has no doubts that Jonson was a "Great Man" and a "Master of Poetry," and he even refers his readers to Oldham's ode to supplement what his own "faint Praise can reach, or describe." At the end of his catalog of Jonson's plays, however, Langbaine follows his citation for The New Inne with both Jonson's "Ode to himselfe" and Owen Felltham's "An Answer to the Ode," clearly ratifying the latter. Langbaine chastises Jonson for the "high Opinion our Author has of his own Performances," and ends this section of his account by providing selections from Suckling's "A Session of the Poets," which "laught at, and railly [Jonson's] unreasonable Self-opinion."

While Jonson's career, and particularly the notorious demonstrations of his hostility towards his audience, cannot be regarded as typical, it is nonetheless revelatory of a problem that concerned almost all Elizabethan and Jacobean dramatists. Drama, Richard Helgerson asserts, "was a bastard child of poetry, an unmistakably illegitimate offspring. Success in such a debased kind could never establish one as a true poet."[33] Playwrights during the first half of the seventeenth century struggle to unite professional success with artistic merit, to construct a theatre within which both art and entertainment might flourish. The success of their efforts depends precisely on their refusal to privilege one term over the other, their failure, as it were, to resolve a contradiction that is the very source of their power.

Congreve, on the other hand, who begins his career less than a century after Jonson began his, fashions a theatrical identity that obviates the necessity to engage genuinely his audience. Almost without effort or regret, Congreve assumes a part already scripted by Jonson that rests on the assumption of a hostile relationship between a dramatist and his audience. D.F. McKenzie, examining the ways in which Jonson and Congreve "fight for the author's right not to be mis-read," describes Jonson as Congreve's "mentor," and speaks of the relation between Jonson's epilogue to The New Inne and Congreve's prologue to The Way of the World as "an acceptance of succession."

While I certainly agree with the establishment of this genealogy, McKenzie, like Jonas Barish, misidentifies the genuine moment of succession. McKenzie can locate this moment in The Way of the World, and describe Congreve as "less tough, more delicate, than Jonson... sensing himself expelled by the misappropriation of his works," only because he accepts and even privileges the mythology of the martyred dramatist.Precisely because of Jonson's example, however, Congreve can be more tough and less delicate than his forebear, for Jonson provided a role that allowed Congreve to generate from the beginning his distance from and contempt for his auditors.

In this elite realm in which popular failure becomes equated with literary success, theatrical authority results not from a contract between playwright and audience, however bitterly and tendentiously negotiated, but from the outright rejection of an audience's right to judge or censure the playwright; its "roaring Gods" silenced, Congreve's theatre acknowledges only the divinity of the aged father and his anointed heir.

Western Philosophers have Theorized About the Nature and Causes of Mirth at Least Since the Time of Plato.

Comedy feeds on incongruity; people laugh even when the joke is cruel because they want to feel a sense of relief that their own follies are not fatal. Indeed, comedy has the power to heighten people's sense of belonging to a common human family. Restoration playwrights understood the value of laughter as a social force, and they used the theatre as a staging ground. With an attitude of detached instruction that was still entertaining, they contrived their plots, fashioned their stock characters (the country bumpkin, the wit, the hero, the fool, etc.), and satirized familiar domestic situations and themes to reflect the ridiculous but nonetheless very human impulses of the times. No playwright was more adept at this in the late seventeeth century than Congreve. And no play better represents his mastery of the comedy of manners than his final play, *The Way of the World*.

Congreve's decision to include lines from Horace, the Roman satirist, on the title page of the printed play immediately alert the reader that his work will relate to the immorality and unscrupulousness of society. These lines, quoted in the original Latin from Horace's *Satires,* cautions adulterers and mocks the fate of those who, caught in the act, must relinquish their dowries. Of course, marital disharmony and sexual intrigue are not new themes. What is of interest is the way these themes are treated in Restoration comedy, where, as Joseph Wood Krutch notes in *Comedy and Conscience after the Restoration,* "the technique of wit" is used to great advantage in "rationalizing debauchery into a philosophical system."

Taking nothing away from Congreve as a master of polished dialogue and a purveyor of wit, it must be observed that this final play was written in answer to one of the most notorious Puritanical attacks on the theatre by Parson Jeremy Collier. The play therefore offers much more than a witty "rationalization," however. It playfully teaches people how to find an antidote to debauchery. In Congreve's dedication of the play to the Earl of Montague, he announces the profound, if comic, intent of his art by placing himself in direct line of ancestry with Terence, "the most correct Writer in the World" who is himself a descendent of the masters of comedy in the classic tradition from Theophrastus to Moliere.

Of this new play, he laments that it will be little understood because it is not animated by the usual characters who "are Fools so gross, that in my humble Opinion, they should rather disturb than divert the well-natur'd and reflecting part of an Audience...." While Congreve is no moralist, nor should his play be read as anything more doctrinal than a well-wrought fable with a moral attached, the heroes of this play nonetheless undertake a "remarriage" of minds that is possible only when both perversely jaded and self-righteously censorious views on marriage are rejected.

In order for the romantic heroes Mirabell and Mrs. Millamant to come together in marriage and to achieve a happy ending for the play, they must first thwart the devious intentions of their foes and character foils Fainall and Mrs. Marwood, who are carrying on an adulterous affair. Moreover, they must undermine Lady Wishfort's falsely pious pronouncements and patently disingenuous hatred of men. It is no accident that the Lady appears in the third act to take her place as the central comic figure of the play when the action reaches a climax. As the dominant matriarch in control of the purse strings, she is also the character who best reflects the sworn enemies of comedy: hypocritical and self-righteousness, with a fashionable but overdeveloped appetite for the opposite sex. Finally, by relying on their intelligence and thoughtful common sense, the two heroes also deflect the tiresome banter of the self-proclaimed "wits," Witwoud and Petulant. These two dandies playfully engage the audience in amusing and often sophisticated dialogues, pointing up unpleasant yet honest insights into the way of the world. But they are essentially shallow, as is the fashionable world they represent, and as such they also serve as foils to the heroes.

In the opening of the first act, when Fainall and Mirabell are gambling (a foreshadowing of the suspenseful battle they will wage for love and money), Congreve establishes the prevailing cavalier attitude toward sexual encounters. Fainall's quip to Mirabell over cards that "I'd no more play with a Man that slighted his ill Fortune, than I'd make Love to a Woman who undervalu'd the Loss of her Reputation" demonstrates the value both he and society place on conquests that will prove disastrous for the vanquished. Congreve would have the audience smile at the sentiment, to acknowledge its compelling force in the way of the world.

But he also finally undermines Fainall and society's libertine attitudes toward adultery and scandal. Both Fainall's "Inconstancy and Tyranny of temper" have led Mirabell to protect Mrs. Fainall's fortunes from her husband by deeding them over in trust to him before she was married. In the final act, this precaution proves to be Fainall's undoing, for without the deed to Mrs. Fainall's property he is without means. He cannot extort Lady Wishfort's estate by blackmail or make good on his promise to set his wife "a drift, like a Leaky hulk to Sink or Swim, as she and the Current of this Lewd Town can agree." He needs his wife's money (which he thought he had "wheadl'd out of her") to survive. Mrs. Marwood suffers a more ignominious fate for her role as a spoiler. She exits the play vowing revenge on Mrs. Fainall. My resentment, she swears, "shall have Vent, and to your Confusion, or I'll perish in the attempt." But her vow is an empty one. She has been revealed as a vicious, grasping adulteress, and she is left without husband or means. Fainall can return to his wife, and Mirabell promises to "Contribute all that in me lies to a Reunion," but Marwood has become, ironically and by her own hand, the "Leaky hulk" that risks perishing.

She has exploited her wit, Congreve implies, at the expense of true feelings. Congreve comically draws out the natural and enduring conflict between the sexes in order to make his audience laugh at human foibles and to poke fun at the posturing associated with romance and sexual intrigue. Early on, Mirabell expresses his mocking disdain of the romantic entanglements that drive the story. The night before the story begins, Millamant has rebuffed him. What can he expect, Fainall asks. The women had met on "one of their Cabal-nights... where they come together like the Coroner's Inquest, to sit upon the murder'd Reputations of the Week." Men are excluded from the gossip circle, and their presence (with the exception of the "coxcombs" Witwoud and Petulant) would naturally stall all conversation.

Clearly Mirabell is too grave, too love-struck, to understand that he has breached "decorum." It is further learned that he cannot win Millamant without first pacifying her aunt, whom he has angered by playing the knave and pretending love to her. Fashion has dictated the rules by which men must pay court to women, and, in the case of Lady Wishfort, Mirabell has paid them only lip service. He has indeed engaged in the "last Act of Flattery with her, and was guilty of a Song in her Commendation."

He tells Fainall he even went so far as to "complement her with the Imputation of an Affair with a "If congreve took exception to the lewdness and over-elaborate artificiality of the times, he also clearly resented the puritanical attacks upon it." young Fellow..." But his attentions have been false. Throughout the exchange of dialogue in act 1, Congreve shines the light of truth on the way things are. The none too subtle implication is that fashionable women and men are victims of their own vanities, that they delight in the weaknesses of others, and that they are blind to their own defects.

For his gravity as a lover and his knavery as a gallant, Mirabell must temporarily suffer. He will be disappointed in his expectations of Millamant until it appears that his gallant efforts to win her have been in vain. For his ability to read the corrupt nature of the world and his desire to circumvent it, even while deploying its methods, he is victorious in the end. He is able to rise above the superficial manners of his peers; furthermore, his deceptions and undisguised attempts at blackmail have been wrought in the name of love rather than greed or artificial gallantry.

He is, as Virginia Birsdall has pointed out in *Wild Civility: The English Comic Spirit on the Restoration Stage,* "a promoter of marriages." The marriages he promotes and also helps to sustain suit his own interests. His arrangement of Foible and Waitwell's marriage secures him the co-conspiracy of Foible against Lady Wishfort. His arrangement of marriage between Mrs. Fainall and her husband and his consequent safeguarding of her estate enable him to foil Fainall, who wants to use his wife's fortune as leverage in the game of extortion. Yet, at the same time, Foible loves Waitwell and is made happy by the union. And Mrs. Fainall, who has been widowed and has indulged in an affair with Mirabell, protects her reputation by marrying Fainall. His ability to be both gallant and wise, both sophisticated and loving render his plots harmless and instructive. It is later left up to Millamant to teach him how to be "enlarg'd" into a proper husband.

In the famous "prenuptial agreement" scene in act 4, Millamant outlines the conditions under which she will "by degrees dwindle into a Wife." The gaiety, capriciousness, and arrogance that has characterized her behavior and conversation with Mirabell are offset by veins of gravity and intelligence, an energetic charm and a desire for profound love that culminate here in a style that reflects her power as a heroine. She has toyed with Mirabell unmercifully, snubbing and teasing him until, at the end of act 2, he can think of her only as "a Whirlwind" and himself unwittingly lodged in that whirlwind. While he allows passion to tyrannize him, she is in complete control. Her airy detachment is a challenge to the despotism of the old marriage code. Indeed, she wishes to establish a new marriage pattern that will look very much like a permanent courtship: "I'll fly and be follow'd to the last Moment," she asserts to Mirabell, "tho' I am upon the very Verge of Matrimony, I expect you should sollicit me as much as if I were wavering at the Grate of a Monastery, with one Foot over the Threshold. I'll be sollicited to the very last, nay and afterwards."

While she is a genius in her manipulation of other characters and while her playfulness borders on cruelty, she is intrinsically aware of her own follies, and she finally cannot deny her own natural inclinations. At the end of the scene she admits to Fainall, "Well, If Mirabell shou'd not make a good Husband, I am a lost thing; for I find I love him violently."

It is fitting to conclude with Lady Wishfort, whose declarations of piety and hatred of men have fooled no one, including herself. In act 3, Mrs. Marwood enters the Lady's house to tattle on Foible whom she has seen speaking with Mirabell in St. James Park. Lady Wishfort knows Foible has gone out with the Lady's picture to show Sir Rowland, the more to incite his passions for her. Of course, she doesn't know that Mirabell has invented the admiring uncle for his own purposes. She only fears here that her own passions will be found out and that she will lose her last chance at marriage, an unpleasant thought at the ripe old age of fifty-five. She laments to Marwood,

"Oh, he carries Poyson in his Tongue that wou'd corrupt Integrity it self. If she has given him an Opportunity, she has as good as put her Integrity into his Hands. Ah dear Marwood, what's Integrity to an Opportunity?"

Despite her willingness to take advantage of her own opportunity, especially at the expense of ruining Mirabell, she falsely insists on her disdain of men in general. Compare the very funny scene with Foible in act 4, during which she readies herself for Sir Rowland:

"In what figure shall I give his Heart the first Impression?... Shall I sit?... No I won't sit... I'll walk... and then turn full upon him... No, that will be too sudden... I'll lie... aye, I'll lie down... I'll receive him in my little dressing Room... with one Foot a little dangling off... and then as soon as he appear, start, aye, start and be surpriz'd, and rise to meet him in a pretty disorder..." to her soliloquy in the final act on the virtues of raising a daughter to despise men:

"I chiefly made it my own Care to Initiate her very Infancy in the Rudiments of Vertue, and to Impress upon her tender Years, a Young *Odium* and *Aversion* to the very sight of Men... she never look'd a Man in the Face but her own Father, or the Chaplain, and him we made a shift to put upon her for a Woman, by the help of his long Garments, and his Sleek-face..."

Her unnatural parenting is not only hypocritical, it has by implication contributed to the unfortunate circumstances in which her daughter has found herself sadly married to a man she truly does hate. And it is Congreve's final "revenge" that she not only be humiliated in her romance with "Sir Rowland," but be the butt of his general joke. For while her fortune is "saved" from Fainall, her reputation as a "superannuated Frippery," a fate she fears most, has indeed come to pass.

If Congreve took exception to the lewdness and over-elaborate artificiality of the times, he also clearly resented the Puritanical attacks upon it. Clearly, Lady Wishfort supplies his comic vehicle for demonstrating the weakness of both extremes. But perhaps the most unconsciously insightful remark belongs to the rude but kind-hearted country bumpkin, Sir Wilfull, who for all his misunderstandings of the "lingo" of London, speaks the great lesson of the play when he denounces Witwoud as a fop and declares that "Fashion" is indeed "a Fool."

The Mourning Bride was Congreve's only dramatic tragedy. Performed in 1697, it was a triumphant success and ran for thirteen days at Lincoln's Inn Fields. Set in the south of Spain, it dramatizes earlier historical conflicts between Granada and Valencia and the part played in this struggle by

Moorish expeditions from the north coast of Africa. But the plot is fictional and characters are drawn not from history but from earlier heroic plays.

When *The Old Batchelour,* Congreve's first play, was printed in 1693, it was an immediate success and its author hailed as John Dryden's successor. Indeed, Dryden helped Congreve, who was only twenty-three years old at the time, prepare the play for the theatre. This first play, like his later comedies, mirrored the manners of fashionable society. It can be enjoyed for its sheer gaiety and youthful energy, but it also provides a contrast to later works where maturity affords him a more original style and a more discerning attitude to the society he evokes.

William Wycherley's play *The Country Wife* is one of the best examples of early Restoration comedy. Born in 1640, thirty years before Congreve, Wycherley is often regarded, along with Sir George Etherege, as one of Congreve's most important literary predecessors. Although there is disagreement about when Wycherley's play was first performed, most scholars put it between 1672 and 1675. The play takes a satirical look at the jealous husband, concluding that jealousy is indeed a monster that consumes those who suffer from it most.

More than any other English playwright, Ben Jonson probably had the most influence on the comic tradition of which Congreve is a part. He was a primary force in the rise of the comedy of "humours" during the Elizabethan period. His play *Volpone,* or *The Fox,* first performed in 1606, provides one of the best examples of comedy at work in the service of social satire.When Jeremy Collier's *Short View of the Immorality and Profaneness of the English Stage* was published in 1698, several playwrights of the period, including Congreve, responded to this attack. Indeed, Collier's book is one of several popular works of Puritan piety that Lady Wishfort tells Mrs. Marwood to entertain herself with when she hides in the closet in the third act of *The Way of the World*. Collier's book is considered one of the most articulate expressions of the Puritanical attempt to reform the stage and purge it from the perceived evils and corruption of the day.

Bibliography

Gardiner, Samuel R., History of the Great Civil War, 1642?1649, London, 1886?1891.

Gardiner discusses the Civil War that temporarily ended the reign of the monarchy in England and replaced it with a parliamentary form of government. The "*Restoration*" of the monarchy took place when Charles II came to the throne in 1660.

Holland, Norman, The First Modern Comedies: The Significance of Etherege, Wycherley, and Congreve, Harvard University Press, 1959.

Holland provides a thorough study of the three Restoration playwrights, their influences, and their heirs.

Johnson, Samuel, "*Preface to William Congreve*" in Lives of the English Poets, 1781.

It is a token of Johnson's eminence that the later eighteenth century is often called the "*Age of Johnson.*" His collection of biographies on the lives of the poets from Cowley to Gray are amusing, often disparaging, but always insightful glosses on the literary giants of the age. The language of the "Preface" is singularly witty, urbane, and acerbic. He outlines the life and work of Congreve from his vantage point only fifty years after Congreve's death.

Loftis, John, Comedy and Society from Congreve to Fielding, Stanford University Press, 1959.

As its title would suggest, this critical work reviews the relationship between social history and culture in the seventeenth and eighteenth centuries. The book is particularly appropriate in its study of moral matters, social customs, and theater values.